Indigenous Identity and Activism

INDIGENOUS IDENTITY AND ACTIVISM

Edited by

Priti Singh

SHIPRA

ISBN: 978-81-7541-488-4

First Published in India in 2009

Indigenous Identity and Activism

Published by :

SHIPRA PUBLICATIONS

115-A, Vikas Marg, Shakarpur, Delhi-110092 (India)

Tel. : 91-11-65277210, 22500954, Fax : 91-11-22458662

Email : info@shiprapublications.com

www.shiprapublications.com

Acknowledgements

Without the encouragement and help of a number of people this compendium would not have been possible.

The project originated at the instance of Professor R. Narayanan with whom I had had extensive discussions on issues of indigenous identity and activism upon which I designed this collection. I am eternally thankful to him.

No less, I am thankful to all the contributors for their support and patience with me.

Among them, I need to thank specially Professor Rodolfo Stavenhagen who not only readily consented but sent his chapter long before others!

I also thank Professor Carlos Montemayor, Dr. Martha Crago and Professor João Pacheco de Oliveira for their gracious kindness in sending their chapters. I record my thanks to Dr. Federico Navarrete Linares and Dr. Peter Gale as they have been very patient with me. Professor Stephen Grant Baines has been a true friend over the years encouraging me and Dr. Ashwani Peetush unstintingly met my demands at a moment's (literally!) notice. A special thanks to Dr. Irene Watson for being always ready to concede to my indulgence. I am obliged to Professor Margery Fee not only for her contribution but also for her useful comments on my arguments.

I also have to record my thanks to Mr. Hari Nair for his timely support with his translation skills. My colleagues and friends at the Centre for Canadian, US and Latin American Studies, School of International Studies have as always been very supportive. My 'thanks-giving' would not be complete without mentioning a few friends who played a vital role in the completion of this book—Mr. Guillermo Puente Ordorica, Professor Raymond Izarali and Dr. Sergio Miranda Pacheco. This entire exercise would not have borne fruition without the constant encouragement of Professor D. Gopal.

I would like to acknowledge my gratitude to Department of Foreign Affairs and International Trade Canada (DFAIT) and Shastri Indo-Canadian Institute for their support which made it possible for me to partially work on this project in Vancouver and Montreal.

And to you Rupa, thank you for standing by me as a pillar of moral and even material support throughout these years and my family for boosting my morale.

I thank Mr. D. Kumar of Shipra Publications for his interest and willingness to take on the task of publishing the manuscript.

Priti Singh

Contents

1

Introduction: Studying Indigenous Identity and Activism

Priti Singh

Articulation and negotiation of individual and collective identities have gained considerable prominence in recent scholarly social science literature. Empirical analyses of identity politics, along with significant yet debatable theoretical studies are prolix on the subject. There is a lively ongoing debate on what constitutes identity between those who subscribe to the 'essentialist' approach and those who support the 'essencialist' view.[1] Arising out of these dichotomized approaches is the question whether identities are to be deemed as constructed or invented. Subtle distinctions are made between 'constructionism' and 'inventionism' to suggest that symbolic 'construction' may be largely unconscious and is an ongoing activity in all human societies whereas 'invention' emphasises creativity and implies a degree of conscious reflection about culture (Handler and Linnekin, 1984; Hanson, 1989; Hobsbawm and Ranger, 1983; Jackson, 1995; Linnekin, 1992; Mato, 1992).

Overall, there is general consensus that social actors taking part in social processes continually make representations of large societal identities. They participate in these processes by advancing their own representations—whether purposely 'invented' or 'non-deliberately elaborated'. However, such identities, it is acknowledged, are by no means fixed; they are formed and are transformed through participation in those processes. The (trans)formation of these representations obviously implies the (trans)formation of the very subjects—social actors—that these identities purport to define. Implicit in this formulation is that identities are without doubt matters of social dispute and contestations.

1. 'Essentialism' refers to discourses of enduring commonalties—common ethnic roots and historical pasts, and experiences that are seen as naturally binding people together. 'Essencialism' is defined in terms of a transcendent spirituality, ties to places, common descent, cultural practices and shared language. These are often asserted as foundational realities.

Changing Course of Indigenous Discourse

Articulated within this more general theory of social formation of identity are the questions relating to the identity and representation of indigenous peoples or, more precisely, the development and exposition of *indigeneity* as a politicized discourse which over time has attained a remarkable centrality. Reasons for this are not far to seek. For one, a multiplicity of indigenous peoples' movements have mushroomed seeking recognition in the public sphere through political manoeuvres that include discursive as well as action-oriented practices. At the same time, new social movements have emerged that defy the traditional class or ethnic criteria, bringing to the fore new processes of individual and collective identity formation.

Nevertheless, available studies on the politics of indigenous identity are somewhat limited in scope and focus. Scholars engaged in the general area of indigenous studies agree that indigenous people without doubt are among the most researched peoples in the world. At the same time, it is widely recognized that there is an almost inexplicable neglect of indigenous activism in the field of social movement studies. Unarguably, there is an urgent need of redress not only because most of the available studies on indigenous politics lack the much-needed comparative dimension both within and across countries, but also because indigenous activism as a subject of research on social movements is yet to mature among scholars.

Admittedly, there is a pressing need to direct future research on studies focussing on the processes of identity construction and mobilization of indigenous activists. Such studies possibly could offer insights not only on the strategic discourse of the activists but develop a necessary theoretical framework for analyzing *indigenist* collective identity processes. After all, in the world of today, *indigeneity* as an emerging expression of local, regional and international collective identity is of deep significance both for an understanding of the process and for developing a vitally needed policy framework. No less significant is the construction and activation of such an identity across tribal, clan, cultural and national differences in the post-colonial context.

Indigenous peoples as place-bound with their identity related to land is, by and large, the general refrain of most past discourse. However, recent writings underline not only the antecedents or the *roots* of *indigeneity* but more importantly the historical trajectory or the *routes* the indigenous peoples have taken over the centuries. The *routes* they have traversed, some scholars stress, have added a new dimension to the meaning and significance of indigenous culture. This view takes cognisance not only of the new trans-ethnic views of culture but also of culture as mobility, communication and action, instead of the traditional anthropological view of culture as tradition (Clifford, 1997). This phenomenon is also treated as displacement of indigenous peoples (Homborg and Kurkiala, 1998).

In turn, some of these studies factored on the new connotation of the term culture emphasise that the historical reality of the colonial encounter is crucial to an understanding of the unique situation that exists between indigenous peoples and the Europeans all across the world. At the dawn of the colonial era human beings with different worldviews and experiences for the first time came in direct contact with each other. From the initial 'discovery' enterprise of Christopher Columbus and onwards, the European colonisers remained—be it in the Western Hemisphere or elsewhere later in Australia and New Zealand—and became citizens after the independence of the nation states. This was not the case to the same extent in the European colonization of Africa and Asia. Therefore, the colonial period is still the 'hidden face' of today's reality.

Apparently a form of internal colonialism has been one way of approaching the relationship between the state and the indigenous population since the beginning of post-colonialism. However, the post-colonial period has largely been concerned with problems of a different character. These include conflicts on geographical, political and ethnic borders between Europeans arriving since five hundred years ago as colonisers of a territory that already was inhabited, and the colonized, whom the intruders conceptualized as 'the other' (Todorov, 1984).

A separation or border was constructed by the colonisers from the first encounter, between the so-called 'civilized' Europeans and the 'primitive' non-Europeans. Ever since, vexing questions on the formation and construction of indigenous identities have surfaced both in scholarly discourse and policy debates. The colonial era spanning five hundred years, therefore, can be seen as a period of establishing new borders and/or crossing of cultural and ethnic ones.

Contrary to the generally held view, indigenous peoples have certainly not lived in isolation during the colonial era. Neither have they remained merely as passive victims of the trauma of colonization. They too were, in a sense, 'shapers of history' as they are today, resisting the political forces that would deny them their identities, nations and future (Fleras and Elliott, 1992). However, their history and knowledge has not been taken into consideration largely on account of the five centuries of turbulent and violent contact with Europeans. During and since the colonial era, the colonisers claimed history writing from their own perspective and forcibly subordinated the indigenous peoples as mere mute witnesses. This state of 'colonial difference' has since that time remained as what Eric Wolf has called 'the people without history', or those to whom history has been denied (Wolf, 1984).

Since the beginning of the colonial era and onwards in the post-colonial period, indigenous identity construction has invariably been about the process of identification and negotiation with the dynamics of evolving historical circumstances. Such attempts at reformulating identities some argue are therefore to be interpreted as the needed strategies of the political struggles that the indigenous peoples had to wage for their own survival and sustenance. In other words, as the indigenous peoples have continually been confronted with the challenge of a process of change, they needed to reinvent, reformulate and recreate their identities, despite obvious language barriers and cultural barriers.

The efflorescence of cultural claims for recognition by indigenous peoples in contemporary times is as much a direct consequence of the homogenizing threats of modernity as the coercive policy of miscegenation—euphemistically labelled as 'assimilation'—that threatened indigenous identity during the colonial era. These threats are so strong that demands for cultural recognition seem to stem from a protective instinct in defence of the familiar and the local. What differentiates the post-colonial era from the colonial is the frequency with which previously insular cultural units are today coming into contact with one another. As Charles Taylor argues "in pre-modern times people didn't speak of 'identity' and 'recognition'—not because people didn't have (what we call) identities, or because these didn't depend on recognition, but because these were then [not] thematized as such" (Taylor, 1994). In the post-colonial era, however, the demand for cultural recognition as some argue springs from a crisis of identity because "under conditions of modernity", it is becoming increasingly "difficult for individuals to develop a coherent sense of self and community" (Benhabib, 1992).

Issues at Stake

One of the most striking features of contemporary indigenous movements the world over is the rapidity with which they have gained momentum in the recent decades and have thus been propelled into international arena as legitimate and widely visible political actors. Rather than being viewed as passive objects of change that dominant history had destined for them, they became active subjects sculpting their own destiny. Indeed, they carved out different strategies and relationships with state institutions and social actors. At times they were viewed within the framework of utopic ideology which revolved around the idea of "revolution" (Escobar and Alvarez, 1992). This view has shifted to more realistic and specific demands like cultural, economic and social rights within the national context. Ultimately indigenous peoples' claims are not that far away from the concerns of other social movements like urban movements, women's movements or peasants' movements. Like any social movement they seek to bring about a change in society and thus a change in the position of their respective communities. Yet, some scholars argue that indigenous movements are unique and upon this claim they have developed a theoretical framework for the study of indigenous ethnicity. Indigenous movements face a class struggle (indigenous/peasants *versus* landlords) and an ethnic conflict (indigenous *versus* non-indigenous people). This means that the indigenous movement has developed a project within its national political context leading to a need to examine its relationship with the state.

From the vantage point of the beginning of the twenty-first century some observers tend to suggest that the brisk pace of world-wide native self-affirmation is not so much a genuine process as more an outcome of the exigencies of our times. To them the gains that these movements have made in the international arena had come about by a sudden volition on the part of those involved—the indigenous and the non-indigenous communities. Also, in some respects, it is the direct outcome of the abrupt and decisive historical conjunctures, which have opened space for the indigenous peoples to assert their identity and rights (Kymlicka, 1995; Taylor, 1994; Walzer, 1997).[2] What they fail to recognise, however, is that the upsurge of the indigenous movements in the past decades is not the direct fallout of the currently witnessed phenomenon of ethnic resurgence across the world. So much so, "indigenism" needs to be delineated as an independent variable of the general discourse on ethnicity, and therefore, its antecedents have to be traced to the currently visible contradiction in the very constitution of modern Western ideology.

Today, the humanist quest for universalism has come to be the hegemonic idiom in which human rights are expressed everywhere regardless of cultural differences. However, at the same time, it is recognized that universalism coexists with the equally humanist quest for relativism, according to which values are not universal but culture-bound. Therefore, the recognition of cultural relativism cannot be subjected to and determined by universalist principles alone. This means that there are certain rights which everyone as a human being may claim, but there are certain 'special' rights, which accrue only to indigenous peoples.

The question here is two-pronged. One is whether the indigenous should be recipients of special rights, which are distinct from those of other minorities. The indigenous peoples' claims can be differentiated from those that can be made for the minorities because the indigenous have special cultural and historical ties with their territory and thus special claims to rights to self-determination in that territory (Bowen, 2000:12). The other argument is whether these special rights should be applicable universally and to all indigenous peoples all over the world. In other words, should indigenous peoples' rights differ from place to place in order for them to have real equality? (Cox, 1994:49). The main question that needs to be addressed here is whether indigenous traditional *usos y costumbres* need to be fully and universally endorsed. The fact that customary practices are not easy to define in non-indigenous terms has added to apprehensions in giving them the kind of recognition required. They have been described as

2. Many theorists like Will Kymlicka, Charles Taylor and Michael Walzer, argue for special rights and recognition for ethnic groups to be given by states.

"rules for the living...backed by religious sanctions [that] also prescribes daily behaviour" (Maddock, 1984:212). It is then a sum of three sets of relationships—people and land, people and deities, and people and people—and of three highly interdependent factors which act upon these relationships: religion, natural environment and social organization/kinship (Berndt, 1981:1–3).

Interestingly, the manifest contradiction between universalism and relativism itself is the immediate result of yet another contradiction—the logic of nationality and the logic of ethnicity. Modern Western ideology is based on the idea that sovereignty of the nation-state is both indivisible and illimitable. The recognition of customary law has necessarily limited this because sovereignty defined thus cannot conceive of an alternative and equal system of law existing within its sphere. Not that indigenous sovereignty has been recognized. Where it questions the legitimacy of the sovereignty of the state, the fear of an independent indigenous nation clouds the issue. Indigenous peoples, however, consider themselves to be nations, and their conception of national security is intimately connected to their survival *as nations.* Thus, in addition to physical security—protection from violence and coercion—indigenous peoples struggle to protect their cultural security, their medium for preserving the indigenous nation as a political, territorial, and societal entity. The most important issue is not only retaining lands they have controlled for generations, but also the right to control that land communally. This is where the problem arises. Stated differently, the principles that undergrid the rule of nation-state and the canons that orient ethnic identity "have indeed produced a social vacuum that is open to a variety of interpretations" (Ramos, 2002:256). In turn, this has led to a variety of demands for self-management, self-determination and internal self-government made by the indigenous communities (Sanders, 1993:14; Coe, 1994:37).

The resulting "cacophony...of discrepant voices", as Alcida Ramos (2002) puts it, is often shown as evidence of the prevailing ambiguities, internal contradictions and built-in tensions within indigenous activism. For, some theorists suggest that disunity triggered by the differing perspectives among the activists more often undermines the movement's strength over time. On the surface, it is true that the internal contradictions in respect of perspectives and objectives in the indigenous movements run along issues such as self-determination and representation; autonomy and dependency; sovereignty and citizenship; tradition and development; individualism and collectivism; indigeneity and hybridity; and unity and regionalism.

The work that indigenous activists are doing in their engagements with one another over these contested issues, however, is deeply important. For, as one scholar argues: "[I]t is these unnoticed contextual struggles of human freedom in the face of techniques of government and strategies of legitimation that have brought the internal colonization of indigenous peoples to the threshold of public attention and critical reflection in our time" (Tully, 2000:59). In many parts of the world even today much of indigenous activism retains a local character in regions and small communities. Neither the specificity of these contexts nor the importance of debate and disagreement between these groups can be underestimated. Related to these local contexts admittedly are the discursive politics of land, identity and political voice as they are deployed in the local and regional context. The content of these tensions concerns the cognitive definitions that frame indigenous activists' goals and strategies. At least for this reason they are both deeply important and worthy of further study. For, after all, in almost all areas there are similar underlying concerns that pull these activists together, even across deep divides around particular issues. Land rights, health, housing, and poverty are universal concerns that impinge on the very survival of indigenous peoples.

Seen from this perspective, the decades-long debates in several international forums including the United Nations regarding the self-representation of the indigenous peoples and the resultant initiatives, however varied, both at the national and international levels ironically make good sense in some respects. International bodies mandated with protection of human rights have paid particular attention to indigenous rights in recent years. The UN Committee on the Elimination of Racial Discrimination, the UN Human Rights Committee, and the International Labour Organization's Committee of Experts and the Inter-American Commission on Human Rights all stand out in this respect. These bodies have contributed to progressive development of indigenous rights by interpreting human rights instruments of general application to account for and protect the collective rights of indigenous peoples (United Nations, 2002).

Indeed, these are extraordinary exercises in universalism and relativism on the part of both the indigenous peoples and the supranational and national organizations. Extraordinary because these exercises, for the first time ever, not only question the traditional policy rationale but also challenge the moral/legal basis of the earlier exercises that ranged from the extermination of native populations, expropriation of their land and labour to "pacification". These policy devices forced them to surrender their lands for the European colonization project. A combination of these policy devices in some countries pushed the indigenous peoples away to the marginal areas of national territory (United States). In some, the state even pretended that they do not exist (Argentina) and in some forced them to be merged with landless peasants (Venezuela). In others, these policies allowed the state to "infantilise" them in order to bring them under the direct ward-ship of the state (Brazil). In some, they permitted the state to recognise them as citizens but without attendant political and economic rights (Australia). The consequence of these long years of forced coexistence with the colonisers/*conquistadores* led the indigenous peoples to experience severe depopulation, dispossession of lands and resources, dependence on dominant cultures, demoralizing social stigma and, above all, loss of their faith and face to live as indigenous peoples.

Seen against this long tortuous historical trajectory, the decades since the 1960s admittedly opened a new chapter in the life and destinies of the indigenous peoples the world over. Far-reaching and transformative changes occurred in the international arena largely thanks to the denunciations aired by the non-governmental organizations (NGOs) of the atrocities perpetrated on the indigenous communities. The first convention dealing specifically with the indigenous peoples of the International Labour Organization, the Convention on Tribal and Indigenous Populations, came into force in 1957 (ILO 107). The first European NGOs dedicated to the indigenous cause were the Danish International Work Group for Indigenous Affairs and the British Survival International as far back as the 1960s. The result was an increasing visibility of the struggle of the indigenous peoples as ethnic collectivities, distinct from that of other minorities. As developments of the subsequent years suggest—in 1971, the UN sub-commission on minorities (Human Rights Sub-commission for the Eradication of Discriminatory Measures against Minorities) distinguished the cases of native peoples from those of other minorities.

In 1974, for the first time an indigenous organization, National Indian Brotherhood, a Canadian organization, was given official voice at the United Nations. In 1977, Canadian Inuit delegates convened in Geneva to reject their inclusion in the statutes on minorities demanding to be classified as "peoples". A host of other developments took place through the 1980s and 1990s. The indigenous movements working with several of these United Nations templates for indigenous rights strove to create political space for groups to make claims on the basis of being distinct "people" rather than as an ethnic group or minority. Significant criticism of ILO Convention 107 by the indigenous peoples led to its revision in 1989 in the form of the Convention on Indigenous and Tribal Peoples in Independent States (ILO 169).[3] In 1985 the Working Group on Indigenous Populations had commenced drafting a declaration on the specific rights of the indigenous peoples. The UN Sub-Commission for the Protection and Promotion of Human Rights approved the draft UN Declaration on the Rights of Indigenous Peoples in 1994. All governments were expected to move towards its early adoption by the General Assembly. This was a major political goal within the UN Decade for Indigenous Peoples (1995–2004). The United Nations General Assembly finally adopted a non-binding declaration on indigenous rights in September 2007. The resolution was passed in spite of countries such as Australia, Canada, United States and New Zealand voting against the declaration.

Concomitant with or as a consequence of these developments, constitutional reforms and court judgements in different countries challenged the dominant imaginary of the nation by redefining the legal status of the indigenous communities and thereby transformed the meaning and substance of citizenship. Most of the Latin American countries saw a spate of such constitutional reform measures along

3. Article 7(1) of ILO Convention 169 provides that: The people concerned shall have the right to decide their own priorities for the process of development as it affects their lives, beliefs, institutions and spiritual well-being and the lands they occupy or otherwise use, and to exercise control, to the extent possible, over their own economic, social and cultural development. This article is one of the general principles of the convention and provides a framework within which other articles can be interpreted. Other general principles of the Convention require participation, consultation and good faith negotiation.

with the democratization process. Some countries adopted new constitutions, other countries amended existing constitutions.[4] In some instances, such as in Argentina's amended constitution, clauses with discrimination of any kind against the indigenous communities were removed. The amended provisions in the constitutions of Panama, Ecuador, Mexico, Paraguay and Bolivia not only recognized the cultural identities of the indigenous communities on the basis of their language, customs and religious practices but some even provided for education and training to the indigenous communities in their respective languages and dialects. Some among these countries proclaimed for the first time in their constitution that the language and culture of the indigenous peoples formed part of the national culture. Further, they enjoined the state not only to protect but also take necessary legal and legislative measures to promote the culture of the indigenous peoples.

One significant instance of the judiciary's initiative was the historic judgement that the High Court of Australia handed down in 1992. Known as *Mabo* decision, it set aside the concept of *terra nullius* (that land belongs to nobody) once and for all and provided the legal basis for the Native Title Act of 1993. Going against the wishes of the powerful mining capital, pastoral and state government interests, it was declared that under certain circumstances common law indigenous title to land had survived European conquest. Native title included other property rights such as usufruct rights like hunting, fishing and gathering rights. It was increasingly argued that since *Mabo* (No. 2) and the Native Title Act two systems of law were recognized in Australia and therefore this approach should be extended from real property to other areas like intellectual property, criminal justice and even self-government (Nettheim, 1995:113; Löfgren, 1995:10; Mercer, 1997). Indigenous rights are *sui generis* and therefore not dependent upon ownership of land. Thus fishing, hunting and gathering rights can survive even when other land-based rights such as native title are extinguished. This implied a renewed phase of indigenous empowerment and self-determination.

---

4. Guatemala (1985), Nicaragua (1987), Brazil (1988), Colombia (1991), Peru (1993) and Chile (1989 with 1997 reform) came up with new constitutions. Those countries with reforms in their constitutions were Mexico (1992), Paraguay (1992), Panama (1994), Bolivia (1994), Argentina (1994) and Ecuador (1983 and 1998).

That indigenous rights are *sui generis* (unique, or in a class of their own) also formed the basis of a decision taken by the Supreme Court of Canada in *Delgamuukw v Queen* in right of British Columbia.[5] It was found that aboriginal title or native title was derived from native occupation prior to assertions of British sovereignty and in part from pre-existing systems of "aboriginal law". So even in Canada aboriginal title was not limited to rights to use of land but included a beneficial interest including mineral rights (Bartlett, 1998:17). While early initiatives provided for basic territorial rights, over the subsequent years the focus has extended to encompass both historical and cultural rights. In the course of Canadian history, a very important development was the creation of Nunavut which became Canada's third territory in April 1999. This most recent boundary change is unique in that it is the result of an initiative by the Aboriginal inhabitants of the Territory. Indeed, eighty-three per cent of the 26,000 residents of Nunavut are Inuit, the aboriginal inhabitants of the area.

The evolving discourse underlines the indigenous "otherness". It also stresses a non-materialist and spiritual relation to the land and related resources, consensual decision-making, a holistic environmentalist approach, and the reestablishment of harmony in the social and physical worlds. Implicit in these values is also a critique of Western forms of authority and the sovereign nation-state model with its accompanying power to define democracy, citizenship, penal codes, jurisdiction and legitimate violence. The emerging indigenous discourse therefore engages the Western/modern state in terms of its political, legal and moral dimensions, with the terms of engagement in constant revision.

Indeed, the current discourse has contributed in significant ways to discussions of how the state itself needs to be restructured. The way indigenous activism plays out to gain strength and stridency with its current discourse undoubtedly varies from country to country. This, of course, is largely on account of the embryonic nature of the indigenous discourses of "difference". What, however, needs to be stressed is that it reflects the plurality of political tactics used by the activists to achieve cultural goals outside the realm of politics of the Westphalian nation-state model.

5. Delgamuukw v. British Columbia, [1997] 3 SCR 1010.

This, in turn, explains yet another novelty that relates to the new weapons with which indigenous movements and leadership defend themselves against the abuses of the nation-state. With some exceptions, inter-ethnic battlefields at the national level have now been relocated in news media, courtrooms and the legislatures. At the international level, the NGOs have been greatly instrumental in opening channels for the indigenous peoples to vent their grievances. Their singular usefulness is precisely in their role as political "switchboards" between local and global. The NGOs empower the indigenous peoples to bypass state resistance and launch their cause in the international arena. The logical chain seems to follow a fairly predictable pattern: the nation-state violates indigenous rights, indigenous people react, the NGOs intervene by submitting their case to international forums, international forums censure the nation-state, and the nation-state then takes measures to ease the pressure, however cosmetic they may be. This phenomenon of the second half of the twentieth century certainly was not available to the numerous indigenous communities who over the centuries have disappeared from the face of the earth, and in a sense, therefore, had become victims of another kind of "stolen generations".

Towards a Theoretical Framework for Indigenous Activism

From the foregoing descriptive analysis, some arguments emerge. The first relates to the dissemination of state concern over indigenous identity and activism. This, as has been pointed out, is in sharp contrast to the historical trend toward extinction, serfdom or assimilation. Some view this attitudinal change as an evidence of the global society's evolving interest in sustainable development. This environmentally wise approach is a recognition of the non-Western systems of knowledge such as those prevalent in indigenous cultures because their non-materialist and spiritual relation to the land and related resources adapts itself to the current discourses on sustainable development. However, there are those who argue that this apparent acquiescence to indigenous cultures is nothing but a strategy to integrate the indigenous communities and their resources into the world economy. In other words, they seem to view that this so called environmentally wise approach, in respect of its thrust, is no different from the same old Western developmentalist bias now cloaked in a "green robe" (Ramos, 2002).

However valid this line of argument, it does not preclude the motivations for the liberalization of indigenist policies throughout the world. Closely associated with the economic component of contemporary neo-liberal logic is the equally perceptible trend toward the reduction of the state. The "de-statizing" trend along side privatization has led, as in other sectors, the indigenous peoples, now allied with entrepreneurial NGOs, to shift their priorities from the advancement of nation-wide indigenous causes to issues such as community and local development. In other words, the "spirit of the age" and the "fundamental locus of human activity" is spun around self-governing community to meet the challenges of globalization. The indigenous peoples are moving away from their contestatory activities and are engaged in raising resources for purely local development (Beilharz, 1996).[6] In doing so, over time, political mobilization may not go well with self-management of local communities.

The second argument relates to the issue of class and ethnicity. Needless to state, this issue once generated heated debates and today, although much less absorbing, is still on the table. However, it is widely acknowledged that there exists a major difference in the ideologies that inform class and ethnicity. In one case—the class, there is quest for the uniformity of interests, and in the other—ethnicity, there obtains the quest for legitimate diversity. Again, ethnic awareness, like class awareness, it is recognized, emerges from specific historical processes, which can initially converge with class. But once created, ethnicity follows its own path. Succinctly stated, ethnicity once objectified assumes an autonomous character and adopts a trajectory of its own. Therefore, to subsume the logic of ethnicity under the logic of class, it is admitted is to miss its most significant attributes as social, cultural and political phenomenon.

6. Beilharz argues that if we are to live with weaker nations, but at the same time not give *carte blanche* to the various multinational unions and common markets that operate ministerially and bureaucratically, then vibrant, self-governing cities must again take a prominent role in government and culture. Beilharz identifies the 'spirit of the age' as the sense that time is right to return to the city as a fundamental locus of human activity from that of the state.

Against these formulations, juxtaposing indigenism as a *dependent* variable of ethnicity poses particular problems. For, indigenism and its attendant attributes such as self-identity and autonomy are rooted in a notion of inherent rights accruing to peoples who were there before the present nation-states arose. Put differently, it is rooted in the concept of "First Nation" underlining not simply social, cultural and political rights but recognizing primarily the inherent or historical rights of the indigenous peoples.

Just as ethnicity once objectified assumes an autonomous character and adopts a trajectory of its own, so with indigenous identity. It seeks much more than the other ethnic formations. It is double-edged in that it addresses the state both as an adversary and as an interlocutor. It seeks the state to endow on the indigenous peoples their inherent historical rights. Through its adversarial role and contestatory activities towards the state it has made positive, if marginal gains in respect of its primordial rights.

With these gains and in their effort towards reorganizing into self-governing local communities to exercise their autonomy, the indigenous communities now need the state to act as an interlocutor to guarantee their right to cultural survival in the wider society. This implies that the indigenous activists aim not only for autonomy in isolation but also for autonomous participation in a democratized polity. And it is exactly this double reflexivity that feeds into a process of reorganization and makes indigenous identity as an independent variable. Until now, this process was not manifest because of the asymmetrical power relations between the state and the indigenous peoples. With the tilt in the balance on account of the recent gains made by the indigenous activists and the simultaneous erosion of authority of the state, indigenous identity has introduced a new idiom viz. "pluriculturality" in the general discourse on ethnicity. What however needs emphasis here is that the delicate balancing act pluralism requires can only be performed in a thoroughly democratic environment that is conducive to intercultural dialogue and mutual accountability. This is necessary to avoid not only the hardening of positions but also a drift to fundamentalisms.

These then constitute the crux of the ongoing debate that informs the writings of most of those engaged in indigenous studies. The underlying objective of the foregoing descriptive analysis is not to close the ongoing debate but to further stimulate their development. After all, indigenous peoples have survived the trauma of colonization spanning five hundred years. Yet, today we see only a strengthening of their ethnic identity formation as they are participating in a variety of processes to negotiate and speak for themselves. No doubt, it is still too early to speculate about the future.

This compendium is intended to make a modest contribution to an understanding of the indigenous construction of self-identity and counter-images through the discourses involved. What it seeks to underline, however, is that further studies on the discursive construction of indigenous identities are indeed needed.

References

Bartlett, Richard. 1998. 'Casenote—Delgamuukw', *Indigenous Law Bulletin*, vol.4, no.9, p. 17.

Beilharz, Peter. 1996. 'Citizens of Cities'. *Thesis Eleven*, Issue 46, August, pp. 89–95.

Benhabib, Seyla. 1992. *Situating the Self: Gender, Community, and Postmodernism in Contemporary Ethics*. New York: Routledge.

Berndt, R. 1981. *Aboriginal Sites, Rights and Resource Development*. Perth: UWAP.

Bowen, John R. 2000. 'Should We Have a Universal Concept of 'Indigenous Peoples' Rights'?' *Anthropology Today*, vol.16, no.4, August, p. 12.

Clifford, James. 1997. *Routes: Travel and Translation in the Late Twentieth Century*. Cambridge: Harvard University Press.

Coe, P. 1994. 'ATSIC: Self Determination or Otherwise', *Race and Class*, vol. 35, no. 4, April-June, p. 37.

Cox, Helen et al. 1994. 'Two Laws, One Land', in Bourke et al, *Aboriginal Australia*. Brisbane: University of Queensland Press.

Escobar, Arturo and Sonia Alvarez E. eds. 1992. *The Making of Social Movement in Latin America: Identity, Strategy and Democracy*. Boulder: Westview Press.

Fleras, Augie and J.L. Elliott. 1992. *'The Nations Within': Aboriginal-State Relations in Canada, the United States and New Zealand*. Toronto: Oxford University Press.

Gutmann, A. ed. 1994. *Multiculturalism*. New Jersey: Princeton University Press.

Handler, Richard and Jocelyn Linnekin. 1984. 'Tradition, Genuine or Spurious' *Journal of American Folklore*, vol. 97, no.385, pp. 273–290.

Hanson, Allan. 1989. 'The Making of the Maori: Culture Invention and Its Logic," *American Anthropologist*, vol. 91, no. 4, pp. 890–902.

Hobsbawm, Eric. 1983. "Introduction: Inventing Traditions" in E. Hobsbawm and T. Ranger eds. *The Invention of Tradition*. Cambridge: Cambridge University Press.

Homborg, Alf and Mikael Kurkiala. 1998. *Voices of the Land: Identity and Ecology in the Margins*. Lund: Lund University Press.

Jackson, Jean. 1995. 'Culture, Genuine and Spurious: The Politics of Indianness in the Vaups, Colombia', *American Ethnologist*, vol. 22, no. 1, pp. 3–27.

Kymlicka, Will. 1995. *Multicultural Citizenship*. Oxford: Oxford University Press, 1995.

Linnekin, Jocelyn. 1992. 'On the Theory and Politics of Cultural Construction in the Pacific', *Oceania*, vol.62 no.4, pp. 249–263.

Löfgren, N. 1995. 'Common Law Aboriginal Property Rights', *Aboriginal Law Bulletin*, vol. 3, no. 77.

Maddock, K. 1984. 'Aboriginal Customary Law', in P. Hanks and B. Keon-Cohen, eds., *Aborigines and the Law*. Sydney: Allen and Unwin.

Mato, Daniel. 1992. 'Disputas en la Construcción de Identidades y "Literaturas Orales" en Comunidades Indígenas de Venezuela: conflictos entre narradores y papel de investigadores y editoriales' *Revista de Investigaciones Folklóricas*. Buenos Aries: Universidad de Buenos Aires. no. 7, pp. 40–47.

Mercer, David. 1997. 'Aboriginal Self-determination and Indigenous Land Title in Post-Mabo Australia', *Political Geography*, vol. 16, no. 3, pp. 189–212.

Nettheim, Garth. 1995. 'Mabo and Legal Pluralism: The Australian Aboriginal Justice Experience', in K. Hazelhurst ed., *Legal Pluralism and the Colonial Legacy*. Avebury: Aldershot.

Ramos, Alcida Rita. 2002. 'Cutting through State and Class: Sources and Strategies of Self-Representation in Latin America', in Kay B. Warren and Jean E. Jackson, *Indigenous Movements, Self-Representation and the State in Latin America*. Austin, Texas: University of Texas Press.

Sanders, William. 1993. 'Reconciling Public Accountability and Aboriginal Self Determination/Self Management', *Discussion Paper No. 51*, Centre for Aboriginal and Economic Policy Research, Australia National University.

Taylor, Charles. 1994. *Multiculturalism*. New Jersey: Princeton University Press.

Todorov, T. 1984. *The Conquest of America: The Question of the Other*, trans. R. Howard. New York: Harper & Row.

Tully, James. 2000. 'The Struggles of Indigenous Peoples for and of Freedom,' in David Ivison, P. Patton and W. Sanders, eds., *Political Theory and the Rights of Indigenous Peoples*. Cambridge: Cambridge University Press.

United Nations Economic and Social Council, Preparatory Committee for the World Summit on Sustainable Development, Second Preparatory Session, 28 January–8 February 2002, E/CN.17/2002/PC.2/6/Add.3

Walzer, Michael. 1997. *On Toleration*. New Haven: Yale University Press.

Wolf, Eric R. 1984. *Europe and the People without History*. Berkeley, California: University of California Press.

2

The Return of the Native: The Indigenous Challenge in Latin America

Rodolfo Stavenhagen

Some years after Cortés conquered Tenochtitlan almost five centuries ago, the chronicler Bernal Diaz del Castillo wrote that had it not been for Malintzin, an Indian woman who served Cortés as interpreter, the conquest of the fabulous Aztec empire might not have taken place. Malinche, as she came to be called, has since been portrayed in Mexico's nationalist historical accounts as a traitor to her people and the term *malinchismo* became synonymous with kowtowing to foreign interests and selling out one's country.

But times have changed: recent appraisals have re-written the story and now Doña Marina, as she was baptized before Cortés gave her in marriage to one of his followers, is hailed as the first exponent of an inter-cultural dialogue that has lasted for half a millennium, a multicultural heroine before her time, who was able to navigate her way among different languages, civilizations, and religions better than any of the accompanying males. She has been turned by some admirers into a feminist icon, the advisor of warrior-chiefs, the interpreter of conflicting interests, the mediator between clashing ideologies, and—why not?—the primal mother of a new race: the mestizos, who came to dominate the history of Latin America in later centuries. Times have changed indeed.

Indian heroes and Indian villains have populated Latin America's symbolic universe for five hundred years. Whereas Tupac Amaru rose against the Spanish overlords in Peru in the late eighteenth century and attempted to reconstruct the Inca kingdom (an initiative for which he was drawn and quartered), Benito Juarez, a son of the Zapotec nation as he described himself, became president of Mexico in the mid-eighteen hundreds, fought the French empire, and has since been revered as one of nationalist Mexico's great civic heroes. He also decreed the disappearance of the communal lands and territories of

Indian communities in the name of progress, sentencing most of the country's peasant population to ruin, poverty and despair.

In 1992 the world commemorated the fifth centenary of Columbus' fateful voyage in 1492, and the event gave rise to acrimonious international debates. The Hispanophiles wished to celebrate the anniversary of the "Discovery of America" and Spain's "civilizing mission", whereas the Hispanophobes denounced the European invasion which resulted in the genocide of millions of natives in the Americas. Historians waged academic battles over the matter, and the media jumped gleefully into the fray. A compromise was reached to name the event the "Encounter of Two Worlds", which gave satisfaction to no one but allowed the United Nations to solemnly celebrate the occasion. Indigenous peoples, who had hardly been consulted about the matter, spoke prophetically of "500 Years of Resistance" and succeeded in having the United Nations proclaim the International Year (1993) and two International Decades of Indigenous Peoples (1995–2014).

Nineteen-ninety two is also the year Rigoberta Menchú was awarded the Nobel Peace Prize for her contribution to the struggle for peace and human rights carried out under conditions of great adversity in Guatemala. Her celebrated memoir, *I, Rigoberta Menchú*, became a world best seller and placed the desperate situation of the Maya people in the limelight of international attention. Yet a few years later a storm broke over Rigoberta and her *testimonio*, when an American anthropologist challenged the factual accuracy of her account. The controversy fueled a minor culture war in American academe and was eagerly picked up by those who were determined to delegitimise the claims of Guatemala's Indians to justice and dignity. What right had a semi-literate young Maya woman to question official truths? In a curious twist of logic, the victim became a culprit and her supporters dupes. In 2007 Rigoberta Menchú, now an experienced and well known actor on the international scene, decided to become a candidate for the presidency of Guatemala.

From Malinche to Menchú, the natives of Latin America have always been seen as a "problem" by members of the dominant society, who typically refuse to recognize that it is this very society that constitutes an unresolved "problem" for millions of indigenous people in the region. Yet in the tangled web of fact and fiction, legends and lies, memory and myth, rebellion and resistance, indigenous peoples have re-emerged in recent decades as new historical subjects, assertive actors in those fragile and incomplete Latin American democracies that brave the tempests of globalisation.

Whilst during the colonial period indigenous peoples had a fixed status in society, ever since the emergence of the region's independent republics, they have been involved in an uneasy and ambiguous relationship with the State and its institutions. As Latin American countries enter the new millennium, they are now faced with the task of reassessing this relationship in the light of the new emerging Indian identities that articulate old grievances and express new demands. The once fashionable theories of social change, modernization and nation-building which dominated social science thinking for over a half-century are now being challenged by the new social movements of indigenous peoples and their developing political ideologies. Will the new millennium bring redemption at last or are we only witnessing one more of those passing social trends that rise and wane in response to external circumstances? Let us attempt to fill in the picture on this amazing development.

Ever since the Europeans first came to the shores of the American continent to conquer and settle, indigenous peoples suffered discrimination, exploitation and racism. Much of the colonial wealth of Europe was based on the use of Indian labor in the mines and fields. Indigenous cultures were destroyed or subordinated to the dominant Hispanic Catholic mold. In some parts of the continent, widespread physical destruction of indigenous societies took place, which is today referred to as genocide and constitutes a crime against humanity.[1] To be sure, the Spanish colonial empire adopted certain measures for the protection of its native vassals, yet they were soon decimated as a result of military conquest, ecological destruction, forced labor and the lethal diseases such as smallpox and measles introduced by the invaders, against which they had no immunity.

The nineteenth century brought independence and a new legal and political system in which Indian populations in most countries were recognized as equal citizens. Nevertheless, the expansion of agrarian capitalism and the modernization of the economy did not bring them many benefits. On the contrary, numerous indigenous communities lost their lands and were forced to provide servile labor on the large estates. Despite holding legal citizenship rights, they were

1. The Convention against the Crime of Genocide was adopted by the UN General Assembly in 1948.

in fact excluded from equal participation in the economic, social and political system. Special legislation often placed them at a disadvantage in relation to the rest of society and in some countries, Indians were treated as minors and legally incompetent until recently.

When the Spanish-American republics achieved their political independence in the early nineteenth century most of them were populated by a majority of Indians, but the power holders were the *criollo* elites, the direct descendants of the Spanish colonial ruling class. Indians remained, as it were, at the bottom of the heap. Indian oppression in the new republics was two-fold. On the one hand, the landowning oligarchies that spread out and consolidated their economic power during the nineteenth century reaped the benefits of the privatization of Crown lands, ecclesiastical estates and traditional holdings of the Indian communities. Soon the remaining Indians were pushed into frontier areas, inaccessible mountain ranges, arid wastelands and impenetrable jungles, while the new *latifundistas* and *hacendados* (large estate owners), and in later years waves of immigrant settlers, took over the best acreages and pastures. In some areas the land was cleared *manu militari* in genocidal "pacification" campaigns. Generations of Indian peasants were forced into peonage and forced labor, and eventually into rural migration circuits and out-migration, a process that has not yet ended.

By the twentieth century, micro subsistence holdings and landlessness had become characteristic of the Indian peasantry, leading to agrarian uprisings and revolutions and to multiple experiments with land reforms. The first such reform came into being after the Mexican revolution (1910–1917) and it transformed the rural landscape in that country. Massive land transfers from the estate sector to peasant communities took place especially during the decades of the nineteen thirties. A later experiment in land reform was undertaken after the 1952 political revolution in Bolivia. A progressive democratic regime attempted to implement a similar transformation in Guatemala in the early fifties, but it ran into the violent opposition of the US-owned banana plantation owners who organized, with the help of the CIA, a military coup in 1954 that introduced almost half a century of violent repression, revolutionary movements and civil wars. In Peru, a nationalist and populist military regime responded to Indian peasant mobilization in the Andean highlands in the late sixties, but the experiment did not last more than a decade, when other military rulers phased it out. In all of these countries, Indian peasantries were at the center of conflict.

The Cuban revolution and its land reform legislation in the early sixties was perceived by the ruling oligarchies of Latin America as highly threatening to their stability because of its influence on the rest of Latin America. In response to this "Communist" threat, the Kennedy administration in the United States proclaimed the Alliance for Progress, a program designed to mollify peasant demands and to stem the appeal of the Cuban revolution through the enactment of mild land reform legislation and some economic aid to a number of Latin American governments.

The Sandinista revolution of 1979 intended to carry out land reform in Nicaragua, which came to naught a decade later when the Sandinistas were voted out of power. A similar fate befell the Chilean land reform during the years of President Salvador Allende, which was cut short by the military coup of 1973. Sometimes Indian communities did indeed receive some land and benefits, in other instances land reforms simply passed the Indians by. Consequently, access to land has become a major claim of indigenous organisations and the subject of continuous disputes between Indian communities and the State in much of Latin America.

A second feature which definitively marked the situation of indigenous peoples within the State, was the non-recognition of Indian cultural and social identity as part of national society. The founding fathers and intellectual elites of the fledgling republics grandly ignored demographics and based the projects of their national societies on their self-perception as a Western, Catholic, racially European people. Indians and Africans were excluded from this project. These ruling groups tried hard to be accepted at the court of Western civilization and to build nations in the image of Western political and economic models. They borrowed their legal systems and public administrations from Spain and France, their political constitutions from the United States, their economic liberalism from Great Britain, their military codes from Prussia. They wished to improve their racial stock in true Darwinian fashion and imported immigrant settlers from Europe. Indians and Africans were considered a burdensome obstacle to nation-building. Wherever it was impossible or too cumbersome to eliminate the latter physically, they were either segregated in the backlands to wither away or remain as an inexhaustible supply of cheap labor, or else they were forced or encouraged to shed their evil cultural ways and become "nationalized" as it were, that is, to turn into useful citizens of the state according to the hegemonic cultural model.

Indians, Mestizos and State Policies

Moreover, the *criollo* elites were gradually challenged by the growing mestizo population, who came to occupy the ethnic middle ranks and frequently became identified with middle-class political parties and nationalist politics. Indians and their cultures were expected to disappear. Acculturation and *Ladinoization* (becoming Ladino or Mestizo) were seen as inevitable processes, a part of the general tendency towards modernization. The latter alternative became official *indigenista* policy in the twentieth century, when governmental programs stressed assimilation and integration of the indigenous through communications and road building, the market economy, education and community development.[2]

Indigenismo became the domestic expression of assertive nationalism and populism in the twentieth century. It was, during the early decades, a generous, inspiring, progressive ideology. Its proponents, mainly mestizo anthropologists, were convinced that they were not only serving their countries well but helping the indigenous overcome their many limitations on the way to becoming modern useful citizens. Directed culture change and applied anthropology were the conceptual tools necessary for this grandiose enterprise: soon our countries would become modern and Indians would be only relics of a picturesque past. Indeed, magnificent museums—such as the one in Mexico City—were built to pay homage to the great dead civilizations of the past and to symbolize the strong Indian roots of the contemporary mestizo nation.

As defined by the then prevailing nationalist ideologies which had arisen during the preceding century, the urban mestizo middle class intellectuals and their political offshoots usually rejected outright the indigenous components of the national culture and actually saw no future for them, except in an idealized past whose privileged locus turned out to be the museums, and more recently as an instrument for earning foreign exchange in the form of tourism and handicrafts. *Indigenismo* evolved into a set of social policies intended to "integrate" the numerous Indian communities and tribes into the life of the nation, as defined by the governing elites. It has always been the instrument of the national state for dealing with the Indians, rather than a process whereby the Indians themselves could determine their own destiny.

2. The first Inter-American Indianist Congress, held in 1940, established continental guidelines for the national integration of Indian populations.

Latin America's ruling classes, unable to wish Indians away, have always been quite happy to build nations without Indians. To their discomfort, as the new millennium unfolds, not only are indigenous peoples still there—and their numbers are rising—but they are actually challenging the very model of the nation-state that the ruling groups have been trying so conscientiously to build up.

Who are the Indians in Latin America, and how many are there? Whereas criteria used in definitions vary from country to country and census data are notoriously unreliable, knowledgeable estimates consider that there are over 400 different identifiable Indian groups, with a total population of close to forty million, that range from some numerically insignificant, almost extinct jungle bands in the Amazon to multi-million strong peasant societies in the Andes. Mexico has the largest indigenous population in Latin America, of between 12 and 15 per cent of the total population of around 100 million. In Guatemala and Bolivia Indians make up the majority of the national population, and in Peru and Ecuador they come close. Though Brazil's Indians represent less than one half per cent, as the original inhabitants of the Amazon basin they have played a significant role in recent years, resisting encroachment upon their territories, claiming land rights and political representation, struggling for the preservation of the Amazon environment and achieving their incorporation into the new Brazilian constitution adopted in 1988.

The rise of indigenous organizations over the last three decades may be considered both as a cause and effect of the transformations occurring in the public sphere regarding indigenous peoples in Latin America. Back in the nineteen sixties there may have been only a handful of formal organizations created and run by indigenous persons and pursuing objectives of interest to indigenous peoples as such. By the turn of the century we are speaking of many hundreds of such associations, of all types and kinds: local level organizations, inter-communal and regional associations, formally structured interest groups, national-level federations, leagues and unions, as well as cross-national alliances and coalitions with well developed international contacts and activities. Indigenous organizations, their leadership, objectives, activities and emerging ideologies, constitute a new kind of social and political movement in contemporary Latin America.

One of the earlier successful organizations, is the Shuar Federation, established in the early sixties to protect the interests of the various dispersed Shuar communities in the Amazon lowlands of eastern Ecuador. The Shuar decided to form their federation to defend their land from encroachment by outside settlers and commercial interests, and in the process discovered that the struggle over land rights could not be separated from their survival as an ethnically distinct people with their own traditions and cultural identity.

Similar organizations emerged during the seventies in several other countries, and they consolidated their activities during the nineteen eighties. While often community based, some were able to build larger units, involving an increasing number of local communities and emphasizing ethnic identity as a unifying bond and a mobilizing agent. A number of ethnic organizations began to appear on the political scene, whose leaders would speak in the name of the ethnic group as such rather than for this or that particular rural community. This level of organization was soon followed by region-wide associations, involving several ethnic groups. Thus arose the Confederation of Indigenous Nationalities of Amazonic Ecuador (CONFENAIE), the Indigenous Association of the Peruvian Jungle (AIDESEP), the Regional Indigenous Council of the Cauca Valley (CRIC) in Colombia, the Indigenous Confederation of Eastern Bolivia (CIDOB), and many others. They all held conferences and congresses, published manifestos and platforms, addressed petitions to state and national governments, as well as the international community, and often organized militant actions such as protest marches, demonstrations, sit-ins, and land occupations, practiced active resistance, or initiated legal proceedings, lobbied legislatures and public officials, to further their various objectives.

A more recent level of organization became the country-wide indigenous confederation. Again, the Ecuadorean Confederation of Indigenous Nationalities (CONAIE) has been in the forefront of political activity, by organizing two major peaceful indigenous "uprisings" in Ecuador in 1990 and 1993 that practically paralyzed the country and forced the national government to negotiate with the indigenous peoples over agrarian and other issues. Later they organized their own political party and in January 2000 they joined a group of army officers, staged a coup and ousted an elected president before they were forced to withdraw. In 2006 they allied themselves once again with a winning presidential candidate. They had finally arrived in Latin American politics.

The Brazilian Union of Indian Nations (UNI), made up of numerous Amazonian tribes, played a crucial role in the political discussions leading up to the drafting of the constitutional article devoted to indigenous peoples in the Brazilian constitution (1988). Similarly the *Organización Indígena de Colombia* (ONIC) took an active part in the national political debates that resulted in Colombia's constitution of 1991, and indigenous movements were actively involved in the drafting of the new Venezuelan constitution of 1999.

Indigenous organizations have also reached out beyond their country's borders to become involved in international activities. Particularly relevant has been their participation in the United Nations Commission on Human Rights (now the Human Rights Council), which adopted a Declaration on the Rights of Indigenous Peoples in 2006. A similar regional declaration is being prepared within the framework of the Organisation of American States. In the meantime, a number of states in the Americas have ratified Convention 169 of the International Labour Organisation that refers to the rights of indigenous peoples.

They regularly attend meetings at the United Nations and have actively supported the establishment of the Permanent Forum on Indigenous Issues and the appointment of a Special Rapporteur on the Human Rights of Indigenous Peoples by the UN Human Rights Commission. They have also successfully sued the government of Nicaragua in the Inter-American Court of Human Rights for a violation of their internationally and constitutionally recognized land rights. This Court as well as the Inter-American Commission on Human Rights have in recent years ruled favorably on the rights of indigenous communities.

A careful analysis of the declarations, resolutions and statements produced by these organizations and congresses would show a progression of ideas and a sequence of issues of concern to their members over time. In earlier years, indigenous manifestos would remind the public at large of their historical victimization and their secular poverty, and demand some kind of overall retribution and justice from governments. At the same time, a persistent theme in many of these documents was a certain idealization of the Indian pre-Columbian past, depicted as a kind of "Golden Age", a period without exploitation, discrimination and conflict, even as Indian cultures are described as morally superior to Western civilization.

In later years, the demands put forward by indigenous organizations became more focused on specific issues such as land, agricultural credit, education, health, technical aid, investments in infrastructure and so forth, issues that the State is expected to solve. More recently, socio-economic demands have been coupled with calls for autonomy and self-determination. Ethnic identity has become a rallying point for many such organizations, concern over the ecology is now a major issue of contention, particularly in the Amazon lowlands, and increasingly there are demands for legislative changes and compliance with recent international legal instruments. At international meetings indigenous representatives are increasingly putting forward constructive proposals involving new legislation and social and economic policies. The new slogan of some of the indigenous movement is: "From Protest to Proposals".

Who represents the indigenous peoples? The traditional village elders are being displaced by a younger generation of cultural brokers. As more and more indigenous professionals appear, an intellectual indigenous elite has emerged in several Latin American countries that is becoming the life-blood of the new organizations. Indigenous intellectuals are actively engaged in developing the "new indigenous discourse" that gives these organizations their distinctive identities. They are not only involved in formulating the political agendas of their movements, they also rediscover their historical roots, are concerned with language, culture and cosmology, and become actively engaged in "inventing traditions" and building "imagined communities". To the extent that this *intelligentsia* participates in national and international networks and is able to mobilize material and symbolic resources, indigenous intellectuals have become indispensable links in the process of organization and mobilization.

In Mexico, for example, the first formal indigenous associations beyond the local level were organized by Indian schoolteachers working for the federal Ministry of Education. They had been trained to teach in bilingual grade schools in Indian villages. A National Association of Writers in Indigenous Languages brings together native students of indigenous oral traditions as well as creative writers, most of whom are at the same time employees of the government or active academics. During the tragic years of civil war and military repression in Guatemala, Indian mobilization frequently took place through innocuous-sounding associations for the preservation and study of Maya culture, by which an emerging Maya identity has become crystallized.

On the other hand, the indigenous leadership also draws support from the "grass-roots", from local activists engaged in struggles against human rights abuses, or for land rights, or over environmental concerns, issues in which indigenous women are often especially active. Sometimes there appears to be a tension between the grass-roots activists and the intellectuals, because the former are concerned with more immediate issues and push for concrete solutions, whereas the latter are more involved in institution-building over the long term. Moreover, whereas indigenous intellectuals are contributing to the development of an "Indianist" ideology and *Weltanschauung*, and also at times find themselves engaged in discussions with various other ideological tendencies in Latin America (nationalism, Marxism, liberation theology, Christian democracy, evangelical protestantism etc.), grass-roots activists do not have much patience for intellectual debates and are more interested in negotiating specific issues with "the powers that be" rather than aspiring to ideological coherence or purity. These various approaches, as well as other factors, have led to not a few disputes over organizational matters, strategy and tactics that sometimes give the impression of a very fragmented and factionalised indigenous movement.

There are a number of factors which may account for the rise of indigenous awareness and the emergence of these new social movements on the public scene. In the first place, mention could be made of the overall disenchantment with, and the failure of, traditional development policies which were assiduously pursued by national governments and multilateral organizations since the end of the World War II. "Economic development" was the magic slogan wielded by generations of government planners and academics, that would bring improved living standards and burgeoning incomes to the poor, the marginalized, the backward populations of Latin America. This did not happen, as the "lost decade" of the nineteen eighties so clearly showed. Indigenous populations were indeed drawn into the "modern" sector of the economy through market mechanisms, labor migrations, expanding infrastructure in means of communication and transport, but they saw the benefits of growth going, as always, to the elites. A World Bank study reports that the indigenous populations are for the most part poor or extremely poor and that their living standards are "abysmal". This fact was not lost on the emerging Indian *intelligentsia* who soon became skeptical of upbeat economic projections, government promises, and predictions about their imminent accession to progress and civilization. Disillusionment with mainstream development strategies was shared widely, beginning in the nineteen seventies, and the search for "development alternatives" often focused on the local grassroots level which would naturally include indigenous communities. Things have not changed since then. The Inter-American Development Bank reports that poverty and underdevelopment has increased in Latin America over the last decade, and a study carried out by World Bank indicates that in ten years there has been no significant change of development indicators among indigenous peoples in the region.

A second factor accounting for the rise of indigenous movements, was the increasing awareness by the emerging Indian intellectuals that the modern nation-state which the mestizo elites had been building so assiduously ever since the nineteenth century was fundamentally flawed. Instead of being all-inclusionary, it was in fact exclusionary: Indian cultures were denied, Indians were victims of subtle or open racism and discrimination; indigenous peoples (even when they constituted demographic majorities as in Bolivia and Guatemala, and in numerous sub-national regions elsewhere), were excluded from economic well-being, social equality, political decision-making processes, and access to justice in the legal system. Indians could not recognize themselves in the prevailing model of the "national" state, as fashioned by the mestizo and white upper-class elites.

European elites, and government assimilationist policies made it clear that indigenous cultures had no future in the modern nation-state. Despite formal citizenship indigenous peoples have in fact been treated more frequently as second-class citizens. Many indigenous persons in fact interiorized the stereotypes and stigmas imposed on them by the dominant sectors, and resorted to self-denial and self-denigration in order to become accepted by non-Indians. Others developed a "culture of resistance", turning inward, avoiding contact as much as possible with the outside world. Still others, realizing that the existing model of the nation-state denies them their identity and their very survival as viable cultures, have begun to challenge the dominant mainstream notion of the nation, by proposing alternative conceptions of a multi-cultural, poly-ethnic state. This is one of the demands that the new indigenous movement has been putting forward in recent years.

The more traditional political parties and institutions of government and the civil society were slow in recognizing the significance of the emerging indigenous movements. During the nineteen eighties, however, a number of processes and tendencies impinged upon public debates. At the international level, cold war ideological confrontation in Latin America came to a virtual end with the break-up of the communist world, although the US still actively pursued it in Cuba, El Salvador and Nicaragua. Secondly, the global economy, which had never been absent from Latin America since colonial times, reaffirmed its impact on the rural areas, including indigenous territories, as in the Amazon basin, Central America, southern Chile and elsewhere, generating tensions and conflicts between Indian peasantries, state institutions and trans-national corporations. Thirdly, a cycle of authoritarian military interventions in politics (which had been linked to the "national security ideology" of the cold war era) came to an end, and a number of Latin American polities began what has been grandly (and perhaps somewhat over optimistically) called a democratic transition, liberating the forces of civil society for electoral competition and opening a formerly restricted political space to new or re-emerging social actors.

The struggle for democracy gave rise in Latin America to an articulate and militant human rights movement, which soon became deeply involved in the issues of indigenous peoples. The Inter-American Commission and Court of Human Rights were increasingly besieged by complaints concerning human rights abuses against indigenous people, and relevant UN committees received reports and complaints on the situation of indigenous human rights. It is almost impossible to chronicle the many associations, caucuses, committees, councils, congresses, conferences, symposia, workshops and meetings that activated Indian agency where none or little had existed before. Many such organizations have not survived, others changed over the years, and still others grew and developed true to the stages and cycles of the various theories of social movements.

The new Indian movement in Latin America has not yet produced a specific coherent ideology, and perhaps it has no need for it. But it is developing a new discourse, which has changed the way the wider society sees the Indians and the way they see themselves. Most of all, the movement and its various expressions are changing the relations between indigenous peoples and the State. In this context must be placed the constitutional and legislative changes that were made in the last two decades of the century in a number of the region's states, legally enshrining indigenous rights, in many cases for the first time. To mention only a few: Bolivia, with a majority of Indian population, amended its constitution in 1994 and adopted special laws recognizing that the country is multi-èthnic, multi-cultural and multi-lingual. In 2005 for the first time Bolivia elected an indigenous president by a large majority, who is pursuing a social and economic agenda geared towards the demands of the indigenous electorate. Brazil's constitution of 1988 devotes an entire new chapter to the Indians. The 1991 constitution of Colombia grants important autonomic rights to its indigenous populations, and in 2007 Ecuador was engaged in a constitutional review along similar lines. The constitutions of Guatemala (1986), Nicaragua (1987), Venezuela (1999), Panama (1972), Paraguay (1992) and Peru (1993) have no less important constitutional statements. The latest constitutional reform on indigenous rights was adopted by Mexico in 2001.

In other countries, such as Argentina and Chile special legislation concerning Indians was adopted in the post-dictatorship years. While these legal advances are surely important in themselves, the open question is how the new legislation will be implemented and how Indian communities will benefit. The answer is not at all clear, because complaints are increasingly heard that the new laws are not being applied as they should, or that secondary legislation has not been adopted after general principles were laid down in the constitutions.

Students of these constitutional reforms point to several commonalities in the process:

1. the rights of indigenous peoples are recognized in the political constitution, rather than ordinary law or decree, giving them a higher symbolic and juridical rank;
2. in some cases (Colombia, Ecuador, Paraguay, and Venezuela) indigenous peoples themselves directly participated in the drafting of some of the new constitutions;
3. the new reforms present a new conception of national identity that is multiethnic and culturally diverse, which replaces a prior homogenizing national myth;
4. the new reforms recognize rights that are collective in nature, and that in some cases grant distinct powers or resources to indigenous communities or populations, as opposed to individuals; and
5. the new reforms restore the colonial tradition of recognizing the public authority and jurisdiction of indigenous authorities (usually at the community or municipal level) and self-

governing structures over some issues, including the exercise of indigenous customary law.

The struggle for indigenous rights is still in its infancy and after the promising beginnings mentioned before, the going will be rough from now on. There are several reasons for this, one being that the opponents to Indian rights have now been able to organise and mount a counter-offensive; another one, that after the first break-through on the political scene, Indians and their allies have not been able to set themselves clear short- and medium-term objectives, nor were they able to develop an effective political strategy to achieve their aims. This seems to have alienated a number of potential sympathisers in the general population and the political establishments. A case in point was the failed civil-military coup in Ecuador in January 2000, in which a prominent Indian leader played a key role. In Guatemala a referendum on the incorporation of indigenous rights into the constitution, as agreed upon in the 1996 peace agreement which put an end to over three decades of brutal civil war, did not receive majority approval contrary to widely held expectations. While there are increasing numbers of indigenous parliamentarians in many countries, who represent different political parties, there is no clear pattern of ethnic voting nor can any political party count on the automatic contribution of an indigenous electoral bloc. In general, it may be said that indigenous demands are channeled in other ways than through traditional electoral party politics, but this may change in the future.

A crucial issue today is the debate concerning demands for indigenous territorial autonomy, as well as access to, and control over their own natural resources. Some of the recent legislation recognizes these rights on paper, but they are difficult to implement. Litigation over such matters has now been taken up in international human rights institutions. In August 2001 the Inter-American Court of Human Rights found that the government of Nicaragua had violated the property rights of the Awas Tigni Indian community in granting logging rights to a foreign corporation on Indian lands in contravention of Nicaragua's own laws.

The Constitutional Court in Colombia has decided several cases in favor of Indian communities against actions of the government, based on the country's new constitution. The demarcation of recognized Indian lands and territories is a lengthy and often conflictive process, as in Brazil and Panama. The Mapuche of southern Chile are involved in a struggle against the privatization of their traditional territories, decreed during the Pinochet dictatorship.

The meaning of autonomy is ambiguous and its complexities are many. Most of the issues are not resolved in the new legislations, and specialists cannot seem to agree on the details. In fact, most governments in Latin America, permeated by a longstanding centralist tradition of authority are leery of autonomy, especially when related to indigenous peoples. The concept of autonomy and the self-determination of peoples has now become a point of honor for the indigenous movement, and self-determination appears at the top of the list of rights claimed in almost every indigenous political document. Progress on the draft declarations on indigenous rights is currently stalled within the United Nations and the Organization of American States in great measure because of lack of consensus on these points.

The Zapatista rebels in southern Mexico, who staged an armed uprising in January 1994, reached an agreement with the federal government after many months of negotiations in 1996, on which the government later reneged. In August 2001 the national congress approved a constitutional amendment that included some of the elements of the peace agreement, but the Zapatistas and the indigenous movement are dissatisfied with the outcome, claiming that the reform does not comply with the major points of the peace accord. An appeal to the Supreme Court by hundreds of indigenous municipalities was unsuccessful. Further negotiations between the government and the Zapatistas were interrupted and the historic conflict in Chiapas is as yet unresolved.

An equally conflictive issue concerns the controversy over individual versus collective rights. Countering the liberal state's assurances that every human being enjoys a packet of inalienable individual liberties, indigenous rights advocates argue that even the best of fundamental freedoms can hardly be enjoyed by ethnic groups and minorities who are systematically discriminated against and excluded by the power structure and the prevailing system of social stratification. Something more is needed, and this would be a bundle of group rights allowing the indigenous to fully live and reproduce their cultures, organise their lives according to their own social norms, maintain and develop their own collective identities, enjoy social, political and legal status as distinct groups in the wider society, and relate to this society and the national state on their own terms as recognized and respected peoples or nations.

No doubt the recognition of these collective rights requires a complete overhaul of the national state, of this "imagined community", the nation, which the *criollo* and mestizo elites created to serve their own interests. Arguably, individual human rights cannot be fully enjoyed by members of discriminated against subaltern groups, unless these are acknowledged as equal and full partners in all their distinctiveness and dignity within a nation-state. Thus the recognition of group rights may be seen as a condition for the enjoyment of individual rights, but they are not easily acknowledged in Latin America's legal systems.

Ethnic Cultures versus National Culture?

Behind many of the controversial issues over which indigenous peoples and the State in Latin America square off, none has raised more polemics than indigenous cultures and identities. The almost bi-centenary old idea of a single national culture has been put to a severe test by indigenous demands for bilingual and inter-cultural education and by the relatively recent legal recognition in some states that these countries are pluri-ethnic and multi-cultural. The current debate in Guatemala expresses these conflicting views rather well.

During the terrible years of the civil war, in which hundreds of thousands of indigenous people were murdered by the army, and many more became refugees, one of the few spaces of resistance of the Maya population were local cultural associations, which grew in numbers and activities after the middle eighties when the military ceded formal power to elected civilian governments. Indigenous intellectuals developed a new discourse of Maya cultural identity, which was strengthened by the signing in 1996 of the peace accord between the government and the guerrillas, the major agreements being the one on indigenous rights and culture. The Pan-Maya cultural movement spread rapidly and has contributed to changing both official discourse and the demands of political and social organisations. In a *Criollo* and *Ladino* dominated state, the majority Maya people have always been considered outsiders, and were effectively excluded *qua* Indians from the society and the polity. The civil war and the ensuing peace accord have changed all that. The various indigenous ethnic groups are now coalescing into a newly constructed Maya identity (including the revival of Maya religion—this in a traditional Catholic country in which Protestantism has made considerable inroads in recent years). Maya intellectuals and activists see themselves as opposing the hegemonic mestizo "national" identity, and claim for their people not only a major cultural role in the redefinition of the nation, but also political representation and access to power.

The Maya cultural movement has developed various theoretical and policy perspectives, and it speaks through different, sometimes dissonant, voices. For example, there is no agreement as to whether the Maya people are to be considered as only one nationality or many. Demerio Cojtí (a Kakchikel Indian who is vice-minister for multicultural education) speaks of 20-Maya nationalities in Guatemala alone (there are others in neighboring countries). Should the new politico-administrative divisions in the country be based solely on Maya ethnic identities, or also include *Ladinos*? Should political representation in congress reflect exactly the ethnic make-up of the country? How many of the Maya tongues should be recognized as official languages, and in what way shall multi-lingual and inter-cultural education be implemented in the school system?

The search for and the construction of a new Maya identity in Guatemala does not enjoy universal approval. The Maya culturalist positions have been attacked, among others, by some who would like to see ethnic identities subsumed in a wider class-based popular alliance, and those who argue from a *Ladino* perspective that Maya "essentialism" is no more than an artificial construct promoted by a host of internationally financed non-governmental organisations. According to this view, there is no such thing as a Maya nation or people, and Maya activists are accused of becoming anti-*Ladino* racists in turn, the only valid solution to Guatemala's problems being the development of an inter-cultural *mestizaje* in which Indians and *Ladinos* would learn to co-exist and interact on equal terms.

Half a century ago, when states in Latin America began to carry out policies for the development of indigenous communities, Indian populations lived mainly in isolated rural villages. Ten years ago, indigenous organizations complained that the celebrations the Western world was organizing around the quincentenary of the misnamed "discovery of America" was for them a time of mourning and remembrance. Today, indigenous representatives sit on United Nations bodies, in national parliaments and government cabinets. An emerging corpus of indigenous law is expressed in international legal instruments and national legislation. Indigenous peoples claim recognition and a distinct place in plural and multicultural societies. The traditional concept of the homogeneous national state has been challenged by the "return of the natives". Far from disappearing in a mestizo melting-pot, over 400 indigenous groups in Latin America demand attention to their rights and problems, an end to racism, discrimination, poverty and social exclusion. Indigenous peoples claim lost lands and territories, respect for languages and cultures, the right to practise their laws and customs, and a measure of autonomy within the territorial state. Above all else, they want to be accorded a minimum of human dignity, which for so many centuries has been denied to them. Surely this is not too much to expect after half a millennium.

3

Identity, Indigenous Insurrections and 'A Different Equality'*

Carlos Montemayor

Ever since the sixteenth century, indigenous people have responded in a variety of ways towards the Indian policies (*políticas de indios*) of the Spanish Crown as well as the indigenous policies of the modern Mexican State. However, these reactions have not always been acts of passive resistance[1] (Montemayor, 2000). The reaction in the form of an armed uprising has posed considerable difficulty towards problematizing indigenous political responses.

Before dealing with our subject matter, let us at the very outset draw up a timeline. Tenochtitlán, the imperial capital of the *méxica*, was captured by the Spanish *conquistadores* in 1521. However, the last *Itzáes* of the Mayan resistance continued fighting over the waters of Lake Tayasal in El Petén as late as 1697. Thus, the conquest of the Mayan peoples was completed *de facto* only as the seventeenth century was drawing to a close, nearly two hundred years after the fall of Tenochtitlán. Meanwhile in northern Mexico, the last reserve of the insurgent Apaches, hitherto unconquered, was defeated by the Mexican army at Tres Castillos in the State of Chihuahua, in 1880. In this long drawn out process of wars against the indigenous peoples, to consider the fall of Tenochtitlan as the consummation of the conquest is merely symbolic, but not real. Between this symbolic date of 1521 and the possibly more realistic one of 1880, a number of armed uprisings took place. Some of these lasted for decades, like the so called *guerra de castas* (the Caste-Wars of Yucatan), or the Yaqui War in Sonora.

---

* Translated from Spanish by Hari Nair, Facultad de Filosofía y Letras, Universidad Nacional Autónoma de México.

1. I have analyzed in detail the evolution of these policies in my book *Los pueblos indios de México hoy.*

Other uprisings broke out frequently, like the insurrections of the Ópatas and the Tarahumaras in northern Mexico, or those of the Mayas in *Los Altos de* Chiapas. Such prolonged struggles demonstrate the capacity of the indigenous peoples to re-structure their armed contingents as well as replace fallen leaders.

There were numerous indigenous rebellions during the colonial era in México. For example, there was one in the province of Pánuco and another in Chiapas in 1524, and yet another one in the very capital of the viceroyalty of New Spain, in 1531. Many of these rebellions and uprisings were either disguised or disqualified by the authorities as commotions or mutinies, depending on the size of the population inhabiting the territory, where such insurrections took place. Whenever the colonial authorities were forced to undertake military action, then and only then, did they recognize an uprising as insurgency. This was also the case with the insurgency of many indigenous communities in Nueva Galicia in 1541. It broke out in the valley of Tlaltenango, in the mountains of Tepic, and in the adjoining areas of Juchipila, Nochistlán and Teocaltiche. Soon, the rebellion was threatening to extend itself towards the central and southern regions of New Spain. The troops of Cristóbal de Oñate were defeated at the fortress of Mixtán, as were the troops of Pedro de Alvarado—the conquistador of Guatemala, who was killed immediately after his defeat at Nochistlán, by the weight of his horse that had lost its footing.

In 1761, there occurred an uprising of the Mayan peoples in Yucatan under Jacinto Canek, a very singular leader who was reputed to be a politician and a *curandero* (doctor of traditional indigenous medicine or *jmen* in Maya). This military campaign was arduous, and often, dangerous. The figure of Canek and the people of Cisteil, who were devastated by the Spanish troops, are landmarks in the history and literature of the province of Yucatan. Two notable Yucatan Creole writers—Ermilo Abreu Gómez and Roldán Peniche Barrera—have penned memorable chronicles of Canek.

Although the principal cause for these insurrections was the defense and possession of land holdings, sometimes the excesses of certain colonial authorities, like the *corregidores* or *alcaldes mayores*, were responsible for the uprisings. Such was the case with the rebellions in Tehuantepec and Ixtepec in 1660, and in *Los Altos de* Chiapas in 1712. On other occasions, an uprising was aimed at opposing government measures, like the hoarding of grains in Mexico City, in 1692. The indigenous miners took over the city of Guanajuato in 1766 demanding the suppression of militias, and against the monopoly of the state in the production and sale of tobacco. The insurrection in Real del Monte was prompted by demands for changes in work timings and salary (labor conditions).

Towards the end of the sixteenth century, the Acaxe Indians of Topia rose up in arms in the mountains of San Andrés in the State of Durango. In 1616, there occurred one of the most important uprisings in Nueva Vizcaya, by the Tepehuan Indians, who were allied to the Acaxes and the Xiximes. This struggle lasted for two years and broke out again in 1621, when the Nonoxes, the Ococlames, the Ocomes and the Cabezas, fiery warriors belonging to Bolsón de Mapimí, joined the fight as new allies. The same year saw the insurrection of the Tobosos and the Conchos in the Valley of San Bartolomé, south of the present-day State of Chihuahua. In 1644, it became necessary to launch an intense military campaign against the Tobosos, the Salineros, the Conchos, the Cabezas, the Julimes and the Mamites, who were devastating agricultural *haciendas*, grazing lands, and *reales de minas* like Mapimí and Parral.

Throughout the sixteenth and seventeenth centuries, the predominant reasons for indigenous uprisings in northern Mexico were also agrarian. Native Indians continued to believe that *hacienda* lands and mining zones belonged to them, and the Spaniards had usurped these. This explains their continuous, almost uninterrupted, insurgency against Spanish domination. The Seris, the Pimas, the Ópatas and the Rarámuris were protagonists of important struggles. The Spanish authorities repressed and brutally punished these northern insurgents, deporting and selling off as slaves those men who had come of age to handle weapons. The captives were shifted to La Acordada, a prison in Mexico City, before being distributed amongst the *hacendados* (owners of *haciendas*) in Veracruz, or, were sent to work in the fortifications in La Habana, Cuba. However, in other parts of Mexico, only the *caudillos* (leaders) were punished, while their 'followers' were pardoned.

During the nineteenth century, protracted and recurring insurrections often spread throughout the entire country. One of the most prolonged and intermittent struggles was the war of the Mayos and the Yaquis. The first rebellion broke out in 1825, under the leadership of Juan Banderas, and it continued till 1868 owing to recurrent uprisings and separatist politics. Since that year, the insurgents were led by Cajeme in their constant battles, until he was shot in Cócorit in 1887. Tetabiate took over command and agreed to surrender in May 1897, although he continued fighting till 1901. The war officially came to an end in 1904, but as late as 1908 the Mexican president Porfirio Díaz was informing the *Congreso* (the Federal Parliament of Mexico) of clashes with small bands of rebels.

The most important uprising by the Mayan Indians in Yucatan began in 1840, gaining singular thrust and turning cruel in July 1847, under the command of Jacinto Pat and Cecilio Chi, the latter being described in official histories as a bloody savage. In April 1848, Jacinto Pat agreed to sign a peace treaty with the governor, Miguel Barbachano. However, in the east of the peninsula, Cecilio Chi opposed the treaty and began warring again. The various stratagems of the authorities in the State of Yucatan gave way to one of the most abhorring aggressions against the American Indians: the sale of Mayan slaves to Cuba with varying tariff rates for bachelors, married men, women and children. The federal government of Mexico opposed these measures and suspended the defense subsidy to the government of Yucatan. On 26 May 1849, the governor protested before the Ministry of Foreign Affairs arguing that 3/5 of the population of the state comprised pure (unmixed) indigenes and it was necessary to reduce their population to maintain peace and equilibrium. The sale of Mayan slaves extended over a long period of time and affected not only prisoners-of-war but also pacific ones. Later, even the *mestizos* became victims of the slave trade. In March 1901, a powerful military campaign was initiated against the insurgents, who dominated the eastern part of the peninsula. The struggle officially came to an end on 1 June 1904, although combats were still being registered in 1906 and January 1909. After the pacification of this zone, it was separated from the State of Yucatan, in November 1902, to form the Territory of Quintana Roo. Two years later, the *Congreso* decorated president Díaz with the *Gran Cordón del Mérito Militar* for having unified the *patria*.

In 1848, yet again for defending their lands, the Indians of Sierra Gorda de Xichú in Querétaro rose up in arms. The insurrection spread to parts of Guanajuato and San Luís Potosí, and even affected Tamaulipas, Puebla and Michoacán. This insurrection coincided with the *guerra de castas* in Yucatan, the war of the Mayos and the Yaquis in Sonora, and with the battles that the natives of Juchitán (1847-51) waged against the owners of the *salinas* and the *haciendas* of the Marquis. The rebellion was put down with an iron hand by the governor of the State of Oaxaca, Benito Juárez, who feared that the *guerra de castas* would spread amongst the people of his region as well.

From 1856 to 1857, owing to *desamortización* (the confiscation of immovable property by the State) of the indigenous communities, or because of a shortage of lands, the Indians of central Mexico, Michoacán, Jalisco, Querétaro, Puebla, Veracruz and Morelos rose up in arms. Later, Manuel Lozada led another important insurrection in the present-day State of Nayarit. In 1868, a powerful rebellion by the inhabitants of San Juan Chamula broke out. It aimed to reinstate their ancient government and religion. A young lady called Checheb was ordained as priestess, and one of her nephews was crucified as the 'new Christ', a theme that Rosario Castellanos deals with in her novel *Oficio de Tinieblas*.

As regards this rebellion, we may affirm anew that the indigenous peoples were repressed in many aspects, not merely in economic and agrarian spheres. The religious data concerning indigenous insurrections are also relevant, even indispensable for understanding the scope of indigenous resistance and its social implications. Christianity exercised tremendous political pressure during the period of conquest, especially in central and southern New Spain; and, through the work of Franciscan and Jesuit missions in northern Mexico. Let us remind ourselves that the Church in Mexico was always Creole, occasionally *mestiza*, but never indigenous. The sequence of these religious elements could give us an additional clue for analyzing the struggle of the native Indians towards cultural vindication.

The most important insurrection during the colonial period in *Los Altos de* Chiapas occurred in 1712 (Montemayor, 1996:118–30). In general terms, it was the first process of *indianización de la religion* (indigenizing the Catholic faith), which was both reproached and persecuted by the civil and religious authorities of New Spain. The story began in 1708, when a ladino hermit vowed that an image of Virgin Mary had descended from heaven to help the indigenes. The Zinacantecos and the Chamulas constructed a chapel for worshipping the Virgin with offerings of food and incense.

The Virgin reappeared a second time in the autumn of 1711, in the Tzotzil region of Santa Marta. Dominica López was the first witness; her husband Juan Gómez had the same experience four days later, as did the traditional authorities of the village, the day after. They erected a chapel for worship at the site of apparition, and also placed images of the patron saints (*los santos patrones de los pueblos*) of the neighboring villages of Chalchiután, Magdalena and Huistán.

The chapel functioned as the principal religious forum during the period of lent in 1712, and witnessed an enormous congregation. The multitude of pilgrims alerted the ecclesiastical hierarchy, which immediately attempted to put an end to the cult and to deny the validity of the Virgin's apparition. Dominica and her husband, who were entrusted by the village with the care of the chapel and the sacred images, were apprehended and put on trial.

While Dominica López and Juan Gómez were being subjected to the trial, the Virgin appeared yet again. This time it was in May 1712, before a Tzeltal adolescent called María de la Candelaría, in the outskirts of the village of Cancuc. The Virgin ordered the girl to place a cross and a candle at the place of the apparition and to construct a chapel later. When the parish priest of Cancuc came to hear of the developments, *circa* 15 June 1712, he removed the cross with the purpose of shifting it to the temple, and ordered that the parents of the girl be flogged with a whip. The apparition was blamed as inventions of the devil. When the priest left Cancuc, the natives built a chapel at the site of the cross. A man called Juan Pérez declared before the authorities on 28 November of the same year that the chapel was built in a single day. On 23 June, the eve of the feast of St. John, a delegation of native authorities assembled at Chamula and pleaded with the bishop for his assent to preserve the chapel, for worshipping the Virgin. The bishop's reply was categorical. He ordered that all those present in the parish-house be arrested, and taken to the prison in Ciudad Real the following day.

It was at this moment that the indigenous insurrection broke out. The parish priest had to escape from the village and seek refuge in Tenango. The Indians wanted to persist with their cult and preserve the chapel dedicated to the Virgin, who had appeared in their defense and *only* to them. In the beginning of July, Sebastían Gómez de la Gloria, belonging to Chenalhó, turned up at Cancuc. He claimed to have spoken with the Holy Trinity, the Virgin Mary, Jesus Christ and St. Peter in heaven, and also claimed to have received their permission so that certain indigenes could act as priests in their communities.

From Cancuc, invitations were dispatched to other villages and the response was profuse. The events that occurred towards the end of June, which initially appeared to be restricted amongst the Tzeltals of Cancuc, were transformed into a grand alliance of thirty-two villages comprising the Tzeltals, the Tzotzils and the Chols. The communities sent their faithful to be ordained as priests and vicars. A majority of them had previously worked as aides to Spanish priests, and were familiar with the Catholic ritual. The literate ones were chosen so that they could maintain a register of the sacraments of baptism and matrimony, which were to be administered. All this meant that the indigenous clergy proposed to fulfill the same functions as those of the Spanish priests without modifying the ritual or the religion.

The significance of this cult was notable. The Catholic religion, which was a prerogative of the Spaniards, was now substantially modified and *it was even becoming indigenous*. The Indians modified the nomenclature of the adjoining cities, as the Zapatistas of the *Cañadas de los Altos* would do, two hundred years later, though for different reasons.

Victoria Reifler Bricker explains that:

> [t]he indigenes had changed the name of Cancuc to 'Ciudad Real', while the Spanish city that carried the latter name came to be called 'Jerusalem'. An Indian *audiencia* was established in Huitiupa, the name of which was changed to Guatemala, and a native was called on to serve as its president. The Spanish monarch was declared dead, and three Indians were crowned as kings of Cancuc, which was in turn named 'New Spain'. The *alcalde mayor* of Chiapas had passed away around this time but the post had remained vacant. The Indians named Sebastián Gómez as their *alcalde mayor*. The natives conceived of the Spaniards as akin to 'Jews', because they had persecuted the Virgin, the mother of Jesus Christ. Besides, the Indians also believed that the Spaniards were forbidden from the 'path to heaven', for they, like the 'Jews', did not believe in the Virgin of Cancuc. Thus, the Bible was reinterpreted in terms of the local ethnic situation, where the Indians assumed the role of the defenders of Jesus Christ and the Virgin, while the Spaniards were identified with the Jews deprived of salvation...(Bricker, 1989:126).

In the nineteenth century, during the *guerra de castas*, the proclamations of San Juan de la Cruz shared a similar discourse, on the basis of the presence of a miraculous speaking stone-cross in the village of Xocén, in the eastern part of the Yucatan peninsula. Instead of the Virgin, Christ himself spoke in this case. For example, the third proclamation of 1850 was as follows:

> That day has arrived, when Yucatan may rise up, once and for all, against the Whites. For this reason, I am giving you a sign, which you may safeguard in your hearts, because am falling at all hours, am being mutilated, am being nailed, am hurt with thorns, am hit with sticks, as I walk through Yucatan to redeem you…(Aban May, 1994:28–29).[2]

In the fourth proclamation of the same year, it was said:

> I order you one more thing, my dear Christian people: You must know that I have visited seven times by day, and seven times by night in the presence of my Father and in the presence of my Lady, the Sweet, Holy Virgin Mary for obtaining permission to initiate a war against the Whites for a second time, the war of my children—the Indians against the Whites … don't brutally kill your neighbours when they kneel or when they cross their arms across their hearts to name my Father, because they must not be killed. Because it is a mortal sin to kill a Christian when (s)he is kneeling and pronouncing the name of my Father. They must not be killed, only disarmed. When they are surrendering they must be set apart, whether they are Whites, Negroes, Indians, Mulattos, or whoever they may be, for they are our neighbors. (Aban May, 1994:29–30).

This means that one of the fundamental principles of the discourse of the Cross was equality, the recognition that all peoples—Indians, Negroes, Whites and *Mestizos*—were equal. Equality was the 'true' condition of all, even before God:

> Thus, my dear human children, don't you see how I am? My feet are hurting because of the nails. Don't you see the chord that is tied around my body, with which I am punished for the beauty of my Father and for you? Don't you see that I am hoisted on the Holy Cross, where innumerable angels and seraphs guard me? I am hoisted two blocks away from the house of my Lord and from there I speak to you. (Aban May, 1994:32).

---

2. According to the text of Santiago Domínguez Aké, in Benito Aban May *et al.*, *Yum santísima Cruz tun.*

At the beginning of the 1970s, in *Los Altos de* Chiapas, there was another important movement for 'equality'. The bishop of San Cristobal de las Casas oriented his pastoral work with the principles of Liberation Theology and prepared eight thousand catechists and four hundred deacons to work in two thousand five hundred communities. This was another kind of indigenous clergy whose origins may be traced to the cult of the Virgin of Cancuc (1712). The deacons could administer certain sacraments, particularly that of matrimony, and often they were the same people, who were at the head of agricultural organizations in demanding land and in settling issues of tenancy. The pastoral labour was based on the belief that Christianity *is* also for the Indians. That poverty, suffering and 'salvation' (liberation) of these people could be understood with the sufferings of the chosen people. In the light of the Bible and a profound notion of Christianity, the Indian was also considered as chosen. The native Indians reassessed themselves and began recognizing that their ethnic condition was not a barrier. This new process of *indianization* of Christianity reached huge proportions, with eight thousand catechists, and hundreds of deacons, *mayordomos*, *principales* and secretaries.

In many aspects, this process nourished a greater part of the contingents that supported or joined the *Ejército Zapatista de Liberación Nacional* (EZLN) on 1 January 1994. This continuous process of reiterating the 'equality' of the human and religious conditions, within indigenous reassessment and reformulation, was also a source that resonated in the uprising in Chiapas. It was relevant not merely because it was the last insurrection of indigenous peoples of the twentieth century, nor because it was the first of the twenty-first century. The 'nation' had periodically changed their historical, juridical and religious conceptions of the 'indigene'. The uprising of the EZLN obliged the country to change its conceptions anew, yet again. Notwithstanding, the Indian peoples did not anticipate that precisely at the end of the century they would still have to confront arguments concerning a 'different equality'.

In 1996, the government signed an accord with the delegates of the Zapatistas in a small village named San Andrés Larráinzar, which is located in *Los Altos de* Chiapas. The Zapatistas also refer to this village as San Andrés Sacamchén *o de los pobres* (or of the poor). The agreement proposed to concretize constitutional reforms with regard to indigenous rights towards conceding to the Indian peoples certain administrative and economic *autonomy* for the exploitation and conservation of lands as well as in their political and cultural organization. The peace negotiations were suspended because the proposals for reform were not being concretised. The *Comisión de Concordia y Pacificación* (Commission for Concordance and Pacification), which was created by the *Congreso de la union* (the Federal Parliament of Mexico) in 1995 to facilitate the peace process in Chiapas, had prepared a legal initiative on the basis of the agreements signed in the village of San Andrés. The EZLN accepted this proposal, but the president of the republic decided to consult a group of constitutional experts, who opposed it. One of them publicised his comments in early 1997, which revealed a total ignorance of the indigenous world as well as racist attitudes that were hardly subtle. It is possible that all the jurists concerned too suffered from this lack of knowledge regarding indigenous cultures and perhaps this was one of the negative factors. Paradoxically, a part of their juridical arguments could be traced back to the defence of the principle of equality before the law, *i.e.*, a 'different equality'.

When this principle was employed by the Constituent Assembly of 1824, 'the equality of citizens before the law' vindicated the rights of most Mexicans *vis a vis* powerful classes, both ecclesiastical and Spanish. But, at the same, this principle also annulled the agrarian and cultural rights of the indigenous peoples of Mexico. This notion of 'equality' served to negate the existence of indigenous peoples and ignored them as subjects of law.

In 1956, during the apogee of Mexican *indigenismo* of the twenty-first century (*indigenismo mexicano del siglo xx*), Alfonso Caso had explained:

> Nothing is more dangerous than considering as equal before the law, those who are not equal given their social and economic conditions .... The principle of equality before the law is just only when it is applied between equals. Proceeding from this principle, liberalism errs fundamentally on dictating laws that aim to restrict, without legislating adequate protective laws .... But, there are social and economic inequalities that can neither nor ought to be ignored, and so long as such inequalities exist, protective laws must be motivated instead of merely [promoting] restrictive ones. An agrarian legislation in Mexico that protects the farmer, [and]

> a universal legislative measure that protects the worker are consequences of a conception that is gaining greater acceptance world over [and, which believes] that there are certain social groups which are less than capable of defending themselves, who need protective laws. The indigene is in such a situation. (Caso, 1958:27–28).[3]

But there was a fundamental contradiction in the official arguments of 1997. Seven years earlier, the Mexican government became a signatory to the 169 Convention of the International Labor Organization. This convention was born out of the simple motivation that in many parts of the world the indigenous peoples and tribes did not enjoy human rights to the same degree as the rest of the so called national population. The convention proposed that the culture, religion, and socio-economic organization of these peoples be respected. The term 'people' is based on the idea that those referred to are neither 'inhabitants nor social sectors', but groups with their own identity and organization. The signatory states, which subscribed to this convention, are committed to reforming their national legislation in accordance with the clauses of the convention.

The convention was discussed in Geneva in June 1989. Norway and Mexico signed it in 1990, followed by Colombia, Bolivia, Costa Rica, Paraguay and Peru. The Mexican senate ratified the convention eight months later. The so called Agreements of San Andrés had incorporated the clauses of this convention. Thus, Mexico had subscribed to this convention thrice: in Geneva, in the Senate, and finally, in San Andrés Larráinzar. We may assume that in these three situations the Mexican government was ignorant that it was recognizing the concept of *autonomy* as the only path available to the Indian peoples. Of course, the Mexican federal government had not consulted with the jurists before signing the 169 Convention in Geneva in 1990, nor for ratifying it in the Senate in January 1991, nor for subscribing to the Agreements of San Andrés in February 1996.

We had noted that in the present-day State of Jalisco there arose for the first time the necessity of resolving a juridical question: 'Who could be considered as an Indian?' Responding to the query of the

3. See Alfonso Caso, 1958. This was initially a part of the preface to the book A. Lipschutz, 1956, *La comunidad indígena en América y en Chile*, Editorial Universitaria, Santiago de Chile.

Ayuntamiento (town council) of San Pedro Lagunillas, the senate of Jalisco had established, on 17 April 1826, that an Indian was one whom the public so considered. Thus, for the first time the Indians were not defined in racial terms, instead as communities that were so perceived *historically and culturally*. This query had sought a concrete answer to recognize and judicially incorporate a *subject of law*. The Agreements of San Andrés, which were signed towards the end of the twentieth century, and which were based on the 169 Convention, did not accede to public perceptions. Instead, the defining point was the self-affirmation of the Indian communities and the perceptible continuity of traditional norms of social and political organization. In 1996, the *Comisión de Concordia y Pacificación* proposed a definition for this 'new' juridical subject in accordance with that of the convention; but, as anticipated, the counter-proposal of the government eliminated such a definition of the indigenous peoples.

The social perspective of the first parliament of independent Mexico (1824) allowed for an internal organization of our country on the assumption that indigenous peoples did not exist. This fundamentally affected the municipal, provincial and national composition. Today, we are incapable of recognizing the real nucleus of indigenous political institutions, within certain social and cultural traditions, which were once inherent to Indian communities for centuries. Their communal vision regarding the possession of lands, collective labor, civil and religious responsibilities, political and family values is based on consuetudinary law, which is surprisingly equitable. These elements which constitute their communal vision form the real basis by which we may recognize their autonomy; not as a new political creation, but as a way of comprehending a part of the Mexican secular (or perhaps millennial) reality.

How must we understand the concept of socio-political 'institutions' as stated in the 169 Convention? For the time being, we must understand this concept with far greater implications than what the common phrase 'customs and practices' would permit. Let us explain this by taking the example of the Rarámuris or the Tarahumaras, which I have commented on elsewhere.

The exercise of justice amongst the Rarámuris is always a public act and is presided over by the *siríame*, who carries a staff or *disora*, signifying authority. The contending parties publicly explain their version of the matter and different members of the community intervene to opine and suggest remedies. If the interventions are successful in achieving a solution that is acceptable to all, it will be so recognized by the *siríame* and by the litigants. When that is not the case, the *siríame* gives his verdict and the traditional authorities issue the sentence. Only the extraordinary contumacy of the accused could call for a higher sanction or a general reprimand, because both the petitioner and the community desire the restitution of a right or property, not punishment.

Towards 1990, in one of his travels to the mountains inhabited by the Tarahumaras (*Sierra Tarahumara*), my son happened to witness a tragic incident in the *Munérachi* community, during the Easter ceremonies. Instigated by other groups, a young Indian killed his companion in a fight. The community was immersed in an enormous consternation, above all because the incident occurred during the ceremonies dedicated to the new sowing season. The authorities of Cieneguita de la Barranca imprisoned the survivor without giving a chance for the Tarahumara system of justice to come into play. It would have asked the survivor to support the spouse and the children of the deceased, since that very moment till the coming of age of the children, when they would be able to look after themselves. With our system of justice, both the families were left in the lurch: that of the assassin as well as that of the victim. My son, who was very young at the time of the incident, thought that it was absurd to leave two families in the lurch. "How could they think that the prison is more just?", he wondered.

In what we could designate as their system of inheritance, there is always a pairing of kinship and moral obligations. I know of this case in Guachochi, where a person had taken care of an old man for many years, and supported him in his house, till the old man passed away. When the wife and daughter of the deceased claimed their inheritance, the decision was the following: As the wife had not bothered at all for years about her husband, the *siríame* thought it fit to disqualify whatever commitment the old man had towards her. The daughter had not worried about her father either, but as she was his off-spring, the commitment of the deceased towards her must remain valid. While the other man, though unrelated, was the only one who supported the deceased, the lands were divided between the daughter and this man.

To understand such a conception of law, it is necessary to keep in mind that this is a case of the thought of the Rarámuris, the thinking of an entire community, not personal opinions. The conception that law is a matter concerning all consequently permits public trials, where everyone can participate, and always demanding the consensus of the community, with decisions and rulings that are collectively accepted.

The law of the Rarámuris seeks reparation of the damages, restitution of what was lent, recognition of obligations and rights, rather than punishing or condemning anyone for a crime. Amongst the Rarámuris, it would be impossible to imagine an idea of law and an application of justice that would not be accepted and recognized collectively. These 'social institutions' are, therefore, more than mere 'customs and practices'. These 'institutions' are based on cultural principles, which provide political and juridical cohesion to these peoples.

This does not involve the creation of a new social structure for the indigenous peoples; rather, the recognition of the reality of their traditional institutions. We must not privilege the law of the State; but must integrate into our juridical system the normative elements that are alive, and in fact, act within the national reality. Validating these systems would not put at risk the normative aspects of the country; on the contrary, it would only be complimentary. Such are the 'institutions', which are at stake in the constitutional reforms and not, as affirmed by one of the constitutional experts consulted, the human sacrifices on the pyramids in Mexico.

The concept of autonomy appeared towards the end of the 1980s as a symbol of struggle in various Indian communities of the continent and had its initial formulation in the *First Continental Congress of American Indians* held in Quito, Ecuador in 1990. Margarito Xib Ruiz and Araceli Burguete suggested in 1992, a couple of years before the uprising of the EZLN, that the Mexican national state was ethnocratic and that the indigenous struggles must modify it. They cited the argument of Rodolfo Stavenhagen:

> The ethnocratic state is not merely a structure within which the dominant ethnicity could exercise power and privileges at the cost of other ethnic communities or nationalities; what is more disturbing is that the dominant ethnic community (the mestizos, in the case of Mexico) tends to appropriate and identify themselves with the nation-state in its entirety. *i.e.,* in a world of nation-states, where cultural pluralism or pluriethnicity are not only condemned but are also frankly discouraged, the dominant ethnic group could present itself with relative ease as the only true nation, the real or authentic, or, at least, as the model to which other nations and ethnicities would have to adjust themselves within the limits of the state (Xib Ruiz and Burguete, 1996:18).

Margarito Xib Ruiz thought that the struggle for autonomy was indeed the path for the indigenous peoples of Mexico, Nicaragua, Colombia, Panama, Guatemala, Chile, Ecuador, Brazil, Bolivia and Canada. Even Europe was approaching a process of transition for recognizing the rights of the peoples in another form of the state. The creation of a multicultural state was the project of the American Indians in the present, and would be their program for the future as well. Spain, for example, had already constituted itself under the multinational format, *i.e.*,

> The state does not represent only one nation ('the Spanish nation'), but [it] represents the interests of diverse nationalities, which live together under the same State: the Galician nation, the Basque, the Andalusian, etc. (Xib Ruiz, 1996:22).

Indigenous organizations in the continent certainly seek the re-founding of a multi-national state. Nonetheless, at the beginning of the twenty-first century, the current projects of the Indian peoples in many of our countries do not merely aim at *autonomy* for indigenous communities; rather, the construction of another entity, historically invisible as yet. That entails the reformulation of the history of indigenous peoples as well as the constitutional reconstruction and the juridical recognition of the legal personae of the Indian communities. Will this history of resistance, restrictions and transformations of the indigenous peoples conclude in the twenty-first century? There are signs of changes in the indigenous movements in Mexico, and in the entire continent. But, there are no visible changes in the two agencies that give birth to indigenous policies: the governments and national communities that form a majority.

Glossary

Alcalde mayor: The governors of Colonial Mexico, especially in the Viceroyalty of New Spain, appointed deputies called *alcaldes mayores*, who acted as their permanent lieutenants in those territories that were located far from the capital city.

Audiencia: The *Audiencia* was the highest judicial office in New Spain and was presided over by the Viceroy.

Cañadas de los altos: The mountainous zone in the State of Chiapas is known as *Los Altos*, equivalent to the word, *highlands*. *Los Altos de* Chiapas has areas characterized by sharp cliffs and deep valleys, which are located inside the Lacandon jungles. These are called *Las Cañadas*, the principal scene of the Zapatista insurgency.

Corregidor: The *corregidor* is a local administrative functionary of the Crown. Although the *corregimiento* was borrowed from Iberia, the role of the *corregidor* in New Spain was different. He acted as magistrate, tribute collector and constable.

Disora: This refers to the ritual baton symbolizing authority amongst the *Rarámuris*.

Itzáes: The *Itzáes* are one of the oldest Mayan subgroups. According to ancient legends, the *Itzáes* were amongst the first Mayas to reach Yucatán, and they established the city of Chichén Itzá.

Mayordomos and *principales*: These terms refer to two kinds of functionaries entrusted with the organization of important religious festivities in their respective indigenous communities.

Reales de minas como el de Mapimí y Parral: The term '*reales de minas*' refers to the concession of the Spanish Crown for founding settlements in and around the zones, where important minerals were being exploited. *Mapimí* and *Parral* are the names of such habitats in the mining areas of northern New Spain, those that remain relevant even today.

Salinas: These are coastal sites, where salt is produced.

References

Bricker, Victoria Reifler. 1989. *El cristo indígena, el rey nativo*. translated by Cristina Paschero. México: Fondo de Cultura Económica.

Caso, Alfonso. 1958. 'La tierra de los indios' in *Indigenismo*. Mexico: Instituto Nacional Indigenista.

Lipschutz, A. 1956. *La comunidad indígena den América y en Chile*. Santiago de Chile: Editorial Universitaria.

May, Benito Aban *et al.*, 1994. *Yum santísima Cruz tun*, (Collection Letras Mayas Contemporáneas), no. 26. Mexico: Instituto Nacional Indigenista.

Montemayor, Carlos. 1996. *Chiapas, la rebelión indígena de México*. Mexico City: Joaquín Mortiz.

Montemayor, Carlos. 2000. *Los pueblos indios de México hoy.* Mexico: Temas de Hoy Series, Planeta Mexicana.

Ruiz, Margarito Xib and Araceli Burguete. 1996. "Comunidades en estados modernos", in Jesús Ortega Martínez ed., *La autonomía de los pueblos indios*, Grupo Parlamentario del Partido de la Revolución Democrática, LVI Legislatura de la Cámara de Diputados, México.

Ruiz, Margarito Xib. 1996. "Los pueblos indios y la refundación del estado", in Jesús Ortega Martínez ed., *La autonomía de los pueblos indios*, Grupo Parlamentario del Partido de la Revolución Democrática, LVI Legislatura de la Cámara de Diputados, México.

4

Crisis and Reinvention: The Redefinition of Indigenous Identities in Contemporary Mexico

Federico Navarrete Linares

Mestizos and Indians

Officially, the population of Mexico is divided between two ethnic groups: Mestizos, who constitute a large majority of 90 per cent of Mexicans, and Indians, who constitute the remaining 10 per cent. Mestizo, an old Spanish term that means "mixed blood" or "mixed race", is applied to most Mexicans because they are held to be racially and culturally descended both from the Pre-Columbian Indigenous population of the country and from the Spanish conquerors and immigrants that have arrived since the Spanish conquest of the sixteenth century. The Indians, in contrast, are defined as the direct descendents of the Pre-Columbian inhabitants of the country and are supposed to have maintained a racial and cultural continuity with their ancestors.

These definitions of ethnic identities are highly ideological, and they constitute a central element of the hegemonic definition of Mexican national identity. As such, they have legitimized State policies implemented through the twentieth century that aimed at achieving the racial and cultural homogenization of the population under the Mestizo category. The Indian "minority", which is constituted in fact by over 60 different ethno-linguistic groups, was defined as different and external to this homogeneous "majority" and the State sought ways to "integrate" it into the Nation. In the past 20 years, as we shall see in this chapter, these categories have entered a profound crisis and Indians have been creatively redefining their ethnic identities and their relation to the State and the rest of Mexican society.

However, before analyzing these transformations, it is necessary to retrace the history of the construction of the dominant ethnic categories.

Who is an Indian?

When the Spaniards conquered the territory that is now Mexico in the early sixteenth century, it was populated by hundreds of different peoples who spoke as many distinct languages, and who belonged to several different cultural traditions. The southern and central regions of the country, known by anthropologists as Mesoamerica, were inhabited by agricultural societies that had developed centralized forms of government and a highly complex religion and cultural tradition. The northern regions were occupied by hunter-gatherer and village societies with a very different cultural tradition, though they were in constant contact with the Mesoamericans.

The Spanish conquerors and colonizers grouped all these different ethnic groups under the category of "Indians", a name that was borne out of a geographical misconception. When he first arrived in the Americas, Christopher Columbus thought that he had arrived in the Indies, i.e. in Asia, and thus considered all the peoples he encountered to be Indians. Although this mistake was rapidly corrected, the name stuck, since the new continent was called the Western Indies, as opposed to the Eastern Indies of Asia, and its inhabitants continued to be called Indians. The term soon acquired a very clear political content, as the Indians were defined as heathens that had to be subjugated and Christianized and in the process turned into purveyors of forced labor and tributes to the Spanish colonizers and to the Spanish government. As Guillermo Bonfil has pointed out, it became a Colonial category that homogenized the highly diverse population of the Americas and defined it as intrinsically subservient to Spanish domination (Batalla, 1995).[1]

The Spanish colony of New Spain was built upon the exploitation of the work force and the agricultural production of the Indians, particularly in the regions of Mesoamerica. Therefore, it was fundamental for the Colonial regime to define and maintain clear ethnic boundaries between Indians and non-Indians. The former were given their own form of government, and were subject to specific laws; in some regions they were even forced to dress differently from the Spaniards, African slaves and other ethnic groups. These ethnic

1. In this chapter I shall refer to the Native population and its descendents as Indigenous peoples, using the term Indians, only when I am referring to the views held about these groups by Mestizos and the State.

boundaries were pretty flexible in practice, since many individuals and groups could change their ethnic affiliation, and there was constant intermarriage between Amerindians, Europeans, Africans and the few Asians who arrived in the country. However, the principle of ethnic differentiation and of the hierarchical superiority of the Spaniards was the foundation of the whole social order (Linares, 2004).

The Spanish conquest and colonization produced a radical transformation in Indigenous societies: the large Pre-Columbian states were dissolved and the traditional religious and political elites lost most of their powers; epidemics produced a "demographic collapse" in which up to 75 per cent of the population died, and the introduction of immigrants, foreign plants, animals and technologies irreversibly modified the landscape of Mexico. However, the Indigenous peoples reacted in creative and complex ways to the imposition of Spanish domination. Many of them collaborated actively with the colonizers and voluntarily assimilated key aspects of their culture, particularly the Catholic religion. This did not mean, however, that they renounced their ethnic identities, but rather that they redefined them in the new political context. As Steve Stern has proposed, Amerindians were able to "colonize from below" the Colonial state, appropriating Spanish culture and using Spanish institutions and laws to ensure their physical, political and cultural survival (Stern, 2000).

Indians, Peasants and the Nation

After the Independence of Mexico in 1821, all the laws discriminating against Indians and Afro-Americans were suppressed and Mexico became the only American country to proclaim the universal equality of its citizens, regardless of race or ethnicity.

In practice, however, ethnic inequality continued, as the *criollos*, i.e. persons of Spanish descent born in the Americas, became the dominant group of the new nation. They established Spanish as the official language of the nation, even though only a minority of the population spoke it, and they defined Mexico as a modern Western nation. Citizenship was made synonymous with Western culture and thus excluded Indians, Blacks and other non-European groups unless they renounced their supposedly "backward" and "inferior" cultures. The *criollos* hoped that the majority of Indians and Blacks in Mexico would eventually be dissolved by European immigration and the nation would be adequately whitened.

In this way, the principle of universal equality became a new tool for discriminating and subjugating the Indigenous groups. This was particularly clear in the matter of land tenure. Throughout the Colonial period, the Spanish government had recognized the collective property of Indigenous communities, since it was interested in extracting the surplus produced by Indian peasants. After Independence, individual property became the only legally recognized form of land tenure, according to the supposedly universal principle of Liberal individualism, and therefore Indigenous communities thus lost legal title to their holdings. The result was a massive land grab that left many communities landless and that sparked a cycle of peasant rebellions that lasted from the 1840s to the Mexican revolution of 1910 (Reina, 1986). For the new national elites, the dispossession of Indigenous and traditional peasant communities was a necessary step for the development of modern agriculture in Mexico and their resistance and rebellions were a sign of their backwardness and their unwillingness, or inability, to participate constructively in the life of the new nation.

However, Indigenous groups did participate actively in the political life of Mexico. As in Colonial times, they colonized the State from below, turning their communities into municipalities under the new constitutional order, and appropriating key elements of the Liberal ideology that was being employed against them. Florencia Mallon has proposed that they developed their own popular Liberalism, one that recognized communal institutions and property, and that defined citizenship in terms that did not exclude culturally different groups (Mallon, 1995). It should be remarked that the communities did not define themselves as Indians, distinct from the rest of the population, but as peasants and citizens who had the same rights as other Mexicans; therefore they did not seek to set themselves apart from the nation, but rather to participate on an equal footing in its construction. The ideology of popular Liberalism became a key rallying point for political mobilization by Indigenous communities through the nineteenth and into the twenty-first century, as we shall see below.

The Rise of the Mestizos

In the second half of the nineteenth century and the first half of the twentieth, the consolidation of the State, the dissolution of communal landholdings, and the development of a capitalist economy, based on the export of minerals and cash crops, such as coffee and sugar, the construction of railways and an incipient industrialization, produced a massive process of cultural and linguistic change: many members of Indigenous communities were forced to migrate to the cities, large farms, and mines, and in that process they adopted Spanish as their main language and abandoned their traditional sense of ethnic identity, shifting their allegiance to the national identity being constructed by the State. At the same time, entire communities also changed their language, and their ethnic self-definition, from Indian to Mestizo.

This linguistic and cultural shift was massive. As Table 4.1 shows, in the beginning of the nineteenth century Indians constituted around 60 per cent of the population, by 1885 they were 38 per cent and by 1921 they were just 29 per cent. Meanwhile the proportion of Mestizos grew from 23 per cent, to 43 per cent and to 59 per cent. In absolute terms it seems that around 3 million people experienced this cultural and ethnic transformation (Linares, 2004).

Table 4.1: Evolution of Indian and Mestizo population between 1808 and 1921.

	Indians	*%*	*Mestizos*	*%*	*Europeans*	*%*	*TOTAL*
1808	3,676,281	60	1,388,706	23	1,097,998	18	6,162,985
1885	3,970,234	38	4,492,633	43	1,985,117	19	10,447,984
1921	4,179,449	29	8,504,541	59	1,404,718	10	14,334,780

Such massive shifts in ethnic identity were not without parallel in the world during that period. In Poland and other European countries the processes of national consolidation and capitalist development produced similar effects among peasant communities. In the Americas however, Mexico's case is pretty exceptional. In other countries with large Indigenous populations, such as Guatemala and Peru, the State and the *criollo* elites have segregated them from national life and they have maintained their distinct ethnic identity until the present. In other nations, such as the United States, Argentina and Chile, the Indigenous populations were militarily subjugated and in many instances exterminated. The transformation of Indigenous culture and identity in Mexico was made possible by the fact that since Colonial times there had been successful channels of intercultural communication and the boundaries separating Indians from non-Indians had been fairly flexible, and were frequently transposed by Indigenous communities and individuals seeking to improve their station in society. Besides, Indians had been long integrated into the economic system, and remained the main source of labor for the developing capitalist economy, and thus they were not regarded as alien enemies to be exterminated or segregated, but as a subaltern population that needed to be integrated in the labor market. Furthermore, Mexico did not receive massive inflows of immigrants that could serve as alternative sources of labor. Finally the Indigenous communities and individuals participated actively in the political and social life of the country: from its war of Independence to the continuous civil wars of the nineteenth century, and the fight against US and French invasions.

Although this was a process of social and cultural change, its contemporaries, who talked of the "mestizaje", or miscegenation, of the Indians, understood it in racial terms. Spanish speaking individuals were held to be racially different from those who spoke an Indian language, even though they may actually continue living in the same territory, engaging in the same kind of maize subsistence agriculture, performing the same rituals and dressing very similarly. Addressing the ambiguity of this characterization, Bonfil has baptized this ethnic transformation as the "de-Indianization" of Mexico, while stressing that there were significant cultural continuities in the communities that experienced them (Batalla, 1990).

The racial interpretation of this process became the basis of a nationalist ideology of "mestizaje" formulated in the late nineteenth and early twentieth centuries, when this massive cultural shift was already well under way, by intellectuals closely linked to the State. This ideology holds that the Mexican national community should be composed of a single race of Mestizos and that national unity will only be achieved when all Mexicans of Indian or European descent intermix and dissolve into this unified race. Mestizos are supposed to inherit the best traits of these two races, with a clear predominance of the "superior" White European elements. They are supposed to be proud of their Indian "past", embodied in the massive constructions and the works of art of their Pre-Columbian "ancestors", while embracing the forward-looking and Modern culture of the White races of the world. Thus mestizaje should be a process of whitening of the Indians, but not of darkening of the Whites.

As formulated by authors such as Andrés Molina Enríquez (1909), Manuel Gamio (1916), and later Octavio Paz (1970), this ideology constructed a compelling historical narrative of how Mexico had managed to overcome the contradictions between its different races, and to achieve harmony through miscegenation, as well as clear prescriptions for completing this process, hastening the integration and dissolution of the remaining Indian groups and the incorporation of European immigrants. Though this ideology was racially tolerant towards the Indians, it ignored the presence of large numbers of persons of African descent in the population, and rejected the incorporation of other immigrants into the racial mixture of Mestizo Mexicans, particularly the Chinese. Thus it helped to underpin blatantly racist policies against these groups (Knight, 1990).

Indigenismo

The peasant uprisings produced by the despoliation of communal landholdings during the second half of the nineteenth century reached their climax in the massive rebellions of the Revolution that started in 1910. As a result, the constitution of 1917 officially recognized the legal title of Indian and Mestizo communities to their land, and in the following decades land reform restituted their traditional holdings or provided them with new lands. While these agrarian policies restored social peace to the countryside, the accelerating urbanization and industrial development of the country after the Revolution hastened the process of cultural change known as mestizaje. As can be seen in Table 4.2, the percentage of the Indian population in the total population of the country declined steadily through the twentieth century, even though its absolute numbers increased dramatically. Meanwhile, the State designed a complex set of policies aimed at achieving their definite "integration" to the nation, known as Indigenismo.

Indigenista policies used the latest advances in anthropological science: leading anthropologists such as Alfonso Caso (1958) and Gonzalo Aguirre Beltrán (1992) applied the principles of culturalist anthropology to devise scientific means of accelerating the cultural transformation of Indians into Mestizos. They identified the aspects of different Indigenous cultures that were most susceptible to change and implemented policies aimed at achieving that transformation, while at the same time looking for ways to preserve the most colorful aspects of Indigenous traditions, such as crafts, rituals and ways of dressing. The State provided Indigenous communities with basic health and education services and using them to foster the dissolution of their particular ethnic identities. Indigenismo also sought to educate a new

Indian elite of teachers, professionals and bureaucrats that would adopt the progressive Westernized values of Mestizos and instill them in the other members of their communities.

Table 4.2: Evolution of Indian Population in the Twentieth Century.

	Indians	%	*Total*
1930	2,251,086	14	16,552,722
1940	2,490,909	12.7	19,653,552
1950	2,447,609	9.49	25,791,017
1960	3,030,254	8.68	34,923,129
1970	3,111,415	6.5	48,225,238
1980	5,181,038	7.8	66,846,833
1990	5,282,347	6.5	81,249,645
2000	6,725,900	7.05	95,429,600

NOTE: In the censuses of the twentieth century, Indians were defined as speakers of an Indian language over the age of 5, and thus these figures actually under-represent the size of the Indigenous population.

Estimates for 2000, place it at 12.7 million, that is 13 per cent of the population.

The defenders of Indigenismo point out that it was a generous policy that used peaceful means to improve the life of the Indians of Mexico and to incorporate them into the progress of the nation (Warman, 2003). However these were not its only objectives: Indigenista policies also sought to co-opt the Indigenous communities into the political networks of the authoritarian post-Revolutionary regime and its ruling party, and thus conditioned basic social services to political loyalty. Besides it was openly paternalistic and never imagined that the Indigenous cadres that it trained would be more than assistants to an elite of Mestizo anthropologists and politicians, and that the Indigenous communities ought to have any kind of voice in the matter of their integration into the nation.

Mestizos and Indians: Historical Realities and Ideological Constructions

The aim of this historical synthesis was to clarify how the division of the Mexican population into a Mestizo "majority" and an Indian "minority" was historically achieved, and ideologically constructed.

In the past centuries Indigenous peoples have been turned into a demographic minority by State policies and capitalist development, and have been simultaneously relegated into a minority status by a nationalist ideology that defines the identity of Mexico as opposed to the ethnic identities of Indigenous peoples. However to state that 10 per cent of Mexicans are Indians is a gross oversimplification.

On the one hand, there are many Mestizos living in traditional peasant communities whose culture is closer to that of the Indigenous peoples than to that of the modernized urban elites, despite the fact that they no longer speak an Indian language. This sector of the Mestizo population could very well "re-Indianize" itself if the legal and cultural circumstances changed. In fact, in many communities such processes of re-Indianization are already well under way.

On the other hand, outside the legal and ideological definitions concocted by the state and the intellectuals, there is really no such thing as an Indian in Mexico. Indigenous peoples speak over 60 different languages and have equally diverse cultures and identities. These identities have traditionally been defined around the local community and its territory, but are currently undergoing a profound redefinition. The only trait that is shared by all these groups is the fact that they are not considered Mestizo.

The ethnic category of Mestizo is even more problematic, since it purports to include groups as diverse as recent immigrants from Europe and the Middle East, westernized urban elites, traditional peasant communities, Catholic, Protestants, Jews and Atheists, and the widely varying regional cultures of Mexico. As in the case of the Indians, the only trait shared by all Mestizos is the fact that they do not consider themselves Indians.

In the twentieth century, artists and ideologues close to the Revolutionary regime sought to give a positive content to the identity of the Mestizos, equated with the national identity, and the State made a concerted effort to instill this identity in the population, through the school system, public art works, the media and other means of propaganda (Bartra, 1987). However, such attempts have been all but abandoned in the past three decades and the Mestizo identity has lost much of its content.

Finally, it must be stressed that the ideology of mestizaje, while overtly promoting the end of all racial differences, actually racialized the social and cultural diversity of Mexico, and has become the basis for a pervasive racism. Mexican racism is not public or overtly political, as in the United States, but it effectively discriminates against those with darker skins and a less Westernized culture in the social and economical realms, thus reinforcing and legitimizing the profound economic inequalities that plague Mexican society. This discrimination has worsened in the past decades, as the momentum of hegemonic nationalism has weakened, and is particularly evident in the mass-media (Linares, n.d.).

Indigenous Strategies of Accommodation and Their Limits

Throughout the twentieth century, most Indigenous communities reached a kind of *modus vivendi* with the Mexican state. The agrarian laws protected their communal holdings, and gave them the hope of recovering some of the land they had lost during the nineteenth century. This meant that their survival was not directly threatened, and they could negotiate accommodations with the State in the political terrain.

These negotiations usually implied accepting the supremacy of the regime, and of local State agents over community governments. In many instances, power centered on a "cacique" a political leader that had the support of the government and that ruled the community in an authoritarian fashion, with frequent resort to force. The acceptance of governmental authority, even in its most repressive forms, gave the communities access to services such as education, health, roads, electricity, etc.

On the other hand, the communities and their members were increasingly integrated to the developing capitalist economy, as they sold their surplus agricultural production, became producers of commercial crops, such as coffee, or migrated to work in the cities.

To preserve their ethnic identity in this context of increased political, social and economic integration, the Indigenous communities reinforced institutions that embodied and ritualized it. The most important were an elaborate ceremonial economy, centered on the rituals celebrating the Catholic saints, and a very complex system of government, consisting of an elaborate pyramid of hierarchically organized political and religious positions. These institutions absorbed much of the economic surpluses obtained by the members of the community in the capitalist economy, since they were expected to invest heavily in organizing the ritual festivities and in performing the duties involved in the government positions they occupied. In this way, they reasserted their allegiance to the community and to its ethnic identity (Hill, 1991). Similarly many communities have strengthened their systems of collective labour, in which all the members of the community contribute their work, or their money, to works for the general benefit.

In this way, many Indigenous communities achieved a kind of equilibrium in their relationship with the State. This situation was in no way advantageous to them, since it meant their subordination to the authoritarian regime. Besides the Indigenous population was usually the victim of political, social and economic discrimination and remained the poorest sector in Mexican society, since its agricultural economy was marginalized by the development policies of the government, and the services it received were usually substandard.

The Current Transformations

In the past three decades the precarious equilibrium reached by Indigenous communities in their relationship with the State, and in their internal life, has been altered dramatically as Indigenous societies, the State, and the Mestizo "majority", have experienced profound crises and undergone deep transformations.

Since the late 1970s the nationalistic and inward-looking model of economic development adopted by the Mexican State entered into a deep crisis, and the subsequent liberalization has not been able to produce sustained economic growth. Simultaneously the State has abandoned most of the policies it had devised for achieving the national integration of Mexico, most notably Indigenismo, and has reduced its role to trying to alleviate the massive inequalities that plague Mexican society. Meanwhile the Mexican economy has been opened to foreign trade and investment, and Mexicans have migrated in increasing numbers to the United States.

These transformations in State policy have deeply affected the Indigenous communities, and their livelihood and traditional ways of life have entered into a profound crisis. It does not seem overly exaggerated to compare this contemporary crisis to the one faced by Indigenous societies in the sixteenth century, after the Spanish conquest. Indeed, the current transformations threaten the very foundations of the ethnic identities of most indigenous societies. Paradoxically, while the most dramatic aspect of the sixteenth century crisis was the precipitous decline in the Indigenous population, in the current, an important element of transformation has been the demographic explosion that has multiplied by three the Indigenous population from 1930 to the present, as can be seen in Table 4.2.

As they did five centuries ago, Indigenous societies are reacting to this dramatic situation by actively transforming their own cultures, by organizing politically, and by making their voices heard in the national and international arena. No doubt, this will lead to a radical definition of their identities and ways of life.

The Complexities of Community Life

Beyond the diversity of Indigenous communities, which range from the small dispersed farms of the Tarahumara in the North, and the Huichol in the West, to the highly dense settlements of the Tzotzil in Chiapas, in the South, and to the town-dwelling communities of traders in Juchitán, Oaxaca, also in the South, the following general trends of transformation can be identified.

First, as Indigenous communities have grown in size, their internal conflicts have intensified. As competition for land and access to government positions has increased, the political systems that traditionally distributed these scarce goods have come under strain. In some instances, an elite has monopolized the best lands and the highest positions and has managed to disenfranchise large sectors of the community. These privileged groups have even distorted the ceremonial economy, and the systems of communal labour, to turn them into mechanisms of exploitation of the disenfranchised groups.

In other communities, the political system has opened up and become more inclusive; therefore, communal assemblies, which include all male members of the town, have gained power over the traditional hierarchical system of positions. In other instances, the traditional system of government has been abandoned and electoral politics, involving the national political parties, have gained ground, usually with an opposition party representing the groups that had been excluded from power.

Since the traditional systems of government were, and still are, closely linked with the traditional religion, a highly modified version of Catholicism, political dissent has often taken the form of religious conversion to Protestant and Evangelical creeds. Disenfranchised groups, particularly women, who were traditionally excluded from all political and religious positions, have turned to Protestant religions in search of different forms of improving their personal and family situation. For instance, traditional religion is linked with high consumption of alcohol among males, which in turn produces domestic violence against women. Thus, women use the new religions' ban of alcohol to improve their domestic situation.

In many communities, the conversions have been massive and have sparked serious conflicts. In Chiapas, and other states, the converts have been killed or expelled from the community. In other communities, however, creative accommodations have been reached, such as separating the political and the religious aspects of community government, so that Protestants can participate in the former. To many observers, religious conversions seem a threat to the unity of the communities; however, it must be stressed that in most instances they simply reflect tensions and divisions that already existed in them.

Gender relations have also become an important issue in the past decades. Traditionally, women were excluded from power and public life in the communities, but lately they have been demanding a greater voice and participation. The crisis of traditional agriculture, a male activity, has meant that in many instances women have become the most important providers for their families. In some cases they have been able to organize into cooperatives and thus have improved the marketing conditions of their traditional crafts; in others, they have found employment as domestic servants in towns, or in factories. Their increased economic weight has given them a greater say in family and community affairs. However, the struggle for female empowerment is far from complete: for instance Indigenous women have far higher rates of illiteracy and systematically receive less education than males.

The End of Subsistence Agriculture?

Another highly significant transformation of the past decades has been the crisis in the traditional form of subsistence agriculture practiced by most Indigenous communities. For 5,000 years, peasants in Mexico subsisted from maize, squash, beans and other associated crops, and using basically the same agricultural technologies.

In the past decades the viability of this form of life has been eroded from inside the communities by the population explosion. As the Indigenous population boomed, their small mostly non-irrigated fields could not increase their production accordingly, particularly since the plots were atomized as they were subdivided among an ever more numerous offspring. Therefore the dependence of most communities on food bought at the market increased, as did the time that their members had to spend working outside them in order to earn the money necessary to purchase them.

Meanwhile, the State considered subsistence agriculture as backward and unproductive and did not support it, while it actively sponsored the development of cash crops. The lack of credits, irrigation works and the artificially low prices imposed on maize made this form of agriculture increasingly unsustainable from an economic point of view. Erosion, deforestation, soil exhaustion and land fragmentation made it increasingly unsustainable from an ecological point of view.

The *coup de grâce* to subsistence agriculture was given by the legal and economic reforms of the early 1990s. The former legalized the fragmentation and sale of communal landholdings, and stopped the agrarian reform that had restituted land to many communities. The latter opened up the country's borders to maize and other agricultural products imported from the United States and other countries, at much lower prices.

These reforms, aimed at modernizing Mexican agriculture and making it internationally competitive, have radically altered the economic and social life of Indigenous and other traditional peasant communities.

Maize agriculture has basically ceased to be an economically viable activity: it is now much cheaper to buy maize than to produce it directly. Thus, many peasants have abandoned this crop, opting for other products; many more, between 5 and 10 million, have abandoned the land altogether and have migrated to seek work in the growing modern farms, in the cities and in the United States. However, maize agriculture has not disappeared entirely, since many peasants continue growing this plant, although in a more limited scale, as an insurance against the uncertainties of cash crop production and the labor market and as a source of better quality food than the one they can buy.

The experience of Indigenous and other peasant communities with cash crops has not been entirely satisfactory. The wild fluctuations in international prices, and the lack of effective compensatory measures from the government, have often led them to economic ruin. Besides the usually poor, eroded, atomized, and non-irrigated land plots of most Indigenous peasants do not allow them to compete with the large agribusinesses from the United States, Brazil, and other countries, nor do they receive the subsidies granted to farmers in the developed countries.

The shift away from the traditional maize subsistence agriculture has meant a dramatic transformation of the life and culture of most indigenous societies. This form of life implies a highly complex relationship with the web of life in and around their communities, one that involved what we would define as economic and technological, as well as religious and supernatural elements. Maize agriculture involves not just the peasants and their land, but also their entire households, the fallow lands that are used for grazing and plant collecting, the domestic animals that feed from the stalks and the corn cobs, the "monte", or wild lands that surround the milpas, the water sources, the weather, the gods and spirits of the maize, the rain and the plagues that afflict it, and other natural, animate, inanimate and supernatural beings. Therefore, its significance goes beyond the alimentary and the economic realms, as the identity of many indigenous people is defined around this plant, which is considered sacred and consubstantial with humankind. For instance, the Maya from Yucatan call themselves "people of maize" and define themselves as "milperos", those who work the maize fields (Burns, 1983).

Besides, being able to produce most, or at least a significant part, of their food provided Indigenous communities with a degree of autonomy from the capitalist economy, which is why they have persevered in planting this crop. Therefore, the erosion of "ecological autonomy", as John Tutino has defined it, has meant, an erosion of the capacity of the Indigenous communities to decide their own future and to openly challenge the State, as they did in the nineteenth and early twentieth centuries (Tutino, 2000). This has upset the precarious equilibrium they had managed to construct in their relationship with the State and the rest of Mexican society, forcing them to seek new forms of relating with them, as we shall see below.

The legal reforms concerning land tenure, and the crisis of maize agriculture, have left Indigenous communities particularly vulnerable to new forms of dispossesion by the State and capitalist enterprises in their endless quest for accumulating capital and resources (Harvey, 2005). Their territories, now apparently deprived of any economic usefulness, are however rich in mineral and forestry resources or are perfectly suited for building dams, or other infrastructure projects. Besides their exceptional biodiversity, among the highest in the planet, makes them the target for prospectors, and the traditional ecological knowledge of the communities has become one more resource to be exploited. Even the genome of these populations has been opened up to dispossession.

Migration and Its Consequences

The crisis in traditional agriculture has led many Indigenous peasants to abandon their land and seek employment elsewhere. By some estimates up to 30 per cent of the Indigenous population is now composed of migrants.

These men, women and children endure terrible work conditions as migrant laborers in the large agribusinesses in the Northwestern regions of the country: they work for more than 8 hours and are paid only by the amount of fruits or plants they harvest; children are made to work since a very early age and often do not have access to education; they are exposed to dangerous pesticides and live in insalubrious quarters.

Other migrants have moved to the city, where many have been forced to subsist in the informal sector of the economy, or as masons and in other underpaid professions. Many more have migrated to the US, to work in farms and in the cities.

While some Indigenous groups, such as the Mixtec, have been migrating for almost a century, other groups have only recently begun doing so. In both cases, the outflow of men, women and children has radically altered the life of their communities.

The absence of males has allowed women to assume many roles from which they had been previously excluded, such as planting the land and participating in the community government. This has produced a redefinition of gender relations. Meanwhile, the migrant laborers' remittances have kept their communities afloat, allowing Indigenous households to acquire consumer goods such as televisions and refrigerators that were previously inaccessible to them.

The migrants have developed highly complex and dynamic networks of communication and travel to keep in touch with their original communities. Many try to go back to participate in the main religious festivals and in important family occasions. Others continue participating in the community government, sending money to purchase their positions and to fulfill their communal obligations. In some instances, the money and the influence of the migrants have managed to topple oppressive "caciques" and have democratized community life.

In their host communities, the migrants seek to reproduce key elements of their community life and their ethnic identities. They celebrate their religious festivals, and try to establish a ritual relationship with their new territory, while preserving and revitalizing their native tongues. However, the pervasive racism against Indians in Mexican towns often forces them to hide their ethnic affiliation and to dress, speak, and act like Mestizos.

Nevertheless, migration has increased the national visibility of Indigenous persons all around Mexico: before the 1970s the Indigenous population of Mexico was concentrated in their traditional territories, but it is now distributed throughout the country, and cities and regions that had no significant Indigenous presence now have growing communities of immigrants.

Indigenous Voices

Political Mobilizations

In the past 20 years the State has abandoned Indigenista policies and has not substituted them by any alternative. As Héctor Díaz Polanco has proposed, Indigenismo has been substituted by "ethnophagy" a kind of *laissez-faire* that abandons any policies of nation-building or social integration and leaves Indigenous communities at the mercy of the forces of globalized capitalism (Díaz Polanco 2006).

The abandonment of Indigenismo, however, was also the result of the mobilization of Indigenous communities, which denounced its authoritarian and paternalistic elements, and demanded a greater say in the definition of government policies directed towards them. This political mobilization was spearheaded by the cadres of teachers and professionals that had been formed under Indigenismo and who were supposed to lead the final and definite integration of their communities into the Mestizo majority. Instead, they became leaders of a new kind of Indigenous political and social movements.

The Indigenous mobilizations of the past thirty years have continued and revived the tradition of peasant mobilization around the central demands of popular Liberalism, as defined in the nineteenth century: political democracy, security in community land tenure, and social justice.

However, the new Indigenous movements have introduced a new set of demands centered on the respect of their cultural particularities and their ethnic identities. Through the recognition of the ethnic particularity of Indigenous communities they seek to establish a new kind of relationship between them and the State, centered on their legal autonomy. These demands have challenged the hegemony of the ideology of mestizaje, and its definitions of Mexico as a culturally and racially unified nation.

The new Indigenous movements have taken many different forms. Some have been centered on the defense of communal lands against dispossession by development projects, such as dams or roads, or by forestry and mining companies. Others have centered on economic demands, particularly for the marketing of the cash crops now produced by many communities. Political mobilization around these apparently narrow issues has had a significant impact on the Indigenous communities involved, leading often to a revitalization of their ethnic identity and their cultural particularities, and new feelings of empowerment.

The best known of the Indigenous movements is the Ejército Zapatista de Liberación Nacional (EZLN), a guerrilla army from the Southern state of Chiapas, that took arms against the State in January 1994 and that has been in an uneasy truce, and protracted negotiations with it, ever since. The Zapatistas, as they are generally known, used the name of the most prominent peasant leader of the 1910 revolution, Emiliano Zapata, thus establishing their link with the popular Liberal tradition. Besides they presented a set of demands centered on the recognition of Indigenous cultures and the granting of legal autonomy to their communities. Their rebellion was publicized all over the world, and they managed to mobilize supporters from many countries.

For many Mexicans, and most foreigners, the Zapatista uprising was the first evidence of Indigenous mobilization and of the demand for a new relation between these groups and the rest of Mexican society. However, it was the result of over 20 years of political experimentation and mobilization in which the different Indigenous societies have managed to find new voices and new strategies for defining and defending their ethnic identities.

The Conflict around Autonomy

Since 1994, the demands of most Indigenous movements have centered on the recognition of legal and political autonomy for Indigenous communities and peoples.

For the Indigenous movements, autonomy means self-government for their communities, with the legal recognition of its traditional authorities and the traditional methods of electing them; it also implies respect for the customary law of the community and for its jurisdiction within its boundaries; it should include too respect and recognition of the cultural particularities of the different Indigenous peoples, which should be reflected in a bilingual and bicultural education, in respect for local medical practices, and in greater access to the mass media. Simultaneously, autonomy would mean that Indigenous communities would have a decisive say in the definition and implementation of government policies aimed at them, including the exploitation of natural resources found in their territories. More generally, the demand for autonomy is a demand for a new kind of relationship between Indigenous communities and the Mexican State and society: one in which Indigenous peoples are recognized as an integral part of the national community, and no longer as an alien minority, and as full legal and political subjects, and no longer as objects of government policies, thus enjoying equal rights to the rest of Mexicans without having to renounce their cultural particularities.

There has been much debate about the limits and forms that this form of autonomy may take. Although all Indigenous movements agree that self-government would not mean independence or sovereignty, non-Indigenous critics have argued that even a limited form of autonomy would threaten the national unity of Mexico and would impinge on the sovereignty of its government. As regards the application of customary law, the defenders of autonomy agree that it would be subordinated to the Mexican laws, particularly in serious crimes, but its critics argue that it would create fiefs within the State, and that many of its precepts are contrary to national laws and human rights. The definition of the territorial rights of the communities is also highly controversial: Indigenous movements demand the recognition of community "territories" that would go beyond the land used for cultivation and include uncultivated zones, such as mountains, forests and rivers, as well as the mineral and oil resources found underground; the State and the critics of autonomy reject such a broad definition, arguing that it limits national sovereignty.

Another theme of debate is the definition of the subjects of autonomy. As we have seen, in Mexico, there are no clear-cut distinctions between Indians and non-Indians, and therefore it would be difficult to decide which specific peoples and communities would have right to autonomy. Indeed the possibility of obtaining autonomy would lead many Mestizo peasant communities, as well as some urban ones, to redefine themselves as Indigenous, something that they have already started to do.

On the other hand, most Indigenous movements argue that autonomy should be granted to individual communities, which have traditionally been the seats of Indigenous government; other observers, however contend that this would atomize the autonomous entities and make them economically and politically unviable, and that autonomy should be granted to Indigenous "peoples", that is whole ethnic groups that share the same language and culture and live in a relative large region; others propose the creation of multi-ethnic regions, whose autonomous governments would include several Indigenous groups as well as the Mestizos living in them.

The debate about Indigenous autonomy started in earnest in 1995 within the framework of peace negotiations between the government and the EZLN, which was backed in this issue by a large number of Indigenous organizations. An early agreement between the parties granted a relatively far-reaching autonomy to Indigenous communities, recognizing them as a fourth level of government, below municipalities. However, it was never made into law and finally in 2001, Congress approved a law that granted a much more limited autonomy and that was rejected by both the Zapatistas and most Indigenous organizations. Since then the issue has been in a stalemate: autonomy exists formally but it has not been implemented.

What has been at stake in this protracted debate is a new definition of Mexico as a nation. There is no doubt that the definition of national identity centered on the ideology of "mestizaje" that espoused the racial unification of the population of the country and the disappearance of Indigenous groups, can no longer be sustained. Indeed, since 1992 the Mexican constitution recognizes that Mexico is a "pluricultural" society. However, the shape that this new definition will take is not clear at all.

The State and many non-Indigenous Mexicans favor a limited form of autonomy according to the Anglo-American model of multiculturalism. This would mean that Indians would be recognized as a "minority", distinct from the "majority" of Mestizos, and would be granted some special rights that would not threaten the sovereignty of the majority and of the State that supposedly represents it. As Slavoj

Zizek has argued, this form of multiculturalism is highly functional for the working of globalized capitalism, since it reduces differences to a meaningless "cultural" realm and precludes any kind of contestation of the system as a whole (Zizek, 1998). In Mexico, this brand of multiculturalism would simply reinvigorate the racialist definitions of national identity proposed by the ideology of mestizaje while entrenching the discrimination against Indians.

In contrast, the more far-reaching form of autonomy proposed by the Indigenous movements and some of its supporters could lead to a true redefinition of the nation, and impose effective limits on the expansion of globalized capitalism into the communities. The recognition of Indigenous territories and of a fuller jurisdiction for Indigenous legal systems, would allow the communities to defend themselves against the dispossession brought on them by the government and the corporations, and would create new *loci* of sovereignty beyond the centralized State. If coupled with other measures, such as the recognition of traditional forms of intellectual property, which we shall discuss below, this would mean a radical redefinition of the relationship between the State and the Indigenous peoples and perhaps allow them to finally surmount the poverty and marginalization that they have endured for centuries.

Indigenous Cultures in the National and Global Arena

In the past 30 years, Indigenous cultures have been profoundly affected by the transformations that we have discussed. As a result of the spread of education, of the crisis in traditional agriculture and of the rise in migration, many of the traditional identifiers of Indigenous identity seem to be disappearing: many Indigenous children are no longer learning the language of their parents; Indigenous men and women are abandoning their traditional occupations as peasants and producers of crafts as well as their traditional communities and moving to the cities to engage in new activities; traditional Indian costumes are being substituted by industrially-produced clothes.

In the nineteenth and twentieth centuries similar cultural transformations led to the abandonment of Indigenous ethnic identities and to the adoption of the National identity by large groups of the formerly Indigenous population within the process of "de-Indianization" brought about by mestizaje. Today, many observers fear, or celebrate, that the contemporary transformations will lead to the disappearance of the last remnants of Indigenous cultures and ethnic identities in the near future.

However, the reality is far more complex. In the past few decades these cultural transformations have somehow decoupled themselves from the ethnic dimension of mestizaje. Many Indigenous persons who have migrated to the cities, learned Spanish and received education, even up to university level, have not renounced their ethnic affiliation to their communities, but have instead sought new ways to express it in the cultural and political realms. Thus the process of cultural change and social transformation that produced the Mestizo majority in Mexico seems to be no longer working in the way it used to work, and in the future may not lead to the dissolution of Indigenous identities, but rather to their redefinition and even revitalization.

In fact, urban-dwelling, educated and articulate Indigenous intellectuals have become important actors in the political and cultural scene of Mexico. These intellectuals, ranging from artists like Francisco Toledo and Saúl Villa, writers like Natalio Hernández and Juan Gregorio Regino, to lawyers like Adelfo Regino, Francisco López Barcenas and Floriberto Díaz Gómez, and academics like Víctor de la Cruz, have given a new projection and visibility to Indigenous cultures, transforming their image in the Mestizo imaginary, from a traditional and static reality, to a dynamic and creative force.

They have also articulated the demands of indigenous movements. Regino and Díaz Gómez, for instance, have formulated a cogent vision of the communal values of traditional Indigenous communities, formulating a political program for the defense of their autonomy and their cultural particularities. The figure and writings of Subcomandante Marcos, the Zapatista spokesman, have also contributed significantly to giving new visibility and vitality to Indigenous culture in the national and international realms.

Besides, thousands of teachers, scientists, engineers, doctors, political activists, and other Indigenous professionals are working in their fields, and within the Indigenous movements, to improve the living conditions of their communities and to redefine their culture and their identity in the changing national and international context.

The role of these new Indigenous élites is fraught with contradictions. Some have reproduced the authoritarian practices of the caciques they have replaced; others have distanced themselves from their communities. Some critics question the relevance of the blooming Indigenous literary movement, which has produced a wide array of novels, poems and dramas written in Indigenous languages, most of them published by the State. They argue that most speakers of these languages do not know how to read in them, and that the literary works do not correspond to traditional oral genres, such as prayers, ritual songs, myths, and folk tales, and thus have no relevance for them. However, precisely because these works go beyond traditional culture, they are modifying and enriching Indigenous cultures.

But educated elites are not the only ones involved in the redefinitions of Indigenous identities and cultures. Women who fight for their rights within their communities, religious converts who seek new ways of defining their individual and ethnic identities, crafts producers and artists who modify their wares to sell them in new markets, political movements that seek to modify community governments, as well as cooperatives and other productive enterprises, all these groups are seeking new ways of defining who they are, and their relationship to their communities, their ethnic identities, the State and national and world society.

Some migrant communities, such as the Mixtecs originally from Oaxaca who now live in California, have also engaged in processes of ethnic revitalization. As undocumented workers in the US, they discovered that they had much more in common with migrants from neighboring communities than they had previously thought. Thus, they have been building a new Mixteco identity that transcends the traditional community rivalries that divided them in their native Oaxaca. They have founded a radio station that broadcasts in Mixteco, and they have also incorporated into their movement members of other Indigenous groups also from Oaxaca. In this process of political mobilization and ethnic redefinition they have actively collaborated with American and Mexican intellectuals and activists (Escárcega, 2002).

Lately Indigenous artists, producers and activists have taken advantage of another phenomenon of globalization: the growing nostalgia for cultural difference and authenticity. Groups like the Maya, particularly the Zapatistas, and the Huichol have been able to reach global audiences that support their political demands and also to find global markets for their agricultural and artistic productions (Nash, 2001). While some critics have derided the lack of authenticity of these globally marketable products and discourses, these opportunities have been extremely valuable for these groups, protecting the Zapatistas from government repression, and giving Indigenous products and artists a degree of prestige and respect that they could not easily obtain in the national arena, given the deep-seated prejudices against Indians among Mestizo Mexicans.

Despite their vibrancy and vitality, Indigenous cultures still face massive disadvantages in their relation with the hegemonic forces of capitalism, institutionalized science and mass culture. This is particularly evident, in the way in which traditional knowledge of Indigenous community, produced by an intimate and a deeply-rooted relationship with the web of life, has been exposed to dispossession by pharmaceutical, agricultural and chemical companies who then recast it into the hegemonic language of modern science and obtain highly lucrative patents. This form of dispossession, known as bio-piracy, is facilitated by the fact that Mexican law offers no protection for traditional knowledge, and the existing international system of intellectual property is stacked in favor of corporations and against traditional communities.

Similarly, the networks of communication that can be built by and for Indigenous cultures, languages and arts, are no match to the mass media, which in Mexico give no space to Indigenous themes and voices and perpetuate many of the racist attitudes towards them.

Towards the Future

There is no doubt that Indigenous societies are adapting to the new realities of world capitalism and the crisis of the Mexican nation-state, that Indigenous intellectuals and artists, producers and activists have been able to redefine their identities and to project them into new cultural and economic arenas. In this way they have emulated their ancestors who in the sixteenth century reinvented Indigenous cultures under Spanish domination and thus ensured their survival after the dramatic crisis produced by the conquest.

However, Mexican indigenous societies face the same dilemmas faced by local cultures all over the world. As the global networks of capitalism incorporate them, as their traditional ways of living and relating to the web of life enter in crisis, and as they are subject to a new wave of dispossession of their territories, their knowledge and even their genomes, the traditional roots of their cultures and identities are being upturned, and they are being forced, as much of mankind has been over the past centuries, to adapt and take part in the economic web of the global market. As a result, their cultures and identities face the risk of becoming merely another brand of picturesque diversity in the marketplace of multiculturalism, as criticized by Zizek. In this new context they could become what Zygmunt Bauman has defined as mere "identifications", rootless definitions of identity that can be discarded and bought and sold in the market (Bauman, 2006).

This is why Indigenous movements defend their communities, and their communal life, which are intimately linked to their territories and to the relationship they have established with the web of life through maize agriculture. In this realm it will be fundamental to recognize that "Nature" as it exists in Indigenous territories is actually a cultural product, the result of hundreds of years of interaction and co-evolution between mankind and other species, and that the "natural resources" contained in such territories, which are among the richest in the world in biodiversity, are part of the patrimony of the Indigenous communities, and must be treated and respected as such. Similarly, maize agriculture should be recognized as an activity that must be revitalized because of its very important cultural and ecological dimensions, beside its economic value.

Indigenous movements have been the most important and visible social movements in Mexico in the past 20 years, and their impact has been felt throughout Mexican society: they contributed to democratization of political life, and they have questioned the nationalist ideologies that marginalized Indians, as well as large groups of Mestizos. However, their adversaries managed to insert them in the straitjacket of multiculturalism, thus casting their demands as minority revindications, dampening their subversive effects for the whole of society. Thirteen years after the Zapatista uprising, and after the fiasco of the autonomy law of 2001, it appears clear that the Indigenous movements alone will not be able to modify the political and social situation of Mexico, and that their fight should not be defined as a minority struggle but as a wider one, aimed at transforming Mexican society as a whole. Since the nineteenth century, Indigenous movements have played a key role in the construction of the Mexican nation, and they should continue doing so into the twenty-first century.

References

Aguirre Beltrán, Gonzalo. 1992. *El proceso de aculturación y el cambio socio-cultural en México*. México, D.F.: Fondo de Cultura Económica (Obra Antropológica, 6).

Bartra, Roger. 1987. *La jaula de la melancolía. Identidad y metamorfosis del mexicano.* México, D.F.: Editorial Grijalbo.

Bauman, Zygmunt. 2006. *Modernidad líquida.* Buenos Aires: Fondo de Cultura Económica.

Bonfil Batalla, Guillermo. 1995 [1972] "El concepto de indio en América: una categoría de la situación colonial", in *Obras escogidas de Guillermo Bonfil.* vol. 1, pp. 337–357. México: INI-INAH.

Bonfil Batalla, Guillermo, 1990. *México Profundo. Una civilización negada.* México, D.F.: Editorial Grijalbo/Conaculta (Los Noventa).

Burns, Allan F. 1983. *An Epoch of Miracles. Oral Literature of the Yucatec Maya.* Austin: University of Texas Press.

Caso, Alfonso. 1958. *Indigenismo.* México: Instituto Nacional Indigenista (Culturas indígenas).

Díaz Polanco, Héctor. 2006. *Elogio de la diversidad: globalización, multiculturalidad y etnofagia.* México: Siglo XXI Editores.

Escárcega, Silvia y Stefano Varese, eds. 2002. *La ruta mixteca.* México: Universidad Nacional Autónoma de México-Programa México Nacion Multicultural.

Gamio, Manuel. 1960 [1916]. *Forjando Patria.* México: Editorial Porrua.

Harvey, David. 2005. *The New Imperialism.* New York: Oxford University Press.

Knight, Alan. 1990. 'Racism, Revolution and Indigenismo: México, 1910–1940', in Richard Graham, ed. *The Idea of Race in Latin America.* Austin: University of Texas Press, pp. 71–113.

Mallon, Florencia E. 1995. *Peasant and Nation: The Making of Postcolonial Mexico and Peru.* Berkeley: University of California Press.

Molina Enríquez, Andrés. 1909. *Los grandes problemas nacionales.* México: A. Carranza.

Nash, June C. 2001. *Mayan Visions. The Quest for Autonomy in an Age of Globalization.* New York: Routledge.

Navarrete Linares, Federico. 2004. *Las relaciones interétnicas en México.* Méxicocity: Universidad Nacional Autónoma de México.

n.d. "Discriminación étnica y desigualdades en México: una reflexión histórica". In *La desigualdad en México: perspectivas interdisciplinarias.* Elisabetta di Castro, ed. México: Universidad Nacional Autónoma de México.

Paz, Octavio 1970 [1950-59] *El laberinto de la soledad.* México: Fondo de Cultura Económica.

Reina, Leticia. 1986. *Las rebeliones campesinas en México (1819–1906).* México: Siglo XXI Editores (Colección América Nuestra, Caminos de liberación).

Stern, Steve. 2001. "La contracorriente histórica: los indígenas como colonizadores del Estado, siglos XVI a XX", in *Los retos de la etnicidad en los estados-nación del siglo XXI.* Leticia Reina, coord. pp. 73–92, México: CIESAS.

Tutino, John. 2001. "Comunidad, independencia y nación: las participaciones populares en las historias de México, Guatemala y Perú", in Leticia Reina ed., *Los retos de la etnicidad en los estados-nación del siglo XXI.* México: CIESAS, pp. 125–151.

Warman, Arturo. 2001. *Los indios mexicanos en el umbral del milenio.* México: Fondo de Cultura Económica.

Zizek, Slavoj, 1998. "El multiculturalismo o la lógica cultural del capitalismo multinacional," in Fredric Jameson and Slavoj Zizek, *Estudios culturales: reflexiones sobre el multiculturalismo.* Buenos Aires: Paidós, pp. 137–188.

5

Contemporary Indigenous Politics in Brazil: Three Modes of Indigenous Political Performance

João Pacheco de Oliveira

Introduction

The existing demographic data about the indigenous population of the Brazilian Amazon[1] point to some changes in its volume and scale that deserve careful consideration. A survey made in 1957 by the anthropologist Darcy Ribeiro, based on the files and reports from the first indigenist agency (the SPI–Serviço de Proteção aos Índios, or Indian Protection Service), concluded that there were 143 native ethnic groups in the Brazilian territory, with an estimated population between 68,100 and 99,700 individuals (Ribeiro, 1970:258). There were 21 isolated peoples, and reliable information could be obtained for only 110 of the ethnic groups. From this universe, 52 indigenous peoples—about half of the total—had a population of less than 250. At the other end of the demographic scale, just six indigenous groups had a population of more than 2000 people.

The most recent statistical data provided by non-governmental organizations and by the present indigenist agency of the Brazilian government (FUNAI—Fundação Nacional do Índio, or National Indian Foundation) show 206 ethnic groups, of which 162 are in the "Legal Amazon". Within this universe, reliable basic information exists

1. The Brazilian Amazon is called by the administration Legal Amazon ("*Amazonia Legal*"); agents in this region have special access to tax exemptions and various kinds of government subsidies, instituted by law since 1971. The region corresponds to about 2/3 of the national territory, and includes the present states of Amazonas, Pará, Acre, Roraima, Amapá, Rondônia, Mato Grosso, Tocantins and part of Maranhão.

for 136 groups, corresponding to about 60 per cent of the indigenous population of the country. There are 49 smaller societies, with less than 200 members, which in absolute numbers is quite close to the figures of the 1957 census. In relative terms, however, they correspond to slightly more than a third (36%) of the total number of ethnic groups. The number of indigenous peoples without contact also did not change much since 1957: FUNAI registers 27 such cases[2].

In the other demographic strata, however, there was a substantial change: today, there are about 50 ethnic groups with more than 2000 members, and this amounts to almost 70 per cent (precisely 68.6 %) of the indigenous population of the Brazilian Amazon. The estimates for the total indigenous population of Brazil range from 270,000 (ISA, 1994) to 306,000 (IBGE, 1991) and 325,000 (FUNAI, 1995). This does not include Indians living in cities (FUNAI believes there are about 26,000 in the whole country, most of them in the Amazon).

These data point to a new demographic profile, and suggest that the societal units and the contact situation of the Brazilian Indians don't conform any more to the older interpretations about isolated tribes and dispersed societies, each one corresponding to a single village, like fragile micro-societies lost amidst the Amazon forest. Communications, land transportation, elementary schools, health stations, various religious confessions, radio, telephone and TV ceased to be rare and surprising elements, and have become part of the villages' daily life. Topics such as land demarcation, indigenous peoples' rights, environmental conservation, sustainable development and even biodiversity and genetic research are discussed in the villages. Words like culture and tradition have been incorporated to the local disputes, often with precise definitions and usage rules, similarly to what happens with definitions of ethnic identity and membership. And in the struggles with the whites, some quite fluid roles have become common, such as "leaders" and "indigenous authorities", as well as complex and ambivalent institutions such as "indigenous movements" and "organizations".

---

2. This is due to the fact that in recent years FUNAI has radically changed its attitude towards the indigenous peoples that haven't been contacted, avoiding the former procedures of "attraction" and "pacification", and adopting an external and protective vigilance.

Today, the indigenous lands that have already been demarcated in the Legal Amazon amount to over 60 million hectares, and in the near future they will correspond to 18 per cent of the region's lands. Given the progressive bias of the Brazilian Constitution of 1988, indigenous peoples have ceased to be populations under tutelage, and have become the aim of various important government policies and programs (concerning environment, sanitation, education, regional planning, and so on).

In this paper my focus will be to identify some organizing principles of this contemporary political universe, searching for constraints and strategies that permit formulating hypotheses about these processes. The present cultural fluxes are very diversified and involve transference and circulation of material resources, people and institutions, as well as new technologies of information and social intervention. What are the general impacts of these fluxes on the indigenous societies, and what new alternatives do they open for them? What meanings can we attribute to verbal categories and social practices that are part of these new discourses?

An Anthropology of Colonialism in Brazil

In Brazilian anthropology, there has been a growing concern in the last few decades to approach indigenous societies not only as "isolates" (in the demographic sense) or as individualized collectivities that produce specific languages and cultures, but also as parts in an interactive process, inserted in a play of dependencies and reciprocities, transversed by cultural fluxes and having to deal with problems of identity definition. Instead of the native as seen by another (supposedly similar) native, the image that inspires this approach is the Indian as seen by other Indians and by the whites, and—based on these perceptions—reflecting about himself and about the whites (Oliveira, 1988).

Some theoretical dialogues have been specially important in this sense, such as those concerning the concept of "colonial situation" (Balandier, 1951), the idea of "encapsulation" (Bailey, 1960) and of "ethnic group" (Barth, 1969). From the fifties to the seventies, Brazilian anthropologists have made a radical critique of the theories of acculturation (Galvão, 1978), have formulated the antagonism between the national society and indigenous societies by means of the idea of "interethnic friction" (Cardoso de Oliveira, 1964), and have tried to describe socio-cultural change conceptualizing it as a process of "ethnic transfiguration" (Ribeiro, 1970)[3].

In this perspective indigenous societies were described in the context of frontier regions, which included different dimensions or faces of the national society[4], that could be studied empirically (Maybury-Lewis, 1965; and Riviére, 1972).[5] The indigenous societies should be understood as parts of a moving frontier[6] and participants in a process of nation building[7].

One of the key dimensions for this approach is territory. How do the lands that the Indians inhabit relate to the agrarian structure and how are they inserted in the regional economic relations? Fundamentally, the answer given by this line of thought in Brazilian social science has not been geographical or ecological[8], but sociological and political. It has included a set of institutional conditions by means of which the state elects a specific mode of incorporation of indigenous populations, and sets limits to departures from this mode. An Amerindian population is recognized as indigenous by an act of state, which assigns them a parcel of the national territory and establishes special procedures for protection and assistance.

---

3. There is a clear parallelism between this idea and the "transculturation" proposed by Fernando Ortiz (1943), which had a wider reception in the anglophone world and received positive comments from Malinowski.
4. Ribeiro (1970) analyzes the differences in the impacts of national society upon indigenous societies as they meet agricultural, pastoralist or extractive "fronts" of the national society.
5. There are ethnographic and analytical studies made in this same period by foreign anthropologists researching indigenous populations in the frontier regions of Brazil or in regions close to the frontier.
6. Velho (1972, 1976) distinguishes "front of expansion" and "pioneer front", while Martins (1976) speaks of "demographic frontier" and "economic frontier", all of them as distinct from the international political boundaries.
7. Mariza Peirano, in her history of Brazilian anthropology, shows the connection between this set of researches and other debates about the formation of Brazilian national identity, which is a central subject in Brazilian sociology and social thought.
8. To assume the spatial dimension as determinant would lead to a static view of the social world, seen as nothing but an extension of an ecological niche, as happens with concepts such as "territoriality" (Raffestin, 1986), very popular among French geographers.

More than just focusing indigenous societies as collectivities that are inserted in a wider regional scale, this approach regards investigating the process of definition of a territory as a privileged analytical key to understand the modes of sociability that are present. This approach in terms of the process of territorialization enables us to describe and inter-relate changes occurring in various levels—social morphology, political roles, cultural traditions and identity building (Oliveira, 1999). The action of the state, however, shouldn't be seen as the sole determinant factor, but as one of the sides of the matter. The other side is indigenous agency—and this means not only reinterpretations and rearrangements but creation and innovation as well. It would make no sense to discard the phonological model based on the search for an unconscious code—supposedly elaborated in a collective, slow and undirected way—just to substitute it by a formal juridical model that assumes predefined norms that would be applied in an obligatory, univocal and self-regulating manner.

The process of territorialization does not express only the reasons of state. It also expresses indigenous conceptions of time, person, and the world. These conceptions are actualized in a specific social context, where meanings and strategies are referred to various scales[9] and may assume multiple meanings. In this context, native and colonial institutions are contrasted, revealing superpositions and differences that constitute a singular experience, which can be subjected to ethnographic vision.

The idea of process of territorialization establishes a dialogue with and incorporates some critical directions in anthropological theory. It takes up the concern with the agency of social actors and with the multiple scales to which social actions are referred. Some recent studies (Oliveira, 1999) also entertain a dialogue with the idea of landscape (Hirsch and O'Hanlom, 1996), which considers territory as the result of a complex social process. Thus, the implicit theoretical dialogues emphasize the exercise of power and the mechanisms of incorporation, the play of mirrors as a constitutive feature of sociability, and the analysis of variation in culture.

9. For instance, intra-family, intra-village, in the ethnical domain, in the regional plane (relating to external agencies), in the national arenas, and even in the international ones.

Concerning the indigenous movements, we favor a socio-genetical perspective that sees the indigenous organizations as singular social creations, which are necessarily intentional and political and should be described and explained according to the forms and functions they assume in each specific context and in each different scale.

An Amazonian Fieldwork

It was with these ideas in mind that I undertook my fieldwork among the Ticuna Indians of the Upper Solimões, close to the boundary between Brazil, Colômbia and Peru. The Ticunas live on the margins of the Amazon River and have been mentioned by most of the numerous travelers (authors of colonial chronicles, naturalists, scientific expeditions, and so on) that have crossed this region. This became a rich source for chronological description and for historical understanding. An earlier anthropological research by Roberto Cardoso de Oliveira (1964) focused precisely this historical dimension, emphasizing the conflictive and adaptive relationship between the Indians and the rubber extraction enterprise.

My research lasted from 1974 to 1988 (after this period, I have often traveled to the region and kept regular contacts, mainly to follow the meetings of the leaders and the processes these meetings have triggered). It enabled me to make a local observation that has theoretical and methodological importance and that can be related to the demographic data presented above. In the Ticuna situation the agencies of contact—amounting to more than ten, including state, religious, economic, military and assistential agencies[10]—could be seen everywhere, and had established diverse forms of interaction with the Indians. The villages could be distinguished by the presence or the absence of each of these agencies and by the time span, the extension and the intensity of their actions. Often these agencies were

---

10. This includes FUNAI, the Catholic Church (Prelacy of the Upper Solimões), the Baptist Mission (Baptists for the Evangelization of the World), the Army (Military Outpost of Tabatinga), the Navy (Maritime Command Office), the State Department of Education, the Projeto Rondon (Catholic University of Porto Alegre), specific medical agencies (such as the National Service for the Eradication of Malaria and Yellow Fever), the police stations, the municipal administrations, besides the economic agents such as the "*patrões*" ("bosses" of the rubber tappers), "*regatões*" and "*marreteiros*" (local commercial agents).

in conflict with each other, producing a dynamic situation to which the Indians were drawn. They brought with them their own concerns (family feuds, witchcraft accusations) and their own forms of action (avoidance, indifference, gossiping, witchcraft, individual fights, collective punishing expeditions, expulsions from the villages and even the death of those considered guilty of offence).

Given the time span of the contact between Ticunas and whites, and the diversity of its dimensions, it seemed of little use, and even misleading, to try to distinguish "traditional" and "modernizing" villages[11]. Undoubtedly, the situation of the Ticunas is very different from the situation of some other indigenous peoples that have inspired very different analytical models. Such is the case, for instance, of the Indians that live in the Upper Xingu region, relatively protected in a "refuge area" and with long-established intertribal connections[12]. The Gê —speaking peoples of the central Brazilian Plateau also had very different conditions in their contact with whites, as they have never been incorporated as an important source of labor by the expansion fronts of the national society. This permitted them to preserve the autarkic character of their institutions, the complexity of their ceremonial life, and even the form of their villages and houses[13].

In the case of the Ticunas, this opposition between "traditional" and "modern" seemed of little operational value for the discourses and strategies of the Indians themselves. It worked only as a replication of the belief, widespread among the Brazilians, in the inevitable extinction of the Indians and their transformation into Brazilians.It seemed better to distinguish them according to the imposition of specific

11. In a similar way the classification of the Ticunas as either "*índios de igarapé*" (Indians from the smaller rivers) and "*índios de rio*" (Indians from the larger rivers), proposed by Cardoso de Oliveira (1964) was understood in this same sense. Oliveira (1977) has explained the relativeness of this distinction and has shown the multiple dimensions that underlie it. The same thing happened with an analogous dichotomous classification proposed by Murphy (1978) in his study of the Munduruku.

12. The same is true for the Upper Rio Negro region and for the area presently included in the Indigenous Park of Tumucumaque.

13. All this in spite of the demographic losses, migrations and the disruption of the basic natural resources they traditionally used, as result of the progressive encroachment by the whites. The latter, however, did not penetrate into the more intimate and daily dimensions of village life.

modes of domination and to the exercise of some kind of hegemony, in connection to the action of those agencies of contact with the whites that had a more totalizing and inclusive intention. The idea of "historical situation"[14], inspired in the works of Gluckman (1968) and Bailey (1960 and 1969) permitted grasping these dimensions. It enabled the construction of a relatively coherent model for the description and interpretation of the diversified play of relationships between native and colonial institutions. When I mentioned the historical situations of the "seringal" (rubber tapping farm), of the "reservas" (Indian reservations), of the "missões religiosas" (Christian missions) and of the "ribeirinhos" (marginal peasantry living along the rivers) I intended to furnish instruments to understand the multiplicity of forms of sociability and mechanisms of self-representation that were acted out by the different social units in which the contemporary Ticunas distribute themselves.

These various models of societal organization which I have called "historical situations" enabled me to distinguish between different modalities of relations of encapsulation (Bailey, 1960). It also permitted me to characterize the diversity of "colonial situations"[15], describing the concrete socio-cultural context in which the indigenous institutions that are the subject of the ethnographies have been actualized. Connecting this to the former discussion, it means that the processes of territorialization are linked to well defined historical situations, creating different sets of interaction patterns and self-regulating mechanisms.

I think that these analytical instruments are still of value for my present interests regarding indigenous movements. However, they need to be adapted to the intention of drawing a comprehensive—thus necessarily schematic—picture of the social conditions from which the new indigenous organizations emerge in the Amazonia and the Northeast.

---

14. A "historical situation" is a construction of the researcher, an abstraction with analytical objectives, which operates with models or schemes of the distribution of power among the various social actors. It is the last product of a situational analysis that brings forth the patterns of interdependency of the social actors, after considering the sources of data and the institutionalized channels of conflict (Oliveira, 1988: 57–58).

15. Stocking Jr. (1991) points to the need of distinguishing the different "colonial situations", to avoid treating very different political processes as if they were homogeneous.

Naturally, this will leave much less space for the analysis of local politics and indigenous ethnopolitics, in comparison with my analysis of the formation of the first Ticuna reservation in the Upper Solimões region and of the related political and religious processes (Oliveira, 1988 and 1999). Focusing on the specific situation of the Ticuna or other Amazonian peoples can be an important method to verify, modify and deepen this analysis. This, however, could not be incorporated into this paper, for reasons of time and opportunity.

An Historic Overview: Three Modes of Territorialization

The first process of territorialization that was imposed on indigenous populations in Brazil dates from the sixteenth century, when peoples of different cultures and languages were gathered in the religious Missions, under the tutelage of different orders of the Catholic Church. In this context, the missionaries promoted the catechization of the natives, and this entailed establishing new forms of labor, new patterns of family and residence, and new forms of sociability and symbolic and identity expression. They imposed a language (the "general language" or "*nheengatu*") to serve as the *lingua franca*; and a new system of "native authority" was developed, based on the selection, by the missionaries, of the "principals" (mediators between the Indians living in the mission and the missionaries).

This process was interrupted in the mid-eighteenth century, with the creation of a new system, the "Indian directory" ("*diretório de índios*"), soon followed by the expulsion of the Jesuits from Brazil. The missions' headquarters were transformed in regular villages or hamlets and the Indians were considered "emancipated" from the religious agents. They thus became subordinated only to the secular authorities. The policies adopted by the Portuguese Crown had a clearly assimilationist outlook, stimulating interethnic marriage and imposing the use of Portuguese language.

The extinction of the missionary "*aldeamentos*" (settlements)[16] and the progressive regulation of capitalist land property rights (with the

16. In the Amazon, the missions had a fundamentally geopolitical nature, serving as witnesses to the growth of the Crown's territories. There were very few private efforts to settle and farm the land. Thus, the old missionary settlements were home to an heterogeneous population, including people that did not see themselves as "Indians". The spearhead for the attack over the lands that were inhabited by

Land Act of 1850) led to a single procedure to have access to land. This procedure had its origins in the colonial institution called "sesmaria", by means of which the Crown handed lands to its protégés, with the condition that they would settle and develop them. But as the state hardly ever inspected these enterprises and rarely took back the lands (except sometimes to turn them over to new protégés), this was the historical root of the land concentration that characterizes Brazilian agrarian structure.

The spearhead of the colonialist enterprise was the farms ("*fazendas*"), permanent units of territorial settlement, much more important than the fragile and dependent rural nuclei (small towns and villages). This is the context for the second process of territorialization of the indigenous population in Brazil. It involved a process of economic expansion that did not recognize any special rights for the native population and its descendants (as they had been legally emancipated from missionary tutelage). The incorporation of Amerindian populations was accomplished by means of clientelistic, individualized relations of patronage, which the Indians and their descendents developed towards the owners of rights of "*sesmarias*".

Indians who weren't under missionary control came from the urban centers, but was executed precisely by the descendants of the Indians from the missionary settlements. They had been transformed in Indian explorers and persecutors (as Indian "directors"—"diretores de índios"—and then later as patrons/bosses—patrões—of the rubber tappers—seringueiros—basing their power on the control over commercial credits they supposedly had). There were good reasons, then, for Darcy Ribeiro to have called the colonial enterprise a "people-grinding mill". The Amerindian population was one of its favorite grinding objects.

In the Portuguese colony of Brazil (outside the Amazon), on the other hand, the permanent occupation of vast spaces was accomplished by pastoralist fronts, while the missionary settlements became focus of agricultural activities. Most of the converted Indians stayed in these settlements until the second half of the nineteenth century, when the Provincial Assemblies decided to declare the extinction of these settlements and of their rights to lands (Carneiro da Cunha, 1992). These lands were then transferred to commercial agents, government officials and other non-Indian inhabitants. After they ceased to be recognized as Indians, for almost a century the populations from the old missionary settlements were not seen as an ethnic group and were culturally invisible. This process started to be reversed only in the twentieth century, mainly in the forties and then since the seventies to the present, with political mobilizations aiming at the recuperation of ethnic territories.

They were permitted to live on the land as "*agregados*" (peasant workers residing in the farms), but without any legal rights to the land. The Indians were part of the multitude of second-class citizens that were politically and economically marginalized[17], permanently dependent on the landowners.

Within this second mode of territorialization faced by the indigenous peoples, assuming the condition of Indian would only lead to jeopardy. It would open the possibility of being overexploited even by other non-Indian clients. Cut off from any kind of collective future and engaged in individual trajectories, trying to avoid the stigmas and to be recognized as "whites" (or at least as "*caboclos*" or "*mestiços*", that is, of mixed blood), the descendants of the Indians tended to disguise their cultural traditions and abandon their language, and to look for interethnic marriages. They admitted the ethnic aspect only regarding their distant family roots.

The third process of territorialization expresses the official indigenist policy that was created in the first half of the twentieth century in connection with republican doctrines. It has been conducted directly by the state, by means of a specialized indigenist agency that, as it defines the lands to which the Indians have access, also promotes peace in the local relations between Indians and the local white populations. In this new situation, state employees manage the Indians' lands, as well as their life rhythms, forms of sociability, mechanisms of political representation and relations with non-Indians. This establishes a tutelary regime that leads to the recognizance, by the subjects themselves, of a generic "indianness", a condition they have in common with other Indians that are subjected to this same relationship of tutelage.

In the history of indigenism the establishment of land reservations—usually described only as a "humanitarian" and "idealistic" procedure—contributed to the regularization of the regional land markets, and led to rising values of the land as merchandise. The complete capitalist regulation of land ownership (Martins, 1975) corresponds to the doctrine of the "siege of peace" (Lima, 1995) proposed by army officer Rondon and adopted by the military positivists.

17. Carvalho (1987) used the category "bestializados" ("the bestialized") to describe this multitude of marginal people, excluded from the political scene.

The indigenist agency has usually been more active in those places where Indian presence or circulation endangered regional interests, or where the Indians could possibly hinder large government projects (such as telegraph lines, railroads, roads, and more recently dams). In this manner, the indigenist agency avoided the physical extermination of the indigenous peoples by the agents of opposing local interests, and permitted a collective solution for the Indians by means of the tutelary protection of the state.

Political Performances in Tutelary Regime

Any possible indigenous strategy of control of territorial and environmental resources has necessarily to take into account the constraints created by the state's tutelary structure. This structure includes 344 *Postos Indígenas*[18], 445 Indian land reservations, 997 schools, and 292 infirmaries, with about 1500 employees in the *Postos Indígenas*, besides 44 regional administrative offices, 32 health stations (usually called "House of the Indian" because they serve as lodgings for Indians being treated in health facilities and their families), an ethnographic museum (with a documentation center and a library) and almost 2000 employees in these facilities. Most of the diversified indigenous demands flow towards this structure, among other reasons because until recent years they were usually ignored by other government agencies (ministries, state and municipal governments).

Thus, there is a tendency for the indigenists to have a monopoly over all the spaces of mediation between the indigenous societies, the state, and the many faces of the national society. As the indigenists have neither a specific training nor a relatively sophisticated and ever present doctrine for action (such as the British policy of Indirect Rule or the Mexican "indigenismo"), they end up establishing a network of personal clientelistic relations with some Indians, who by their turn mobilize and direct the others. The function of representation in the historical situation of the Indian reservation tends to be exerted by chiefs (called "*caciques*" or "*capitães*") that often have clientelistic relations with local civil servants (people with jobs on the local *Postos Indígenas* or in the Regional Administrations). The surest way of

18. Posto Indígena is the local headquarter of the government's indigenist agency, which may have multiple functions: bureaucratic, economic, social and health assistance, supervision and vigilance, etc.

involving the Indians is to make them employees of the agency, and then use them as mediators for the administration.

How is it possible for the Indians facing this structure of tutelage to interfere on the processes of territorialization and to exert their power of initiative and their agency, so as to widen their range of options by acting in various scales? Empirical observation shows us that this is done by means of four strategies. These strategies work as idioms for the expressions of their will and interests, as well as for the consolidation of different indigenous political projects.

As they face this tutelary structure, the Indians have three options to accomplish their interests. The first option we will call shortly, for simplicity's sake and to distinguish it from the others, "Indians as civil servants". It happens when the Indians enter the game of clientelistic relations with the indigenists. This gives them access to collective resources and leads to accumulation of material goods and prestige. The second option we will call "indigenous movements", and involves mobilization for land and assistance. The third option we will call "indigenous organization", which aims at creating mechanisms for territorial management and development. The fourth, which I will not focus here because it is rarely connected to collective strategies, involves breaking up with the relation of tutelage and searching for material and institutional support elsewhere: in other government levels, in private companies, or in contacts with private persons. This means looking for the same kinds of solutions that are available for any Brazilian, establishing relations of clientage outside the indigenist field.[19]

In the first alternative the Indian is absorbed by the structure of tutelage, and becomes a civil servant (usually in the lower levels), ruled by the same bureaucratic norms[20]. The trajectories of these Indians show a clear individualization in face of the original collectivity, and the progressive adaptation to roles and personality models exported by the whites. "Indians as civil servants" can be found in many local *Postos Indígenas* and in Regional Administrations of

19. As Darcy Ribeiro has already observed, the strong concentration of land ownership, the low wages and the precarious social security network available to the common citizen in Brazil make the complete integration into the national society quite unattractive from the Indians' point of view.

20. These rules, however, are applied with a certain laxity, because they are Indians.

the indigenist agency, but they are specially common among certain ethnic groups (among others, the Fulniô and Pankararu in the Northeast, the Kaingang in the South, the Terenas, Karajás and Xavantes in Central Brazil).

When these trajectories take some individual Indians outside the village and the local *Postos Indígena*, they need to master ever wider and more diversified abilities, and only a few exceptional persons are able to meet these requirements. The bureaucratic spaces, however, are limited, and in the upper echelons usually the non-indigenous officials have the first choice. Protests by indigenous civil servants are highlighted by the means of mass communication and appeal to the public opinion, resulting in that some Indians become widely known. This ends up creating a channel for the expression of indigenous claims, which is frequently used by the press, by the state and by international organizations to give the impression of indigenous participation in debates and decision-making processes[21]. This is, however, a highly personal and individualized process of representation, almost a native version of the career of some of the more illustrious "sertanistas"[22].

The Rise of the Indigenous Movements

In the later decades of the twentieth century indigenous claims and projects related to territory received wider attention. These initiatives are connected with the tutelary regime and with the system of Indian reservations. But they are also connected with the simultaneous presence of new actors, forms of action, themes and priorities. Such initiatives establish a game with specific constraints that opens new

---

21. Marcos Terena is the most impressive example of an Indian that, even though he is an employee of the indigenist agency, was able to carve out a special place through the means of mass communication as speaker for the Indians in general. Initially he was an airplane pilot, then he was one of the organizers of the UNI/União das Nações Indígenas—Union of the Indigenous Nations—and later he was chosen as representative for various international events. There are many other examples of Indians that are civil servants but appear widely in the regional press and are recognized by government agencies.

22. "Sertanistas" is the name given to those who act as something like "frontier pacifiers", usually employees of the indigenist agency who specialize in contacting and establishing peaceful relations with the Indians living in the "frontier".

spaces for the Indians, very different from the spaces that exist within official indigenist policy. Thus, we may consider them to form an articulated set of constraints and strategies that generate organizational models (that is, forms of association, social roles and linkages, as well as claims and mottos). We will now focus on the two strategies connected to this new situation.

The first context is the one I called "indigenous movement". This is a central operational category in the discourse of the Indians and of the actors and institutions that interact with them in this situation. The central belief here is that to have their rights recognized by the state, the Indians should mobilize themselves politically instead of waiting or demanding the protection of a "patron". They should create representative mechanisms, establish alliances and make public claims. Only if they created a system of pressures could the Indians force the state to act—identifying and demarcating indigenous lands, enhancing assistance, or solving administrative problems that had been pending for years.

The seventies and eighties were the time of wider visibility for this mode of political action. It was like a negative replica of the official indigenist policy, opposing state and civil society and proposing the amplification of citizenship. A survey of the non-governmental organizations that worked with protection and diffusion of indigenous peoples' rights points to the predominance of religious organizations (mostly connected to the Catholic Church and to the doctrines of "liberation theology"). In 1981, 15 secular associations were active, with very diverse histories, composition and aims; at the same time, there were 21 local groups of Catholic missionaries, articulated in one centralizing organization (CIMI, *Conselho Indigenista Missionário*—Missionary Indigenist Council[23]) and linked to other regional Catholic organizations (such as the OPAN/*Operação Anchieta*[24]) or to organizations connected to other religions (such as the GTME/*Grupo de Trabalho Missionário Evangélico*—Missionary Evangelical Work Group, and the IECLB/*Igreja Evangélica de*

23. CIMI was, by its turn, connected to the CNBB—Conferência Nacional dos Bispos Brasileiros (National Conference of the Brazilian Bishops), which had wide visibility and political influence and was one of the cornerstones of the re-democratization of the country along this period.

24. OPAN congregated former Jesuit seminarians, working initially in Mato Grosso, then later in other parts of the Amazon.

Confissão Luterana no Brasil—the Lutheran Church), which maintained 7 other local groups (respectively, 3, 3 and 1)[25].

The form of articulation proposed to the Indians was mobilization by means of successive meetings of various scales, from meetings in villages to large meetings in regional centers and state capitals. Beginning in Mato Grosso in 1974, meetings that became known as "Indigenous Assemblies" ("*Assembléias Indígenas*") spread to other regions of the country in the following years, always backed up by religious organizations. There were 15 such "Assemblies" before the end of the seventies, and they were very important to bring forth a number of Indians who served as speakers in behalf of their peoples' claims, most emphatically demanding land demarcation. In the beginning of the eighties this movement became even stronger and more visible. The meetings started to bring together also non-governmental organizations, anthropologists and other people who were interested in the indigenous question. From 1980 to 1984, a period of only four years, 42 such meetings were held.

The Indigenous Assemblies were inspired in the model of the "Ecclesiastical Base Communities" ("*Comunidades Eclesiais de Base*"), which were a form of action favored by the progressive sectors of the Catholic Church to recuperate the Church's popular support. They worked as open political forums, without any bureaucratic structure or continuous forms of action. The category that unified the procedures, and was never put into question, was "indigenous leader". This expression could be used to define any participant to these meetings—any Indian that would speak about "the problems" (needs and claims) of his people or village. This category could refer to chiefs of Indian reservations, or from a single village, as well as any influential persons (sometimes the chief's local opponent) or literate Indians that could express themselves better in Portuguese.

The mode of action of the Indigenous Assemblies was always the creation and legitimization of a mediation—assumed individually by a "leader"—towards the world of the whites (NGOs, human rights organizations, public opinion). This mediation should result in responses to collective claims (with emphasis on the demarcation of lands) to be fulfilled by the government's indigenist agency, FUNAI.

25. Besides this, there were occasional partnerships with secular organizations, universities, anthropologists, etc.

The "leaders" became speakers on behalf of their people, bringing forth accusations and claims, being interviewed (by government authorities, prestigious organizations or the press), and mobilizing committees that would go on pilgrimage to FUNAI's regional headquarters or the national headquarter in Brasília to exert "pressure" for the recognition of indigenous rights.

Thus, the action of the leaders consisted of intermittently proposing and inspecting the official initiatives, working as a trigger for indigenist action. To do this, they were backed up by the non-governmental organizations, reinforcing a dichotomous division (between "official indigenism" and "alternative indigenism") and the mechanisms of exclusion and mutual accusations between the FUNAI and the NGOs (NGOs accused FUNAI of omission and inefficiency, FUNAI argued that the NGOs focused only on the problems but did not help solving them). The process of mobilization triggered by the "Indigenous Assemblies" excluded the traditional authorities, which were more connected to themes and forms of action typical of local ethnopolitics and were often accommodated and linked to the structure of tutelage. Contrariwise, the category "leaders"—referring to those mediators engaged in the struggle for rights and having domain over the vocabulary of participation and political conscience—became more and more accessible to the Indians that acted as external mediators (even if they were usually distant from the daily life of the villages and took no part in the local level decision processes).

The "Indigenous Assemblies", the committees, and the protests made visible a new political actor, who appeared to the public opinion as "indigenous movement" (a movement composed and directed by "indigenous leaders"). Even though the political demands that were raised (such as the demarcation of the lands) were accepted by society and legitimized by the native authorities, political initiative was not controlled by the collectivities. Rather, the indigenous mediators and the NGOs (that furnished the resources for the accomplishment of the meetings and elaborated the schedules of these meetings and activities) controlled it.

Even though there were important impacts on public opinion[26]

26. The insistence of the press in consulting a few "leaders" created a hall of fame of Indians that became "public persons", serving as authorized speakers for all questions connected to indigenous populations.

and on the restructuring of official policies[27], the results of this process were small regarding the mode of political organization of the villages and the mode of control over ethnic territories. The indigenous mediators have an external source of power and often escape the mechanisms of control exerted by the collectivities they are supposed to represent; however, they are fragile facing the power of the state and the attacks of powerful sectors of national society.

Being specialists only in functions of external mediation, many of these "leaders" after some time were captured by the structure of tutelage. They were hired as unqualified manual workers, directors of local *Postos Indígenas*, bilingual teachers, health assistants, or maybe even regional directors or councilors (in Brasília). Some others were transformed in to political candidates (most of them running for local municipal councils) by all kinds of political parties (even the most conservative ones, which are consistently opposed to all indigenous movements' claims). Others, still, were hired for positions in the local municipal governments. Recently, some of them are being absorbed into evangelical churches, which have trained them as professional "preachers". All this reminds us of integrationist strategies and political projects (that I have mentioned as the fourth political alternative).

Political Indigenous Performances in New Globalized Settings

In this context, few indigenous organizations were formed. Between 1982 and 1987, there were only nine indigenous organizations with an ethnic or regional basis, most of them around the Amazon and Negro rivers. The oldest one is the CGTT/*Comando Geral da Tribo Ticuna* (General Command of the Ticuna Tribe), created in 1982 as a forum that congregated the chiefs ("*capitães*") of Ticuna villages, united around the claim for demarcation of their lands. The *Conselho Indígena de Roraima*/CIR (Indigenous Council of Roraima) was created in 1987. It seems to be connected to the "Indigenous Assemblies" that brought together Makuxi and Wapixana Indians. The FOIRN/*Federação das Organizações Indígenas do Rio Negro* (Federation of the Indigenous Organizations of the Negro River) was born in 1987, congregating cooperatives and associations that were

27. In 1982, indigenous lands amounted to 13 million hectares; today, this figure has risen to more than 60 million hectares, reflecting a new stance of the government regarding the issue.

active along some of the rivers in this region (such as the ACITRUT/ *Associação das Comunidades Indígenas do Rio Traíra*—Association of the Indigenous Communities of the Traíra River—and the AUCIRT/ *Associação Unificada das Comunidades Indígenas do Rio Tiquiê*—Unitary Association of the Indigeous Communities of the Tiquiê River, which were created in 1986 and 1987 respectively).

Some of these associations were active before being registered as a legally recognized body. The CGTT, for instance, was legally registered only when a dissident faction tried to jump ahead and register it in its own name in the local public notary. The Constitution of 1988 recognized the legal capacity of the indigenous communities to represent themselves, independently of the governments' indigenist agency. This contributed for the growth of indigenous organizations in the following years: in 1988, five of them were created, and eight in 1989.

The context has changed radically since 1991. Concerned with the fact that the Second World Conference on Environment and Development (1992 World Summit) was going to be held in Brazil, government agencies accelerated the demarcation of indigenous lands and opened the way for many environmental protection programs (including the ones that concerned the indigenous areas). Many of these programs were supported by international agencies (World Bank, BID, EEC, G-7, etc.) and are seen with sympathy by the international public opinion.

Progressively, the Brazilian government started to participate in the international forums that work towards combining environmental protection and development. Within a planet-wide macropolitics, the indigenous areas are seen as important conservation units. Internally in Brazil, adaptation to this new context has been much slower, and has lasted most of the decade. Recently, the most affected ministries (such as the Ministry of Environment and the Ministry of Science and Technology) and foundations (such as the FUNAI and the IBAMA—organ responsible for the environmental conservation units) finally established new procedures and engaged specialized teams, supported by programs funded by international resources.

Taking up the year of 1992 as a mark, the NGOs have moved faster: they changed their forms of action, themes and rhetoric. The main concerns of the seventies and eighties, such as human rights and democracy, ceased to be a priority, and the main focus now is on natural resource conservation. The NGOs personnel assumed a more specialized and technical profile, and the organizations took up a dialogue with government organs and international cooperation agencies. The militant and critical stance that predominated in the earlier decades became rare.

Another decisive factor for this new political configuration was the decision of the cooperation agencies to handle resources directly to local communities and initiatives, giving preference to partners seen as closer to the groups which would put the project in practice. The indigenous organizations became the best candidates for development and environmental protection projects, and the NGOs were admitted rather as partners that should furnish technical counseling.

The new rules and directives connected to this political context soon caused a multiplication of indigenous organizations. Already in 1991, there were 48 organizations; in 1996, there were 109, and in 1999 they amounted to 290! Of this total, 195 (that is, more than two thirds) were in the Amazon, reflecting the priority given to this region by the international support agencies. In the survey made by MARI (1999) a significant number of these organizations (76, corresponding to almost one quarter) did not have addresses, which probably means they are very recent.

There are however some very positive aspects in this new context, if compared to the clientelism that is typical of the tutelary structure or to the individual mediation made by the "leaders" and the "Indigenous Assemblies". First, because for the first time the importance of the incorporation of indigenous culture and traditions to the development projects and the political mediation processes is overtly recognized. Second, there is an emphasis on the local management of resources and on the local initiatives, with a concern that the projects should be adapted to the collective and local procedures. Third, there is a concern with accountability and rationality in the decision-making processes, as well as in the planning and evaluation of the results.

There are many risks involved, however. The first one is that the state, which now has other priorities, might destroy the tutelary structure without at the same time creating institutional solutions that can absorb and redirect it, and without defining any controlling and supervising mechanisms. The second risk concerns the economic and political viability of the few existing experiences. Are the alternative projects only laboratories for innovative practices that would have to be assumed by government structures, or can they be self-sustaining, with a capacity to generate sufficient revenue to maintain the older assistential network, while correcting its vices? The third question concerns the de-politicization of the actions of the NGOs and indigenous organizations, as they tend to adopt a strictly technical idiom and to act upon aims and means that are often supposed to be consensual. Even without external funding, some of the state governments in the Amazon region, such as the governments of Amapá and Acre, have supported a few projects and programs directed to the Indians, because of their political principles. On the other hand, many economic and environmental plans with good funding and sound technical directives are ruined by bureaucratic and political mechanisms. As Ferguson has observed, there is great danger in naively assuming a "anti-politics" attitude based on the NGOs (Ferguson, 1995).

Diversity and Dynamism in Contemporary Indigenous Movements

In the Brazilian juridico-political context, recognizing a collectivity as indigenous implies encapsulating it in a specific territory, which is controlled and regulated directly by the state. During the last two decades forces and possibilities linked in different scales resulted in the appearance of three strategies for the political expression of the indigenous populations. These strategies are connected to different sets of categories, roles, dynamisms and demands that we have named shortly as "Indians as civil servants", "indigenous movements" and "indigenous organizations".

All these strategies and projects point to the construction of an indigenous citizenship, having an ethnic territory as its base. The latter two strategies, however, value the process of strengthening civil society, which distinguishes them from the more corporatist and statist stance of the "Indians as civil servants" strategy. Each of these two, however, has different conceptions and modes of action. In one of them, what is most important is the recognition of rights and opposition to the state (at least the state in its present form), demanding alliances with other excluded sectors of society. In the other one, what matters most is the management of territory, combining environmental conservation and development. These distinctive social origins and projects are at the root of the conflictive interpretations given by the indigenous associations and speakers to the facts that happened in southern Bahia, during the celebration of the "500 years".

About 2000 Indians gathered in this event, from the most diverse ethnic groups, regions and organizations in Brazil. The aim was to produce the first national conference of the indigenous peoples. Locally, the more tense and dramatic moment was in a march, with confrontation with the Military Police of the state of Bahia, richly covered by the press. In the evaluation of these events, the differences between the two strategies, we have distinguished in this chapter, came clearly expressed (included through public documents and evaluations made by them after the fact).

On the one hand, there was a document presented by COIAB/ Coordenação das Organizações Indígenas da Amazônia Brasileira – Coordination of Indigenous Organizations in Brazilian Amazonia), which represents the indigenous organizations of the Amazon, that accuses the catholic missionaries of manipulations and interferences on indigenous affairs.

On the other hand, there were documents prepared by the CAPOIB/Comitê de Articulação dos Povos e Organizações Indígenas do Brasil (Committee of Articulation of the Indigenous Peoples and Organizations in Brazil), which has a strong representation of the indigenous peoples from the Northeast, usually excluded from the international cooperation programs, that accused Amazon Indian leaders to be passive and clientelistic to the government.

I have focused my analysis on a political dimension still little investigated: the construction of different and sometimes opposed strategies and political projects by leaders, intellectuals and representatives of Indian people, based in a set of constraints, alliances, and agency that can be observed and described through ethnographic work.

To better understand this, we had to bring into focus the colonial relationship, in its diversity and its constitutive contradictions. If instead of treating the native and the colonizer as categories that are totalizing, self-evident and diametrically opposed, we explore their internal variability, the different historical contexts to which they are connected, and the multiplicity of linkages that are established between these partial categories, we might open up a new field of research. Maybe so the notion of a single indigenous voice (or a native model), frequently active on activists discourses, could be substituted by an effort to bring out the different social strategies that make this voice so diversified and contradictory.

References

Bailey, F. G. 1969. *Stratagems and Spoils: A Social Anthropology of Politics.* New York: Schocken Books.

Bailey, F. G. 1960. *Tribe, Caste and Nation: A Study of Political Activity and Political Change in Highand Orissa.* London: Manchester University Press.

Balandier, Georges. 1951. "La Situation Coloniale: Approche Théorique". *Cahiers Internationaux De Sociologie,* XI, pp. 44–79.

Barth, Fredrik. 1969. 'Introduction,' in *Ethnic Groups and Boundaries.* Boston: Little Brown & Co.

Cardoso de Oliveira, Roberto. 1964. *O Índio E O Mundo Dos Brancos.* 2 Ed. São Paulo: Difusão Européia do livro. (Há Uma 4ª Edição Da Editora Da Unicamp, De 1994, Incluindo Um Posfácio).

Carvalho, José Murilo de. 1987. *Os Bestializados: O Rio De Janeiro E A República Que Não Foi.* 2. Ed. São Paulo: Companhia Das Letras.

Cunha, Manuela Carneiro da (org.) 1992. *História dos índios no Brasil.* São Paulo: Companhia das Letras.

Ferguson, James. 1995. *The anti-politics machine: "development, "depoliticization, and bureaucratic power in Lesotho.* Cambridge: Cambridge University Press.

Galvão, Eduardo. 1978. *Encontro De Sociedades.* Rio De Janeiro: Paz E Terra..

Gluckman, Max and Devons, E. 1968. Ïnter-Hierarchical Roles: Professional and Party Ethics in Tribal Areas in South and Central Africa", in Marc J. Swartz ed., *Local-Level Politics.* Chicago: Aldine.

Grupioni, Luís Donizete Benzi. 1999. *Diretório De Associações E Organizações Indígenas No Brasil.* INEP/MEC E MARI/UIP.

Hirsch, Eric. 1996. 'Introduction: Landscape: Between Place and Space', in Eric Hirsch and Michael O'Hanlon. *The Anthropology of Landscape: Perspectives on Place and Space.* Oxford: Clarendon Press, pp. 1–30.

Hirsch, Eric and Michael O'Hanlon, eds. 1996. *The Anthropology of Landscape. Perspectives on Place and Space.* Oxford: Clarendon Press.

Lima, Antônio Carlos Souza. 1995. *Um Grande Cerco De Paz.* ANPOCS. Petrópolis: Ed. Vozes.

Martins, José De Souza. 1975. *Capitalismo E Tradicionalismo.* São Paulo: Livraria Pioneira.

Maybury-Lewis, David. 1965. *The Savage and the Innocent.* Cleveland: World Publishing Company.

Murphy, Robert. 1978. *Headhunters Heritage: Social and Economic Change Among the Munducuru Indians.* New York: Octogon Books.

Oliveira, João Pacheco De. 1977. *As Facções E A Ordem Política Em Uma Reserva Ticuna.* Brasília: Universidade De Brasília.. Dissertação De Mestrado Em Antropologia Social.

_______. 1988. *"O Nosso Governo": Os Ticuna E O Regime Tutelar.* Rio De Janeiro: Marco Zero/Cnpq.

_______. 1999. *Ensaios Em Antropologia História*. Rio De Janeiro: Editora UFRJ.

_______. 1999. *A Viagem Da Volta: Etnicidade, Política E Reelaboração Cultural No Nordeste Indígena*. Rio De Janeiro: Contra Capa.

Ortiz, Fernando. 1943. *Etnia Y Sociedad*. Cuba: Editorial De Ciencias Sociales, (Pensamiento Cubano).

Peirano, Mariza. 1991. The Anthropology of Anthropology: The Brazilian Case. *Série Antropologia, 110*. Brasília:Unb.

Raffestin, Claude. 1986. "Écogénese Territoriale Et Territoriale" in F. Auriac and R. Brunet eds., *Espaces, Jeux & Enjeux*. Paris: Gallimard/Le Seuil, pp. 173–185.

Ribeiro, Darcy. 1970. *Os Índios E A Civilização*. Rio De Janeiro: Civilização Brasileira.

Riviere, Peter. 1972. *The Forgotten Frontier: Ranches of North Brazil*. New York: Holt, Rinchart and Winsdon.

Stocking Jr., G. W. 1991. "Colonial Situations", in *Colonial Situations: Essays on the Contextualization of Ethnographic Knowledge*. Madison: The University of Wisconsin Press.

Velho, Otávio Guilherme. 1972. *Fontes De Expansão E Estrutura Agrária*. Rio De Janeiro: Ed. Zahar.

_______. 1976. *Capitalismo Autoritário E Campesinato*. Rio De Janeiro: Ed. Difel.

6

Indigenous Identity and Activism in Brazil After the Federal Constitution of 1988

Stephen G. Baines

In this article, I examine some general questions on the specificity of indigenous identity and activism in Brazil since the promulgation of the Brazilian Federal Constitution of 1988. I then go on to briefly mention some ethnographic examples of ethnic reconfiguration: among the Waimiri-Atroari people in Amazonas and Roraima states; the Makushi and Wapishana along the international border between Guyana and Brazil; some other indigenous peoples in the Amazon region, and the Tremembé indigenous peoples on the northeast coast of Brazil, who are re-organizing themselves politically and culturally as indigenous peoples in relation to the State, to illustrate just a few examples of the immense diversity of situations in Brazil.

The Brazilian Federal Constitution of 1988 brought several changes to the legal rights of indigenous peoples, some marking a clear advance over previous Constitutions such as the right for indigenous peoples to legally represent themselves. Other changes are polemic, such as the right for private mining companies to operate on Indian lands with the previous consent of the indigenous peoples impacted and with Congressional approval.

In the case of the Waimiri-Atroari, encapsulated within an indigenist[1] programme which depends on the economic interests of giant companies which undertake large-scale regional development projects—the Balbina Hydroelectric Scheme and the Pitinga mine — the possibility of political activism is circumscribed by an assistance programme of entrepreneurial indigenism which imposes a regime of

1. I use the term "indigenist" to refer to policies or assistance programmes planned for indigenous peoples by the State, the church, companies, or non-government organisations, distinct from "Indian policies" which are the policies which indigenous people plan for themselves.

surveilled freedom over this indigenous people and rigidly controls their access to information, their access to the indigenous political movement, and prohibits access to their area by anthropologists who are independent of the programme (Baines, 2000). After decades of interethnic conflicts and violence from the regional population, lethal epidemics, drastic depopulation, and capitulation to powerful military forces in the 1970s, the survivors were incorporated into an "attraction front" administered by the FUNAI[2] and submitted to attempts at re-socialization (Baines, 1991). In the case of the Wapishana and Macushi on the border between Guyana and Brazil, these two indigenous peoples interact with two national States which have different indigenist policies. Other descendants of indigenous populations who suffered colonisation and enslavement, losing their original languages, are re-identifying as indigenous peoples through participation in ethno-political movements. In the case of the Tremembé in the northeast of Brazil, indigenous identities emerge in different local contexts and through claims to territorial rights (Valle, 1999), facing large companies of industrial coconut production, in Varjota, Tapera and Almofala, in the municipalities of Itarema and Acaraú, and as a strategy of defence against the proposed implantation of a giant tourist city, "Nova Atlântida", by a consortium of transnational companies in Buriti and São José, in the municipality of Itapipoca.

In the 1960s, Fredrik Barth (1969), proposed that ethnic groups should be treated as forms of social organisation and no longer as cultural unities, as was the custom in most studies in Social Anthropology at that time. Barth transferred the emphasis from the study of ethnic groups themselves to the study of ethnic boundaries and laid emphasis on the organisational aspect of ethnic identity, culture being an important but not a determining factor. Roberto Cardoso de Oliveira, in dialogue with Barth, introduced the notion of "contrastive identity...which implies the affirmation of *we* in relation to *others* .... It is an identity which emerges by opposition.... In the case of ethnic identity, it is affirmed 'negating' the other identity, which is 'ethnocentrically' visualized" (Cardoso de Oliveira, 1976:5–6).

---

2. Fundação Nacional do Índio (FUNAI—National Indian Foundation) is the Brazilian government indigenist agency. FUNAI was created in 1967 to substitute the Serviço de Proteção ao Índio (SPI—Indian Protection Service), which had been created in 1910.

In anthropological research with indigenous societies it is important to examine and to give value to the native viewpoints about the historical processes in which they are enmeshed, calling attention to their role as active subjects who claim ethnic identities. The two principal theoretical lines of approach which emerged in Social Anthropology in the study of ethnic identity in the 1960–70s—the primordialist and the instrumentalist—are no longer capable of dealing with the new situations in which Indians have become subjects of their rights and protagonists of their own histories. The primordialist perspective of analysis seeks references in ancestral origins, in elements which refer to consanguinity, and to the idea of historical continuity, treating ethnic identity in an essentialist way. The instrumentalist perspective focuses the claim to an ethnic identity in relation to land rights, differentiated education and health attendance, and ethno-development projects. However, studying the ways in which indigenous people identify themselves, we perceive that these two lines of approach merge, since indigenous people often claim a primordial essence to make effective their political struggle as an ethnic group, while at the same time they politicise their ethnicity, through participation in ethno-political movements.

In this article, I focus ethnicity in relation to territory and differentiated rights among indigenous populations in Brazil, showing that ethnicity encompasses many different situations, from those which can be classified as paradigmatic for government indigenist policy as, for example, an "attraction front" of the FUNAI in the Brazilian Amazon region, to situations of ethnic re-elaboration centred around the indigenous political movement itself, such as the Macushi and Wapishana on the Brazil-Guyana border, and yet other situations of cultural re-elaboration (Oliveira, 2004) or ethno-genesis, among peoples such as the Mura in the municipality of Autazes in Amazonas State, the Baré on the Rio Negro, the Nawa (Correia, 2007) in Acre state, and the Tremembé on the northeast coast of Brazil.

I shall first raise some general questions about the specificity of processes of ethnic re-configuration and indigenous political activism in Brazil which have occurred, especially, since the promulgation of the Brazilian Constitution of 1988. The growth of the indigenous political movement since the 1970s, and increasing political pressure exerted by indigenous leaders, both at national and international levels, to guarantee their rights, and an intense mobilization of Indians in the constitutional process together with support organisations, led to several changes in the Brazilian Constitution of 1988, which at least brought the potential to bring about changes in the relations between indigenous peoples and the State. Two very important innovations compared to the previous Federal Constitutions are the recognition of indigenous rights to their lands as "original" rights from the fact that the Indians were the first inhabitants of Brazil, and the abandonment of the assimilation perspective which understood Indians to be a transitory category destined to disappear. The Federal Constitution of 1988 spells the end of attempts at assimilation and integration of Indians by the State, by establishing the principle that indigenous communities are constituted as collective subjects having collective rights. Another important innovation is that in Article 232, it has been recognized that "Indians, their communities and organisations are legitimate parts to go to court in defence of their rights and interests, the Attorney General Department intervening in all the acts of the process", ending the situation in which they could only be represented by the FUNAI. Indigenous peoples become recognised as active subjects in legal proceedings, following the international tendency to incorporate indigenous rights into national constitutions. One consequence of this has been an efflorescence of indigenous organisations (Albert, 2000).

The rapid growth of indigenous organisations has played an important role in exerting pressure to consolidate indigenous rights. Indigenous political organisations opened the door for many leaders to become political actors in interethnic relations with the national society, occupying political spaces in which they seek visibility and recognition. One strategy of the indigenous political movement has been to seek formal school education as a way of preparing young people to face the national society using its own instruments to demand that their rights be respected. Many present-day leaders who participate in the administration of indigenous organisations are people who have gone through formal school and university education. The formation of an indigenous intelligentsia has also led to contradictions, since indigenous teachers have acted, in many cases, both as reproducers of national ideology and as agents who formulate and modernize ethnic ideologies (Alves, 2007:298).

On the one hand, according to Alves, the transit between government institutions and indigenous organisations is seen by many Indians as something positive which strengthens the leaders and gives them power and influence with politicians and bureaucrats. On the other hand, this transit between jobs in public institutions and political posts in indigenous organisations can lead to potential conflicts between Indians, involving them in political party disputes, accusations of betraying the Indian cause, of having capitulated to political pressure for personal interest, to be playing a double game, leading to possible fragmentation of the indigenous political movement. Often, indigenous leaders, as a strategy to face segments of the national society which are immensely more powerful, hide or suppress these conflicts as a way of obtaining a consensus to guarantee the viability of political representation at the regional or national level, although the consensus may be weakened as a result.

The term "traditional populations" reflects the attempt by the national State to recognise the fact, emphasised by Oliveira, that "the indigenous peoples of the Northeast do not fit into the generic representation of Indians as primitive; neither can they be thought of according to the conventional schemes of Brazilian indigenism" (Oliveira, 1993:vii). Oliveira adds, "It was the situation of attraction and pacification, where the State had to face groups of isolated Indians, which maintained control over or disputed with expansion fronts significant parts of the national territory" (ibid), which moulded the paradigms of government indigenist policy.

With the emergence of new indigenous identities and the re-emergence of ethnic identities which were considered extinct, Oliveira affirms:

> The diacritical signs usually used to delimit cultural boundaries...cannot be applied with any success at all...the Indian cannot easily be distinguished in terms of cultural characteristics from the rural population descended from Indians, black people, slaves or fugitives, and white people of lower social condition (Oliveira, 1993:vi).

Taking into consideration the fact that there is not any cultural distance from the regional population "that might be used to justify the creation of a tutelary regime aiming to isolate the Indians and manage their heritage" (Oliveira, 1993:viii), Oliveira stresses that this "indigenous peasantry (Oliveira, 1979)...claims...the guarantee of access to land, source of their political mobilization and basis for a re-composition and/or ethnic elaboration" (Oliveira, 1993:viii).

Several "emergent" or "resistant" indigenous peoples have appeared during recent years because they have only recently chosen to emerge from invisibility and manifest their identity, demanding their rights in a society in which they have traditionally been discriminated. Arruti refers to this process, which some anthropologists have called "ethno-genesis", as "the construction of a self-consciousness and of a collective identity against an action of disrespect (generally produced by the national State) aiming at recognition and the conquest of collective objectives" (Arruti, 2006:51). Indigenous peoples taken to be extinct and/or unknown are reappearing and claiming the right to difference (Arruti, 1997).

This process, as Oliveira (ibid) emphasises, "results from a set of pressures and alliances within the field of indigenist policy action, populated also by other banners, institutions and ideologies as well as the FUNAI" (The Indigenist Missionary Council—Conselho Indigenista Missionário [CIMI]—of the Catholic Church and other non-government organisations). Although the emergent ethnic identities in the Amazon region are appearing in a geographically and culturally different context than the Northeast, we can agree with Oliveira, based on Hobsbawm (1984) and Bourdieu (1984), that

> [i]t is under the sign of the invention of culture that we must consider the indigenous peoples of the Northeast, with a resolute movement to discard the ethnological bias of looking for authentic cultures in the present (or even specific cultural sources of ethnicity). It does not matter how much the symbols and values effectively come from outside, what matters is that they are lived and thought of as if they were branded on the bodies and sentiments of individuals... (Oliveira, 1993:viii).

In the case of the Waimiri-Atroari, the official government indigenist policy aimed to transform this indigenous people into sedentary farmers, with the aim of preparing them for a redefinition of the use of their territory, through assistance programmes planned within a logic of indemnifications aimed at mitigating the impacts of the Balbina Dam (Baines, 1996).

Referring to the process of ethnic re-elaboration of an indigenous population, Oliveira affirms: "In the description of everyday life in an attraction front, facts appear not as denunciations, but because it is impossible to describe the real behaviour omitting the factors of domination and violence" (Oliveira, 1989:30). The indigenist policy in this area, which imposed the sedentarisation of the Waimiri-Atroari in settlements made up of an Indian village and a government Indian Post, and their submission to a controlled agricultural work regime (Baines, 1991, Chapter VII), was permeated by a concern in mitigating, verbally, its coercive character and presenting the drastic changes imposed as if they were being undertaken according to Waimiri-Atroari traditions, through a rhetoric of "respect for traditions" (Baines, 1991:26, 137–138, 173–175). To try to justify the domination of the Waimiri-Atroari by the FUNAI employees, the indigenist policy makers of the attraction front had to invent new traditions, called by Ranger in his study of colonialism in Africa "neo-traditions of subordination" (Ranger, 1984:236–237). The process of invention of traditions in the Waimiri-Atroari attraction front incorporated all the contradictions of an indigenist policy which aimed to "integrate" the Waimiri-Atroari to the national society and, at the same time, "preserve their traditions" (Baines, 1991:301).

After the Indian political movement had been consolidated through the 1970s, 1980s and 1990s, and new legal rights recognised for indigenous peoples in the Brazilian Constitution of 1988, the possibility emerged of establishing interethnic relations that are less asymmetrical than in the past. Cardoso de Oliveira, basing his argument on the notion of "ethno-development" of Rodolfo Stavenhagen, mentions the possibility of "creating conditions for a real community of communication to be established by the parts involved in the interethnic conjunction and, with this, a community of intercultural argumentation" (Cardoso de Oliveira, 2000:222), with the theoretical possibility "of the emergence of a common nexus within this new community of communication, or of a knowledge fruit of a 'fusion of horizons'...where the parts might establish a minimal universe of rules that guarantee free and productive interlocution" (ibid).

Cardoso de Oliveira, referring to the Apel-Habermas theory of discourse ethics, points out some of the difficulties which seem to be inherent to the interethnic dialogue. Without taking these difficulties into consideration it would be impossible for any indigenist practices to make this dialogue viable (2000:224). He emphasizes that the main difficulty is that "the dialogue is compromised to the rules of hegemonic discourse; that is, in dealing with relations between Indians and non-Indians, the hegemony of the institutionalized rules of the discourse of the dominant pole over the dominated pole, of the non-Indian over the Indian" (ibid). Cardoso de Oliveira argues that:

> [i]n the relation between indigenous and non-indigenous peoples, mediated or not by the State (FUNAI), even if an interethnic community of communication and argumentation could be created, which presupposes democratic dialogical relations (at least this is the intention of the dominant pole), *the dialogue would be compromised by the rules of hegemonic discourse* (2000:225)

Thus, a "'distorted communication' between Indians and non-Indians would persist, compromising the ethical dimension of the argumentative discourse" (Cardoso de Oliveira, 2000:226).

The Waimiri-Atroari (Ki'in'ja) and Ethnicity

Despite a long and violent history of interethnic contacts, well documented from the nineteenth century, the Waimiri-Atroari (Ki'in'já) indigenous people have had continuous contact with agents of the national society since 1979. The names "Waimiri" and "Atroari" are a historical social construction of government indigenist policy. I shall examine the way the government indigenist administration has dealt with the Waimiri-Atroari indigenous population through local administrations—the Waimiri-Atroari Attraction Front (FAWA) of the FUNAI (1970–87) and the "Programa Waimiri-Atroari" (FUNAI/ ELETRONORTE[3]) which has succeeded it since 1987—in relation to the construction of ethnicity. During fieldwork (1982–85) with this indigenous people, I witnessed a process which was in many ways the inverse of what is happening in cases of the emergence of new indigenous identities in other areas, including parts of the Amazon Basin and especially in the Northeast of Brazil. In the case of ethnic emergence or re-elaboration, especially in the Northeast, "the 'Indians' were poor rural workers without access to land, and also did not present a strong cultural contrast with other rural workers" (Oliveira, 2004:20).

3. "ELETRONORTE", or "Centrais Elétricas do Norte do Brasil S/A", created in 1973, is a concessionary of public service of electrical energy, a society of mixed economy, subsidiary of "Centrais Elétricas Brasileiras S.A.—Eletrobrás", which aims to undertake studies, projects, the construction and operation of generating plants and systems of transmission and distribution of electrical energy, as well as commercialization of the energy generated by the company.

The construction of ethnicity is occurring through popular movements in relation to land claims, based on a re-composition and/or ethnic elaboration.

Citing Oliveira:

> If, in the Amazon, the worst threat is the invasion of indigenous territories and degradation of their environmental resources, in the case of the Northeast, the challenge to indigenist policy action is to *re-establish indigenous territories*, promoting the removal of non-Indians from Indian areas, *de-naturalizing* the 'mixture' as the only way to achieve survival and citizenship (ibid:20).

The Waimiri-Atroari were submitted to government indigenist policies, under pressure from large companies which operate in their traditional territories (Mineração Taboca, a mining company of the gigantic Paranapanema Group and ELETRONORTE, the government company responsible for constructing and operating large hydroelectric schemes in all the Amazon region), which aimed at rapidly re-socialising this indigenous people so that they did not present an obstacle to large scale economic development. In a violent process of entrepreneurial indigenist policies (Baines, 1991, 1993a, 1993b) which incorporate the dynamic of large company pressures over the Indians, the administration, through an "official theory", aimed at redefining the Waimiri-Atroari as "civilized Indians", obedient executors of orders, recruited as spokespersons of the administration itself. This social invention of ethnicity, controlled at that time by the FAWA, through the imposition of a disciplinary work regime, following the working hours of the FUNAI employees, was part of a larger plan, articulated at the level of the federal government, to redefine this indigenous territory with the object of installing large-scale regional development projects—the Pitinga mine (Paranapanema) and the Balbina Hydroelectric Dam (ELETRONORTE).

Despite the fact that its supervisor presents the "Programa Waimiri-Atroari", implanted in 1987 when the dam was in the final stage of construction, and a few months before a vast area of traditional Waimiri-Atroari lands were flooded (Viveiros de Castro e Andrade, 1988), as an example of "alternative indigenist policy", the incorporation of Waimiri-Atroari leaders in its administration certainly does not represent "the emergence of a 'community of communication and argumentation', created in the process of 'planning, execution and evaluation', mentioned by Rodolfo Stavenhagen (1985) (Cardoso de Oliveira, 1994:24–25), in his concept of ethno-development. Nor does it guarantee the possibility of bringing into effect interethnic relations in symmetrical terms, as ELETRONORTE would like to make it appear in its publicity films and propaganda. On the contrary, the images of Waimiri-Atroari leaders published by ELETRONORTE through the media hide extremely asymmetrical social relations established by an indigenist administration which subordinates the Indians to decision processes of planning, execution and evaluation, incorporating them in its publicity campaigns. Since 1987, when it was implanted, the company has been constructing images of a model programme of indigenist policy, manipulating demographic data to present it as having "saved the Waimiri-Atroari from extinction" (Baines, 2000), with the implicit message to the public that the noxious impacts of giant hydroelectric schemes which flood large areas of Indian territories can not only be overcome, but turned into advantages for the indigenous peoples through assistance programmes. In this way, the company aligns the compensatory actions of the "Programa Waimiri-Atroari" with the energy policy to expand the construction of giant hydroelectric schemes in the Amazon which, if constructed, will flood other Indian territories and seriously affect other indigenous peoples, such as ELETRONORTE's latest and most profitable project, the Belo Monte Hydroelectric Scheme on the River Xingu.

Macushi and Wapishana on the Border of Brazil and Guyana

I shall limit my comments here to those Macushi and Wapishana who live on both sides of the international border between Guyana and Brazil, from Jacamim Indian Land in the south, passing through Pium, Bonfim, Lethem and St. Ignatius, Normandia, to Uiramutã and Willimon in the Raposa Serra do Sul Indian Land, and Kamapang. These indigenous peoples who have been involved in interethnic contact with segments of the national populations of these two countries since the eighteenth century, and have passed through great changes in their culture and society as a result of this long history of contact.

Despite the existence of networks of kinship which spread out linking villages on both sides of the border and deep into these two national States in all the region of savannah, and an intense flow of migrants which, in recent years, is predominantly from Guyana to Brazil, the dialogue between the indigenous political organisations which have most influence in this border region, the Indigenous Council of Roraima (Conselho Indígena de Roraima—CIR) in Brazil, and the Amerindian Peoples Association (APA) in Guyana, is still incipient. However, in both Brazil and Guyana, indigenous leaders through indigenous organisations, following the legal systems of their respective countries, are making land claims for their lands to be officially recognized to permit the cultural survival of indigenous peoples who have been living in this region long before an international border was imposed[4]. On the Brazilian side of this border, the indigenous peoples are organizing themselves, above all, through indigenous political organisations, while on the Guyanese side political participation has been more through leaders running as candidates within the national political parties. In a post-colonial society with enormous inequalities and many Indians living in a situation of marginalization in border regions far from the densely populated coastlands, neglected by the State which is far more concerned in trying to manage the ethnic conflicts between the majority of Afro-descendents and East Indian descendents, the indigenous peoples along the border look more to Brazil as a possible way out from the apparently insuperable political and ethnic conflicts of Guyanese society.

In this border situation between two States, in which indigenous matters reach the international media, such as the indigenous claims for the demarcation and homologation of the Raposa Serra do Sol Indian Land, which was finally homologated by the Brazilian federal government on 15 April 2005, after many years of conflicts, and the present-day struggle to remove the rice-producers from this Indian land, indigenous leaders who live along this border exert pressure over the national governments, as Catherine Howard observed among the Waiwai, further to the south on this same international border (Howard, 2002:38–39). The Macushi and Wapishana, together with other indigenous societies, through indigenous leaders and organisations such as the Conselho Indígena de Roraima (CIR),

4. The dispute over this border was only solved in 1904, after Brazil and England sent the matter to the arbitration of the king of Italy, who announced his decision drawing the border along the River Maú/Ireng and River Tacutu (Riviére, 1995).

are bringing into effect their rights which are guaranteed in the Brazilian Constitution. In Guyana, claims are being made through the Amerindian Peoples Association (APA), although more timid compared to the situation on the Brazilian side of this international border.

Re-ethnicization Processes and Indigenous Peoples Who Were Made Invisible

The Mura have lost their language after more than three centuries of slavery and speak Portuguese. Their culture is similar to that of the regional population, however, since the 1990s, they are identifying as Mura and demanding that the Brazilian State recognises their rights as Indians, with the creation of the Mura Indigenous Council (Conselho Indígena Mura—CIM) which has its headquarters in the town of Autazes on the lower course of the River Madeira. Their population was estimated to be about 300 persons in 1997, and had grown to more than 5,540 by 2000[5], by the adhesion of more people to this ethno-political movement of re-identification. Their leaders sign agreements following legal norms, they meet publicly to deal with government and non-government organs, and constitute part of the movement of indigenous protagonism.

Some indigenous peoples of the Amazon, especially in the Rio Negro basin, on the River Uaupés and River Içana, use the Amazon "Língua Geral" or "Nheengatu"[6]. As well as being the mother tongue of part of the rural "caboclo"[7] population, it is used as a lingua franca

5. Instituto Socioambiental http://www.socioambiental.org/pib/epi/verbetinho/comfoto/mura.htm Access on 12/10/2007.

6. The Amazon "Língua Geral" was a language created during the Portuguese colonisation of Maranhão from the first half of the seventeenth century. Contact between the colonizers and Tupinambá Indians on the coast of Maranhão led to the creation of this "Língua Geral", based originally on Tupinambá, which was spoken by the soldiers and in Catholic missions during the colonial occupation of the Amazon Basin. It became the language of colonial occupation of the Amazon in the seventeenth and eighteenth centuries until the nineteenth century. Today it is spoken mainly on the Rio Negro, and on the River Uaupés and River Içana. (Rodrigues, 1986:102).

7. "Caboclo" or "Caboco" is a term widely used in the Amazon region of Brazil with many different connotations, including: mixture of Indian and non-Indian, mestizo, degraded Indian, civilized Indian, rural dweller, etc. Nugent states that

between Indians and non-Indians, or between Indians who speak different languages, and is an instrument of ethnic affirmation for peoples who have lost their languages, such as the Baré, the Arapaço and others. Ricardo Pereira (2007) informs that "the Baré live along all the course of the Rio Negro from its mouth up to the Cassiquiare canal in the south of Venezuela, and also in the urban centres of Manaus, Barcelos and Santa Isabel" (2007:43). This author notes that,

> over the past ten years, the number of individuals who identify as Baré has grown enormously, principally in the middle and lower course of the Rio Negro. Within the context of the ethno-genesis process on the Rio Negro, it can be observed that the term Baré has also become an 'identity symbol' in cases in which an individual knows that he is Indian, but does not know his origins or those of his ancestors (ibid).

Pereira looks at a specific case of a much wider process of ethnic affirmation and the construction of collective identities on the middle course of the Rio Negro. Starting with a study of the history of regional frontiers, he aims to show the Canafé community as a collective identity historically constructed by indigenous migrants at the centre of processes of expansion and retraction of expansion fronts in the twentieth century. This author discusses the multiplicity of situations and agents involved in this case through an ethnography based on the apprehension of values and meanings shared by collectivities of indigenous people and "caboclos" who live in the rural zone of the municipalities of Barcelos and Santa Isabel. Pereira argues that "the ethno-genesis process in the middle course of the Rio Negro is strongly influenced by this macro-process which the Aruak protagonize throughout their traditional territory" (2007:18), and points out elements which characterize the middle course of the Rio Negro as a regional frontier, focus of distinct processes of ethnocide, ethno-genesis and radical social changes (ibid:19).

Pereira affirms that:

"For my purposes, *caboclo* refers to an historical Amazonian peasantry which has emerged amidst the abandoned colonial apparatus of empire and state" (1993:23). Carmen Rodrigues asserts that "If caboclo is not an ethnic category in the strict sense of the term, then it is in the game of difference, as well as other anthropological subjects/objects" (2006).

> The contemporary period situated between the creation of the community and its involvement in the Indian movement in the region was crucial in the ethno-genesis process in the middle course of the Rio Negro, since the dispersed and invisible rural population started to concentrate in 'community' spaces and to be recognised as organized collectivities, related to specific areas and objects of administrative actions of local governments. Within this new context many family groups of caboclos have made an effort to stay in 'their' areas and guarantee common access to basic resources for their reproduction in relation to more traditional agents of the region and new agents which come 'from outside' (Pereira, 2007:93).

This author stresses that one aspect of regional ethno-genesis which promotes the visibility of this process is "the engagement in the ethno-political movement of the Rio Negro" (2007:110).

The Baniwa anthropologist and intellectual, Gersem Luciano, observes that:

> In the case of indigenous peoples of the upper Rio Negro, their cultural changes have been marked by strong processes of deculturation and acculturation, which have occurred simultaneously, phenomenon that I call, in the case of the Baniwas, ethnic up-dating, in which ethnicity has been forced to symbolically re-articulate as a passage from *savage Indians* to *civilized Indians*, or from *tribal Indians* to *modern Indians*, just like other ethnic processes in Brazil, without this constituting integration or assimilation to the national or global society.

In fact, we observe that there has not been any type of change in identity reference, even among the Barés, who for a time started to identify themselves as "caboclos" (Luciano, 2006:26).

In Acre state, in the southwest of the Amazon Basin, Cloude Correia relates that the Nawa in Acre state affirm "that they were victims of a huge massacre when they entered in contact with the rubber extraction fronts on the Upper River Juruá ... the Nawa were practically exterminated at the time of the expeditions to drive Indians from their lands and enslave them, there remaining only a 'seed', a few survivors" (Correia, 2007:175). The survivors were incorporated into the productive system of rubber extraction. This author adds, "After a gap of several decades in which there is no mention of the existence of Nawa Indians in the region of the River Juruá, in 1999, after representatives of the CIMI visited the River Moa, FUNAI informed of the existence of a people who call themselves Nawa..." (Correia, 2007:181).

The Tremembé of the Northeast of Brazil: Reactivating an Indigenous Identity

In the case of the Tremembé of Ceará state in the northeast of Brazil, indigenous identities are (re)-emerging in different local contexts through claims to land rights, as strategies of defence from large companies, especially "DuCOCO"[8], that operate coconut farms, in Varjota, Tapera and Almofala (within the municipality of Itarema). In Córrego João Pereira (within the municipalities of Itarema and Acaraú), a Tremembé identity has emerged as a strategy of defence against people who invaded their lands and tried to establish themselves as landowners, subordinating the traditional inhabitants. In 2003, the Córrego João Pereira Indian Land was homologated by FUNAI, being the first Indian Land which has been fully recognised by the Brazilian federal government in Ceará state. More recently, a Tremembé identity has been re-activated as a strategy of defence against the proposed installation of a mega-tourist resort by a consortium of international companies in Buriti and São José (within the municipality of Itapipoca).

Nowadays, the Tremembé of the coast of Ceará state make up a population of well over 5,000 people. In the sixteenth and seventeenth centuries, the Tremembé occupied the coast of Brazil from Pará state to Ceará state. With European colonisation, mission settlements were created, such as Tutóia and Aracati-Mirim. In 1766 the Aracati-Mirim mission became a "freguesia de índios" (administrative division) and was renamed Almofala (Valle, 2007). In 1858, the "Diretoria dos Índios" (legislation created in 1845 by the "Regulamento das Missões") was abolished by provincial law and by the end of the nineteenth century the indigenous settlement and church at Almofala

8. DuCOCO was established in 1982, nowadays having seven farms and two factories, distributing products both nationally and internationally. DuCOCO is the largest exporter of coconut milk in Brazil.

were being engulfed by sand dunes. Having been made invisible as an ethnic group by the end of the nineteenth century, Tremembé identities have been re-emerging over the past decades, a process which has been studied by the anthropologist Carlos Guilherme O. do Valle (1999), who uses the notion "semantic field of ethnicity" to analyse processes of ethnic re-elaboration. The persons who nowadays identify themselves as Tremembé Indians live in Almofala, Tapera, and Varjota at the mouth of the River Aracati-Mirim; in the Indian Land Córrego João Pereira; and in Buriti and São José. The Tremembé are frequently accused of not being authentic Indians by people who have economic and political interests in their lands. They are deploying culture as an important resource in this land struggle, projecting the "torem", a circular dance, with songs that mix Portuguese and indigenous words, as their most important diacritical cultural expression (Valle, 2007). The "torem" dance has become recognised as an original folkloric expression and constitutes a powerful semantic field.

The communities of Buriti and São José have emerged since 2000 as Tremembé, since when they have been facing the attempt, by a consortium of companies, to install a gigantic residential tourist city called "Nova Atlântida"[9] on their traditional lands, and to confine the Indians within two small enclaves in the midst of the hotels and tourist installations. In the words of Erbene Veríssimo, leader of the Buriti community:

> Buriti and São José together make up 3,225 hectares. There are more than 200 families.... They wanted to give 1,000 hectares for the whole community ... to live and to work ....This would be impossible, one house joined to another like in towns .... A simple house, without any land to plant on. They pay a wage which is not sufficient for a family to live on.... It would be impossible to plant, we would have to buy everything. (Declaration of Erbene Rosa Veríssimo, July, 2007).

9. On its site, the Nova Atlântida Project, http://www.gruponovaatlantida.com/english/index.htm presents itself as being made up of 17 companies, occupying more than 32 square kilometers, and claims to be the world's biggest tourist residential complex, with "almost thirty luxury hotels, luxury residential areas and seven golf courses".

Social agents of the Consortium which plan to build "Nova Atlântida" are paying wages for the people to work as guards to protect what the company has constructed, and to co-opt individuals among the original population of this region to deny the existence of Indians:

> They earn four hundred reais (about US$200) each month. The payment comes every 15 days, illegally without a signed work card. No one knows if they will ever have any holidays. The work is as guards in the planted areas (watering and putting fertilizers on the plants), looking after areas of land and buildings. Others work on the prawn farms. They employ most people as guards (Declaration of Luzia Carneiro, January, 2007).

The question of identifying as Tremembé or not, in this particular situation, is closely related to the struggle to have their traditional lands recognised, their only source of subsistence, in the case of a traditional population that sees its existence threatened by a transnational large-scale development project in the tourism sector.

Conclusions

This short article reveals that there are many different and contrasting processes of ethnic re-configuration among indigenous peoples in Brazil in recent years. Adolfo de Oliveira affirms that,

> It can be said that there is a *field of dialogue* within indigenist policy in Brazil. If until recently the relations between Indians and the State were characterised by an ideal of monopoly of interlocution by the federal indigenist organ ...with the return of the civil State in Brazil—and especially after the promulgation of the new constitution, the relation between Indians and the Brazilian State has become fragmented by a number of institutions (ministério público federal—Attorney General's Department, the ministries of education and health, as well as corresponding institutions in states and municipalities). In addition, the so-called "third sector", made up of non-government organisations (NGOs) and whose presence has been felt among indigenous peoples for a longer time, has increased its role, leading to a diversification of possibilities of interlocution, nowadays no longer only with

> the State and the encompassing (national) society, but also with the international sphere... (Adolfo de Oliveira, 2002:118–119).

In the case of the Waimiri-Atroari, an indigenous people who have only been in continuous contact with the national society since 1979, this society is encapsulated by an indigenist administration, subordinated to the ELETRONORTE company and also dependent on indemnification resources from Mineração Taboca of the Paranapanema Group. Under an indigenist regime in which their freedom is under constant surveillance, the Waimiri-Atroari leaders have learnt to play the rules of the game of a highly authoritarian entrepreneurial indigenist administration, simulating discourses of indigenous autonomy which represent the interests of the administration.

The Macushi and Wapishana who live on both sides of the Brazil-Guyana border, with more than two hundred years of interethnic contact with the respective national/colonial societies, are achieving an ethnic re-organisation over the past three decades to vindicate that their rights be respected by the national societies. On the Brazilian side of the border by way of indigenous organisations such as the CIR and, on the Guyanese side of the border, through the APA and through participation in political parties of that country. In the cases of peoples like the Mura, the Nawa and the Baré, in the Amazon region, and the Tremembé in the Northeast of Brazil, processes of political organisation are emerging around ethnic identities and cultural differences through the establishment of dialogical relations with the State and NGOs in the form of ethno-political movements.

In recent years, and especially since the promulgation of the Brazilian Constitution of 1988, ethnicity has taken on new meanings for many indigenous peoples, although the complexity of these processes of cultural re-elaboration can only be understood through ethnographic research at the local level, and using theoretical perspectives which take into account the local within the globalised context that characterizes the indigenous political movement and indigenous protagonism.

References

Albert, Bruce. 2000. "Associações indígenas e desenvolvimento sustentável na Amazônia brasileira" in Carlos Alberto Ricardo ed., *Povos Indígenas no Brasil, 1996–2000.* São Paulo: Instituto Socioambiental, pp. 197–207.

Alves, Jean Paraizo. 2007. Em Busca da Cidadabia: Escolarização e Reconhecimento de Identidades Indígenas em dois Países Americanos Brasile México. PhD dissertation presented at the Centro de Pesquisa e Pós-Graduação sobre as Américas: Doutorado em Ciências Sociais, CEPPAC/Universidade de Brasília.

Arruti, José Maurício. 1997. 'A emergência dos 'remanescentes': notas para o diálogo entre indígenas e quilombolas'. *Mana*, vol. 7, no. 2, Rio de Janeiro, pp. 7–38.

__________. 2006. "Etnogêneses Indígenas" in B. Ricardo and F. Ricardo, eds. *Povos Indígenas no Brasil: 2001–2005*. São Paulo: Instituto Socioambiental, pp. 50–54.

Baines, Stephen G. 1991. *'É a FUNAI que sabe': a frente de atração Waimiri-Atroari*. Belém: Museu Paraense Emílio Goeldi/CNPq/SCT/PA.

__________. 1993a. 'A Política Indigenista Governamental e os Waimiri-Atroari: Administrações indigenistas, mineração de estanho e a construção da 'autodeterminação indígena' dirigida'. *Revista de Antropologia*, vol. 36, São Paulo, pp. 207–237.

__________. 1993b. 'O Território dos Waimiri-Atroari e o indigenismo empresarial' *Ciências Sociais Hoje*, São Paulo, pp. 219–243.

__________. 1996. "A Usina Hidrelétrica de Balbina e o deslocamento compulsório dos Waimiri-Atroari", in Sônia Barbosa Magalhães, Rosyan de Caldas Britto and Edna Ramos de Castro. *Energia na Amazônia*, Vol. II, Belém: Museu Paraense Emílio Goeldi/ Universidade Federal do Pará/ Associação de Universidades Amazônicas, pp. 747–759.

__________. 2000. 'Imagens de liderança indígena e o Programa Waimiri-Atroari: índios e usinas hidrelétricas na Amazônia'. *Revista de Antropologia*. São Paulo, USP, vol. 43, no. 2, pp. 141–163.

Barth, Fredrik. 1969. *Ethnic Groups and Boundaries: The Social Organisation of Cultural Difference*. Boston: Little Brown & Co.

Bourdieu, Pierre. 1984. 'La Délègation et le Fetichisme Politique'. *Actes de La Recherche en Sciences Sociales*, Vol. 52/53, pp. 49–55.

Cardoso de Oliveira, Roberto, 1994. 'O movimento dos conceitos na antropologia' *Revista de Antropologia*, São Paulo, vol. 36, pp. 13–31.

__________. 1976. *Identidade, Etnia, e Estrutural Social*. São Paulo: Livraria Pioneira Editora.

__________. 2000. 'Ação indigenista, eticidade e o diálogo interétnico'. *Estudos Avançados*, vol. 14, no. 40, pp. 213–30.

Correia, Cloude de Souza. 2007. *Etnozoneamento. Etnomapeamento e Diagnóstico Etnoambiental: representaçõies cartográficas e gestão territorial em terras indígenas no estado do Acre*. Tese de doutorado em Antropologia Social, DAN. Brasília: Universidade de Brasília.

Hobsbawm, Eric. 1984 [1983]. 'Introdução: A Invenção das Tradições' in Eric Hobsbawm & Terence Ranger, eds., *A Invenção das Tradições*. Rio de Janeiro: Paz e Terra.

Howard, Catherine V. 2002. "A domesticação das mercadorias: estratégias Waiwai" in Bruce Albert and Alcida Rita Ramos, *Pacificando o branco: cosmologias do contato no norte-amazônico*. São Paulo: Editora UNESP, Imprensa Oficial do Estado, pp. 25–56.

Luciano, Gersem José dos Santos. 2006. 'Projeto é como branco trabalha; as lideranças que se virem para aprender e nos ensinar': experiências dos povos indígenas do alto rio Negro. Dissertação de Mestrado apresentada ao Programa de Pós-Graduação em Antropologia Social do Instituto de Ciências Sociais da Universidade de Brasília, Brasília, DF.

Nugent, Stephen. 1993. *Amazonian Caboclo Society: An Essay on Invisibility and Peasant Economy*. Oxford: Berg.

Oliveira, Adolfo Neves de. 2002. 'Fragmentos da Etnografia de uma Rebelião do Objeto: indigenismo e antropologia em tempos de autonomia indígena' *Anuário Antropológico,* Vol. 98, pp. 109–130.

Oliveira, João Pacheco de, ed. 2004. *A Viagem da Volta: etnicidade, política e reelaboração cultural no Nordeste indígena*. 2ª ed. Contra Capa Livraria/ LACED.

__________. 1979. A Fronteira e a Viabilidade Do Campesinato Indígena. Rio de Janeiro: PPGAS.

__________. 1989. 'Expedições Científicas em terras Indígenas'. *Boletim da ABA*, Vol. 6, Associação Brasileira de Antropologia.

__________. 1993. "A Viagem de Volta': reelaboração cultural e horizonte político dos povos indígenas no nordeste in *Atlas das Terras Indígenas do Nordeste*. Rio de Janeiro: PETI-Museu Nacional, pp. v–viii.

Pereira, Ricardo Neves Romcy. 2007. 'Comunidade Canafé: história indígena e etnogênese no Médio Rio Negro', Dissertação de mestrado em Antropologia, Universidade de Brasília.

Ranger, Terence. 1984. "A Invenção da Tradição na África Colonial" in Eric Hobsbawm, and Terence Ranger, eds. *A Invenção das Tradições*. Rio de Janeiro: Paz e Terra.

Riviére, Peter. 1995. *Absent-minded Imperialism: Britain and the Expansion of Empire in Nineteenth-century Brazil*. London: Tauris.

Rodrigues, Aryon Dall'Igna. 1986. *Línguas Brasileiras: para o conhecimento das línguas indígenas*. São Paulo: Edições Loyola.

Rodrigues, Carmen Izabel. 2006. 'Caboclos na Amazônia: a identidade na diferença'. *Novos Cadernos NAEA*, vol. 9, no. 1, pp. 119–130.

Valle Carlos Guilherme do. 1999. "Experiência e semântica entre os Tremembé do Ceará" in João Pacheco de Oliveira Filho, ed. *A Viagem da volta: etnicidade, política e reelaboração cultural no Nordeste indígena*. Rio de Janeiro: Contra Capa Livraria, pp. 279–337.

Valle, Carlos Guilherme do. 2007. Tremembé. *Enciclopédia: Povos Indígenas no Brasil*, Instituto Socioambiental, São Paulo: ISA. http://www.socioambiental.org/pib/epi/tremembe/hist.shtm access on 15/10/2007.

Viveiros de Castro, Eduardo, and Lúcia M. M. de Andrade. 1988. "Hidrelétricas do Xingu: o Estado contra as sociedades indígenas" in Leinad Ayer de O Santos, Lúcia M. M. Andrade eds., *As Hidrelétricas do Xingu e os Povos Indígenas*. Comissão Pró-Índio de São Paulo, pp. 7–23.

7

Assimilation Agendas of the State: What Space Remains for Aboriginal Law and Culture?

Irene Watson

In 2007 a *World Health Organisation Commission on Social Determinants of Health* report confirmed that the health of Aboriginal peoples currently remains one hundred years behind white Australians' expected standards of health. To some this was already well known. Dr Jackson Pulver of the University of New South Wales Muru Marri Indigenous Health Unit contributed a chapter to the WHO report highlighting the after-effects of colonisation on the lives of Aboriginal peoples. It was argued that colonialism continues to contribute to the poor health of Aboriginal peoples (World Health Organisation, 2007).[1] Over the past decade there have been shifts in Australian government policy to advance and further fast track the assimilation of Aboriginal peoples, yet under these 'advances' by the Australian state, the health and well-being of Aboriginal peoples continues to worsen. The most recent phase of the assimilation project has failed in its attempt to merge and absorb Aboriginal people into the same health paradigm as white Australians. One might ask: has there ever been a good time for Aboriginal peoples since the advent of colonialism? Our health has continued to erode and deteriorate from the time of invasion; it is 100 years behind white Australia. Some commentators have argued that colonialism is not the root of Aboriginal disadvantage. These same commentators have stated that the pre-1970s were better times for Aboriginal peoples; they have deemed Aboriginal communities were more 'functional' then than they are today (Cape York Institute,

1. See the Commission on Social Determinants *Achieving Health Equality From Root Causes to Fair Outcomes,* World Health Organisation (2007), and for a media discussion of the report see, Mark Colvin, ABC PM, Monday 30 April 2007, *Aboriginal Health 100 years Behind: Report.*

2007).[2] The pre-1970s were seen as times when Aboriginal peoples were free from a welfare system which fostered idleness and substance abuse. This view has been promoted by Noel Pearson and is embraced by the current Australian federal government (Pearson, 2005; Education and Health Standing Committee, 2007:43–53).[3] A number of commentators have expressed similar sentiments towards the 'good old mission days', but those days were not good for all, particularly the non-Christians, the resisters of colonial violence, and the advocates for the protection and care of country.

It is my view that the impact of colonialism is central to the contemporary position of Aboriginal peoples and de-colonisation of the Aboriginal position is central to the healing of that condition. De-colonisation processes are in the realm of what is yet to come, to be imagined and negotiated between the colonized and the colonizer. While assimilation into white Australia might be the choice of some individuals what choice is available for Aboriginal peoples wanting to re-build Aboriginal communities on traditional lands; to rebuild and embrace Aboriginal world views: caring for country and resistance to developments which are potentially destructive of the environment. What possibilities exist, for the survival of an Aboriginal world? Who are we to survive as: Aboriginal peoples living in relationship with Aboriginal territories, or another kind of Aboriginal peoples absorbed and mutated into something else? Can we have justice or the possibility of de-colonising the past injustices of colonialism when the state is

---

2. See Cape York Institute, *From Hand Out to Hand Up*, Cape York Welfare Reform Project (2007) for an analysis of the proposal on welfare reform of Aboriginal communities.

3. Pearson critiques the past 30 years of Australian policy for its failure to deliver capacity building within Aboriginal communities. See also Education and Health Standing Committee (WA) *Initiatives in the Remote Indigenous Communities of Cape York* Report No. 7 (2007) pp. 43–53, for a discussion on the views of Noel Pearson and the tension between an assimilationist and a rights perspective agenda. Following the release of The Northern Territory Government, *Broad Inquiry into the protection of Aboriginal Children from Sexual Abuse,* Report of the Northern Territory Board of Inquiry into the Protection of Aboriginal Children from Sexual Abuse (2007); the federal government proclaimed a state of emergency and responded through their introduction of the *Northern Territory National Emergency Response Bill* (2007). This legislation empowers the Commonwealth to privatise and to also open up Aboriginal lands to public access.

committed to a one dimensional universal world order, which disallows for the diversity of peoples? (Watson, 2006:256–271).

During the public debate known as the history wars,[4] Aboriginal peoples were advised to move on, give up the 'blame game', to quit blaming colonial Australia for the massacres, dispersal, and removal of peoples from traditional lands into institutions where Aboriginal children could be trained as a cheap/slave labour force (Windschuttle, 2002). Instead of engaging in conversations on how to provide a basis for the restitution of these injustices Aboriginal peoples were expected to simply move on with their lives. That is to move on without the expectation that the state should take responsibility for the provision of essential services and resources or the return of our traditional land base. Windschuttle and others argued that the blame was not based on truth but fabrication (Watson, 2005:15). While Aboriginal voices and perspectives on Australia's black history have gained some volume, the marginality of that voice remains relegated by the dominant colonial view. The dominant colonial view continues to assert racist ideologies and mis-representations and constructions of Aboriginality, for example that violence is 'inherent' within the cultures of Aboriginal peoples (Watson, 2007a). This dominant conversation never engages the view of inter-generational trauma and its source—colonialism, and while the conversation is stuck, the complexity of Aboriginal traumas will also stay stuck in the colonial paradigm of blaming the "backward native" and our "failure to adapt to modernity".

In this paper I would like to explore the tensions between cultural relativism and universality and how those tensions are engaged and used by the colonial state Australia to legitimize its assimilationist initiatives.

I have argued that violence against Aboriginal women has been constructed and mis-represented throughout Australia's colonial legal history as being inherent in Aboriginal culture and law (Watson, 2007). Recent proposals of the federal government in the *(Cth) Crimes Amendment (Bail and Sentencing) Bill 2006,* to remove the courts' discretion to give consideration to Aboriginal law and culture

4. Keith Windschuttle questioned the validity of recordings which documented a violent colonial history of massacres, cultural genocide and the overall violence of the colonial frontier.

when making sentencing determinations,[5] is an indication of its thinking, that is, that Aboriginal law condones violence against Aboriginal women and children (Parliamentary Debates, 2006:27).[6] However when the federal Attorney-General's Department was asked to identify cases where the consideration of customary law had resulted in a more lenient sentence they 'failed to provide a single case to the Senate committee'.[7]

The volume on the idea that Aboriginal culture is inherently violent was turned up recently when the Commonwealth government publicly opposed collective Aboriginal land ownership, while promoting the idea that Aboriginal families' lives were at risk while they lived in communities where land was held under communal land ownership.[8] These views supported the idea that collective land ownership contributes to the vulnerability of Aboriginal women and that private ownership of land would provide greater protection for women. However, there is no evidence to support this position. Does Aboriginal culture have anything to do with it or are other dynamics at work? For example, to what extent might powerful lobby and property development groups have influence over how Aboriginal culture is perceived and constructed? Why blame Aboriginal culture in isolation of the impact of colonialism and the socio-economic effect of displacement and dispossession? Does the discrediting of Aboriginal culture and law aid in the absorption and commodification of our

5. (Cth) *Crimes Act, Section 16A*, which currently allows the court to consider any 'relevant' matter, the proposed amendment would direct the courts to exclude from consideration of relevant matter, the cultural background of the defendant. In reality this legislation is unlikely to apply to crimes in Aboriginal communities, as the legislation effects only federal crimes.

6. See the Commonwealth. Parliamentary Debates House of Representatives, 28 November 2006, in particular at p. 27, Michael Keenan MP.

7. Ibid comment by Nicola Rixon MP at p. 25.

8. For further comment on proposals to privatize see, Commonwealth of Australia, *Parliamentary Debates*, House of Representatives, 31 May 2006, Minister Brough, Minister for Families, Community Services and Indigenous Affairs and Minister Assisting the Prime Minister for Indigenous Affairs, in his second reading speech, Aboriginal Land Rights (Northern Territory) Amendment Bill. It is also interesting to note the Prime Minister John Howard's position has always been opposed to land rights, and a commitment to dismantle the *(Cth) NT Aboriginal Land Rights Act*.

lands into Australian 'real property'? Through the demonisation of Aboriginal culture the state is able to appear crusader-like in its 'rescue' of Aboriginal women and children from 'cultural practices' the state deems harmful. The state becomes keeper of Aboriginal cultural knowledge while Aboriginal peoples and communities are positioned as mere players, acting out a deemed and 'known' cultural practice. The state and its agencies as the knowers of 'objectionable practices' have power to construct that which is Aboriginal culture and to analyse, demonise and ultimately undermine the right of peoples to self-determination.

The most evident site in this debate is the setting of violence perpetrated by Aboriginal men against Aboriginal women. Spivak (1999:284) has identified these public outcries as, "white men rescuing brown women from brown men", or perhaps otherwise the "white crusader complex". But as I have argued in earlier writings that the reality of the crusader-like intervention is more one of entrapment, that is, of being hunted into a confined space, or removed from collectivity to become assimilated into the isolation of individualized spaces. The abolition of collective land ownership in favour of individualized land ownership is a parallel. It should be noted that Aboriginal land rights legislation does not apply across Australia and that the Northern Territory is the site of the only extensive Commonwealth land rights legislation.[9] The Australian government's aversion to Aboriginal collective land ownership must be viewed within the context that within Australia, for the vast majority of Aboriginal peoples there is no provision for land rights or collective land ownership. The majority of Aboriginal peoples are housed through public housing, within urban assimilated spaces where the majority live in overcrowded conditions. Violence in these assimilated Aboriginal enclaves does not attract the same level of attention from the state, because the connection between violence, Aboriginal peoples

9. Not all states of Australia have implemented legislation in recognition of Aboriginal rights to land, in New South Wales *Aboriginal Land Rights Act* (1983) represents a very small percentage of the state. Similarly the South Australian *Pitjantjatjara Land Rights Act* (1981) and the *Maralinga Tjarutja Land Rights Act* (1984) refers only to the north-west region of the state. The other states have more limited forms of recognition or none at all. Native title laws provide for the recognition of a beneficial right to land that a small minority of the population are likely to make for a successful claim.

and collectivity is in truth the basis for a land grab by a state that posts its future on the development of the natural resources contained within these Aboriginal lands. For more than 200 years the state has built itself upon the lands grabbed from Aboriginal peoples. How it is that the privatization of Aboriginal lands and the assimilation of Aboriginal peoples will benefit women and children eludes me, particularly when the state fails to alleviate violence against non-Aboriginal women and children who occupy what is considered that 'privileged' private space.

Implicit in this debate is that violence is constructed as being inherent within Aboriginal culture. But what is the evidence? It is not possible to examine Aboriginal culture in isolation of the power relations which have existed for more than 200 years between Aboriginal peoples and the dominant Anglo-Australian culture. Any attempt to understand 'Aboriginal violence' in isolation of these would be flawed and incomplete. The real picture is complex. The violence of colonialism cannot be excluded from the analysis, an analysis which must also include inter-generational traumas and their internalisation by Aboriginal peoples and their communities. These colonial traumas leave little space to heal. What Aboriginal space which might exist for healing is targeted and demonised as barbaric and uncivilized, and the state offers no healing beyond assimilationist options. Mainstream spaces in which one could live, work and heal provide only for those who can endure the inherent white racism in them (Moreton-Robinson, 2007).[10]

Traditional Cultures and the Other Criminals

Australian courts appear to have shown 'sensitivity' towards Aboriginal men in matters of rape where the cultural background of the offender has been considered while determining sentencing options. Sherene Razack (1994) suggests that at these moments consideration 'is often about the culturalization of rape: how cultural and historical specificities explain and excuse the violence men direct at women.' In taking what is perceived to be Aboriginal law into consideration, the courts contribute to 'making invisible the harm that is done to Aboriginal women' while at the same time constructing or deeming Aboriginal men as inherently violent (Razack, 1994:899–900).

10. See Moreton-Robinson (2007) for a critique on the possibility of surviving the racism of an Australian work environment.

Benhabib suggests that the court's use of the cultural defence so that it '...imprisons the individual in a cage of univocal cultural interpretations and psychological motivations;' produces stereotypes of race and culture. 'Traditional culture' is viewed as being pure and unaffected by colonialism, frozen in time. In the following Northern Territory Supreme Court decision *The Queen* v. *GJ* (2005), CJ Martin stated:

> I appreciate that it is a very difficult thing for men who have been brought up in traditional ways which permit physical violence and sexual intercourse with promised wives, even if they are not consenting, to adjust their ways. But it must be done.[11]

The assumption is that 'traditional culture' sanctioned violence. The anthropological evidence of violence within 'traditional culture' is mostly taken from a colonial context and presented to the courts. The violence of colonialism itself and the effect that it has had upon Aboriginal peoples does not enter the frame when the court is constructing 'traditional culture', nor is the process of how this representation is translated from Aboriginal to non-Aboriginal settings questioned or analysed. Douzinas (2000:137) suggests that in looking too simplistically at questions of culture and seeing culture as inherent can be unhelpful and risks negating how history impacts upon how culture is constructed. The whole life position of persons coming before the courts should be considered, along with the diminishing and demonized spaces which Aboriginal culture occupies in the 'real' world. The reality of colonial violence, its effects and its creation of injustices, inequality, displaced sovereign power and dispossession of peoples from traditional lands should be considered for its impact upon the construction and finally the translation of Aboriginal traditional culture and law into the contemporary context. There is no space where Aboriginal culture is unaffected by the inroads of colonialism, and attempts by the state to accommodate Aboriginal law and culture do so in ways which fail to accommodate Aboriginal peoples' core principles.

---

11. *The Queen* v. *GJ* (2005) SCC 20418849.

The Accommodation of Aboriginal Laws

The High Court in *Mabo*[12] accommodated the recognition of Aboriginal law as being a beneficial use of land such as would benefit hunting and gathering peoples. It was recognition 200 years after the British invasion, and was an accommodation that is to sit within the frame of 'modern' Australian mainstream law. With a recognition of 'native rights' which arrive at a time when the natural world is no longer able to sustain a hunter and gatherer lifestyle, the possibility of our survival as Aboriginal peoples is not recognized in a 'real' world context. While our position as sovereign peoples was not pleaded in *Mabo*, it was negated by the court when it affirmed the legitimacy of the violence of Australia's colonial foundations (Watson, 2007b).[13] In finding a space in which to heal or invoking a decolonized space we are left with the decision in *Mabo* (No. 2), and the court's failure to provide a remedy beyond the possibility of a meagre acknowledgment of a lesser right to land, or one that falls outside the common law of man and by the 'good grace of the common law' has been brought inside for recognition.[14] What does it mean for the survival of Aboriginal peoples to be brought into the common law, particularly when we know *Mabo* offers so very little more than the right to be 'native' in relation to our traditional lands? Benhabib (2002:43) reviews John Lockes' concept of a 'state of nature':

> Psychologically, the state of nature metaphor is an affirmation of individualism, autonomy, independence, and self-reliance. The male is seen as one who owes nothing to others for the rights to which he is entitled; it is not his historical community of birth and entitlement which endows him with these rights; rather, it is his "Maker" and the law of nature, which all men of sound reason and good will can consult in order to discover this radical message of equality and autonomy.

---

12. *Mabo* v. *The State of Queensland* (No. 2) [1992] 175 CLR 1.
13. The colonial foundations of Australian law in relation to the *Mabo* are discussed in the special edition on *Mabo* in 2002 13(3) *Law and Critique*, and in Watson (2007b).
14. In reference to the ideas of John Locke in the *Second Treatise on Civil Government*, in particular the 'state of nature'.

The universal centre is 'God-male'. Community is displaced. The universal is man's becoming and community's demise. Benhabib sees that the fact that we are not all "...similarly equal, rational, and deserving in the eyes of God" is a limitation on Locke's "universalistic portrait of bourgeois freedom" (Benhabib, 2002: 43). Locke defined political society as excluding Aboriginal governments for he saw them as being located in a "state of nature", and less "progressive" than modern forms of government. Aboriginal relationships to land were not recognized by Locke as a form of property; instead he viewed these relationships as being similar to those of an earlier stage of European development. This particular view of 'backwardness' became a justification for colonization.

...Amerindians become just like the Europeans; their otherness is buried in the early stages of our own past. But because we are like them, or rather were like them, the order of the government and property that we bring upon them is not alien to them, but simply a better and higher version of what they lack. Thus colonization becomes an act of speeding up a developmental process toward consensual government and a regime of private property. (Benhabib, 2002:46).

To achieve those ends the assimilation of Aboriginal laws and cultures into the common law should occur and as CJ Martin states in his sentencing comments in *The Queen* v. *GJ* (2005):

> The process of reconciling traditional Aboriginal laws with the Northern Territory law is a difficult process that has been occurring for many years. It is an ongoing process, and no doubt will continue for many years. Two of the more controversial areas where there is a conflict between traditional Aboriginal laws and Northern Territory laws concern traditional punishment and promised marriages. In both areas a lot of work towards reconciliation of the laws has been done. Fortunately, in many communities the traditional laws have been modified in order to achieve reconciliation with Northern Territory laws. It is to the credit of those communities that they have been successful in this limited reconciliation of laws.[15]

---

15. The Queen and CJ (Sentence) Martin CJ, in the Transcript of Proceedings at Yarralin, Thursday 11th August, 2005, In the Supreme Court of the Northern Territory SCC 20418849.

In the reconciliation of laws focus is given to those which are deemed barbaric, for example Aboriginal marriage laws and traditional punishments. But what does reconciliation of laws entail? Does it mean that Aboriginal laws suffer their complete absorption? Locke saw Aboriginal laws had no place in the modern world of law and governance; he argued for their disappearance into the 'darkness' of an early stage of 'human development'. So what place might Aboriginal laws on land and the environment have for the future relationship of Aboriginal peoples to country? Will they also be considered repugnant and to be engulfed? Possibly so, if Australian governments continue to pursue the line of the seventeenth century apostle Locke. But why would they be seen to have no place in this 'modern' space particularly when they hold solutions to the survival of the planet against ongoing environmental disasters? Aboriginal laws recognize the relationships between humanity and the natural world and emphasise sustainability. Australian laws[16] make way for the use of huge water quantities for the mining of uranium in one of the driest regions of the state at a time when the country faces the worse drought on record. The laws which benefit the profiteering motives of large corporations such as BHP Billiton are not laws that ensure sustainability but rather the destruction of the largest source of a huge tract of country and the poisoning of an enormous amount of underground water.

Benhabib suggests the absorption and assimilation of Aboriginal law and culture might translate as part of a "developmental process toward consensual government and a regime of private property". What constitutes consent to such a process is an important consideration, and is a question I don't have the space here to develop further, other

---

16. One example of state laws is the *Roxby Downs (Indenture Ratification) Act* 1982 (SA), this legislation allows for the exemption of 1.5 million hectares in central South Australia, including the Roxby Downs mine and surrounding areas, from both environmental and Aboriginal rights legislation. The Indenture Act provides BHP Billiton the legal authority to override the following South Australian legislation: *Aboriginal Heritage Act* 1988; *Development Act* 1993; *Environmental Protection Act* 1993; *Freedom of Information Act* 1991; *Mining Act* 1971; *Natural Resources Act* 2004 (including the *Water Resources Act* 1997; for further discussion on impact upon the environment see, Peter Burdon (2006).

than to simply dispute the characterization of the Australian relationship between colonizer and colonized as being a relationship which could constitute consent. How can a people consent to their own genocide; why would you? What's at stake for Aboriginal peoples in respect of taking care of country is something Benhabib does not consider in her analysis; perhaps it is a forgone conclusion that the state will take on this role. But as we have seen, the state is empowered to make lawful laws instruments which are to the detriment of future environmental sustainability. And meanwhile the Aboriginal laws remain dis-empowered to effect their ancient custodial role of taking care of country.

Who Holds the Centre: And What's Culture Got To Do With It?

In a moment of being able to disconnect from the world of the 'real', I would sing of love, love, love. A love of the land—that is our Aboriginal centre from which we came into being and connect as Aboriginal peoples with each other. But in the 'real' world that holds the power to remove Aboriginal peoples from our centres, the colonial project continues to grow, to occupy and control all of our spaces, until the only ones we can occupy are those we fit into as assimilated subjects. What is the possibility of Aboriginal peoples finding spaces that nurture and make possible for us to hold a love and connection to land? Is there a possibility that Aboriginal views of the world will survive and become more central to our lives? If indeed it exists there are many tensions and oppositions to it. So what's culture got to do with it? Perhaps it has everything and nothing to do with it. Douzinas (2000:139) argues that the tension between a universalist and cultural relativist position is difficult to reconcile, particularly when both sides are convinced of the truth of their own position and committed to both a fear and a demonisation of the others' position. These tensions may be advanced by what Benhabib (2002:7) describes as the insiders' cultural space around which the boundaries of culture are "…securely guarded, their narratives purified, their rituals carefully monitored." Benhabib (2002:8) further points out:

> Struggles for recognition among individuals and groups are really efforts to negate the status of 'otherness', insofar as otherness is taken to entail disrespect, domination, and inequality. Aboriginality and the struggle to re-engage with

> our responsibility to care for country is concerned with more than the negation of otherness. I maintain that the Aboriginal struggle is to re-engage as sovereign peoples and as empowered carers for country.

Benhabib does not consider the colonial project and the extent to which those tensions between Aboriginal aspirations and the colonial order of things have the potential to collide and crash. I see a situation where the Aboriginal subject is the only crash victim. The Aboriginal quest to protect country is mostly lost to the more powerful objectives of farmers and corporate development, while the state sanctions the destruction of Aboriginal lands as being in the national interest. Assimilation of Aborigines is in the national interest. But who will guard the interests of the country and the possibility of sustaining it for future generations? The state might say: the farmers and corporate interests, but the record of the last 200 years does not inspire confidence.

(Im)possibilities for the Survival of the 'Mob'[17]

Consider the link between the politics of collective difference and the recognition of one's individual, unique identity, and ask: why should an individual's search for authenticity, for the expression of one's unique identity, take the form of a search for collective self-expression? (Benhabib, 2002:52) Perhaps it is because whom we are as Aboriginal peoples is about relationships, which we have not only with other humans but also with the natural world. So without essentialising, an Aboriginal identity is about the expression of relationships to kin and country and to speak as the individual is to detach oneself from those relationships and obligations.

What is the relationship of the collective identity of Aboriginal peoples to the Australian state? Is it one of 'voluntary' as opposed to 'forced' integration? If voluntary what might constitute an act of voluntary participation, an act of recognition? Does the difference matter? I think it does, because the basis of all political legitimacy must be some form of consent of the governed. So the question is: within what framework could we the Aborigines have consented, to our absorption and assimilation and the abandonment of our obligation to care for country?

17. A term that is frequently used by Aboriginal peoples to describe the peoples they come from.

The possibility of recognition under native title law is limited. I will not spend time here going over an area which is covered extensively in other works,[18] but I point out that it is failure of native title processes which have been used to advocate against the recognition of collective rights. The following is from the Western Australian media:

> But there is increasing understanding, not least among Aboriginal communities themselves that the real problem lies with the nature of the title obtained. Title is communal; title is inalienable. The property rights it contains are more or less useless (Rutherford, 2006).

Here again the pressure is for Aboriginal laws and cultures to assimilate into the dominant Australian property law. Aboriginal title is deemed useless as a commodity within a capitalist framework. The thinking of Locke reappears: Aboriginal cultures are not yet sufficiently developed to fit into private property frameworks. The problem is seen to be inherent in Aboriginal culture and our methods of holding land, and not in the Australian legal system's inability to give greater recognition to Aboriginal sovereignty claims. Meanwhile under current native title laws for those communities who desire to continue to hold onto communal title the struggle to keep the mob and the land together is one that is being whittled away at by the commonwealth government. The latest push is a pressure to convert lands held collectively to lands that will be leased back to the federal government. We are yet to see the impact this will have on communities and their ability to continue to care for country.

In conclusion I ask: is it possible to relax the guarded borders of culture so as to navigate a peaceful settlement where the principles of co-existence are given a more powerful presence, particularly in regard to Aboriginal relationships to country? I am not convinced there can be a peaceful settlement when we are locked into protecting positions and where the positions being protected are undermined by fear, ignorance and misrepresentations. We need to critically examine who is locking whom into position? To what extent do Aboriginal people have voice over the representation of our culture and the call for recognition of our humanity? Who holds the keys to the castle?

18. See special edition of 2002 13(3) *Law and Critique.*

Clearly not Aboriginal peoples. Do we need individualized castles anyway? As an alternative what are the possibilities for Australian society to evolve into a place where all spaces are filled with empathy for both the collective and individual belonging, and perhaps more importantly for the future: a collective loving for the land?

References

Benhabib, S. 2002. *The Claims of Culture: Equality and Diversity in the Global Era.* New Tersey: Princeton University Press.

Burdon, Peter. 2006. "Above the law? Roxby Downs and BHP Billiton", *Friends of the Earth* Adelaide, 1 May 2006, <http://www.geocities.com/olympicdam/indenture1.html>

Douzinas, C. 2000. *The End of Human Rights: Critical Legal Thought at the Turn of the Century,* Portland: Oxford.

Education and Health Standing Committee (WA). 2007. *Initiatives in the Remote Indigenous Communities of Cape York,* Report No 7.

Moreton-Robinson, Aileen. 2007. 'Witnessing the Workings of White Possession in the Work Place: Leesa's Testimony', *Australian Feminist Law Journal*, vol. 26, pp. 81–93.

Pearson, N. 2005. *The Cape York Agenda.* Cairns: Cape York Institute for Policy and Leadership.

Razack, Sherene. 1994. 'What is to be Gained by Looking White People in the Eye? Culture, Race, and Gender in Cases of Sexual Violence', *Signs,* vol. 19, no. 4, pp. 894–923.

Rutherford, Tony. 2006. "Native Title Hostility Pointless" *The Western Australian,* 18th October 2006; <http://www.thewest.com.au/default.aspx?MenuID=77&ContentID=10238>

Spivak, Gayatri. 1999. *A Critique of Postcolonial Reason: Toward a History of the Vanishing Present.* Cambridge, MA: Harvard University Press.

Watson, Irene. 2005. 'Illusionists and Hunters: Being Aboriginal in this occupied space', *Australian Feminist Law Journal,* vol. 22, pp. 15–28.

Watson, Irene. 2006. 'Internationalising, Humanising and Diversifying: The One Nation State', in Baden Offord and Elisabeth Porter eds., *Activating Human Rights* Bern: Peter Lang European Academic Publishers.

Watson, Irene. 2007a. "Aboriginal Sovereignties: Past, Present and Future (Im)Possibilities" in Suvendrini Perera ed., *Our Patch, Enacting Australian Sovereignty Post-2001,* Network Books Symposia Series, Australia Research Unit, Curtin University of Technology, pp. 23–43.

Watson, Irene. 2007b. 'Aboriginal Women's Laws and Lives: How Might We Keep Growing the Law?' *Australian Feminist Law Journal,* vol. 26, p. 95.

Windschuttle, Keith. 2002. *The Fabrication of Aboriginal History: Volume One Van Diemen's Land 1803–1847.* Sydney: Macleay Press.

8

Fear and Outrage: The 'Problem', the Politics, and the National Emergency in Australia

Peter Gale

While there is a long history in the struggle for Indigenous rights in Australia, Indigenous politics begun as a concerted social movement in the 1960s leading up to the referendum to remove the discrimination against Indigenous Australians in the Australian Constitution in 1967 (Grossman, 2003). There was overwhelming support for the 1967 national referendum on Indigenous citizenship in Australia. It significantly changed the history of exclusive nationalist practices associated with previous policies of segregation and assimilation. However, 40 years on Indigenous Australians remain the most disadvantaged group within Australian society.

Since the early 1990s, the policy of reconciliation between Indigenous and non-Indigenous Australia, and the High Court judgments on native title in 1992 heralded a new era in Indigenous politics (Gale, 2005). However, Goot and Rowse (2007) argue that following the inclusive referendum in 1967 the Australian public have been divided on Indigenous issues such as land rights and reconciliation. Indigenous rights to land had become the focus of both media scrutiny and political debate following the High Court decisions on Indigenous native title rights during the early 1990s. Langton (1997) argues that wedge politics became a significant feature of political discourse on Indigenous rights over the past decade, in what Manning (2003) and others refer to as dog whistle politics.

There have been contrasting responses to what can be identified as a cluster of issues around the politics of division. For example, the national panic associated with heightened border protection and national security in response to perceived increased levels of global terrorism stands in contrast with the moral outrage against the treatment of asylum seekers leading up the 2001 federal election. The former is seen as a form of moral panic or crisis surrounding a perceived threat to "our" national heritage and culture. This contrasts with the outrage associated with the latter in the public response to the apparent contradiction between Australia as a First World nation and the perceived harsh treatment of asylum seekers (Gale, 2004).

During the Australian Prime Minister, John Howard's first period in office he argued that the overwhelming majority of Australians are proud of the achievements of the nation and that "Australians of this generation should not be required to accept guilt and blame for past actions and policies over which they had no control" (Howard, 1997). Ten years on in a speech on 'Australian Achievement' John Howard (2006) stated that "...compared with a decade ago, fewer Australians are ashamed of this nation's past." However, a year later John Howard (2007), described the "...abuse of children in indigenous communities in the Northern Territory" as a crisis and 'national emergency'.

Media reporting on violence in remote communities began in May 2006 when there was an unprecedented level of coverage of what was described in newspaper as a crisis of "violence in indigenous communities", with abuse, and neglect of Indigenous children.[1] In what can be identified as a first wave of reporting on Indigenous violence in remote communities there were two significant political and media responses, that of "moral panic" over such violence against women and children, and "moral outrage" over why 'white' Australia has allowed such violence to occur (Gale, 2006). One year later following the release of the report by Rex Wild and Pat Anderson (2007) on the 'Northern Territory Board of Inquiry into the Protection of Aboriginal Children from Sexual Abuse', there was a second wave of reporting and associated moral outrage and panic heralding a national emergency.

Michael Morrissey (2006) argues that Australian governments have constructed the 'Aboriginal problem' of poverty and inequality

1. For example see: Russell Skelton, Nassim Khaddem, and Melissa Fyfe (2006). "Urgent call: send troops now to NT – Doctors say 1500 vulnerable children are at risk of abuse by warring gangs", in *The Age*, 20 May, p. 1; see also Overington, Caroline, and Ashleigh Wilson (2006) "desperation that forced a hand", in *The Weekend Australian*, 20th May, p. 1; Khadem, Nassim (2006). "Aboriginal sex Abuse row grows—Call for evidence on pedophile claims", in *The Age*, 18th May, p. 3.

while seeking to avoid the perceived electoral disadvantage of resolving the 'problem'. Morrissey claims that the Howard Government has abandoned any social justice approach to Indigenous issues. Even under the previous Labour Government there had not been any appreciable improvement or even increased levels of disparity in the indicators of inequality between Indigenous and non-Indigenous Australians in areas such as health, housing, education and employment. Morrissey (2006) clearly argues that there has not been any appreciable level of resources allocated to address such indicators of inequality while under the Howard Government there has been a further deterioration in indicators of inequality. Analysis on the level of funding on Indigenous programs which have not kept pace with inflation and the increase in the number of Indigenous Australians between 1996 and 2006 highlights how under a Howard Government there has not been substantive improvement in the disparity between Indigenous and non-Indigenous Australians in areas of health and education (Harin, 2006:37).

Professor Larissa Behrendt (2003) provides a comprehensive review of Aboriginal Affairs under the Howard Government, describing Indigenous Australia as an "impoverished minority" where average life expectancy is at least twenty years less than the general population. Behrendt (2006) also highlights the disparity between Indigenous and non-Aboriginal Australians with death rates among Indigenous under thirty year olds four times that of non-Aboriginal people, infant mortality is three times that of other Australians, and the rate of infectious diseases twelve times higher than non-Indigenous Australians. Lower levels of educational attainment, higher unemployment rates, and Indigenous income at only 65 per cent that of the general population, highlight the indisputable socio-economic disparity between Indigenous peoples and other Australians.

Tracey Bunda (2006) argues that self-determination is not just a legal definition but is part of a broader rights framework that includes government funding of institutions and communities. Bunda also includes values of hope and care as part of analysis into the extent to which self-determination is and can be exercised. As such the level of funding cannot be separated from values such as hope and care as expressions of community or institutional based self-determination in contrast with processes of assimilation.

Cunneen (2007) highlights the 'moral panic' associated with what is represented as 'Indigenous lawlessness'. The notion of moral panic has been applied to the analysis of what is seen as the deviance of behaviour of social groups in many western nations most commonly applied to young people and crime. Cunneen (2007) focuses on the alarm associated with 'riots' following incidents of Aboriginal deaths in custody, however the perceived Indigenous lawlessness contributes to increased levels of policing rather than a review of the relationship between Aboriginal communities and law enforcement policies and practices.

Aileen Moreton-Robinson (2006) draws on the work of Michel Foucault as an analytical framework to explore racism as a form of biopower as race became a means through which the state became a colonizer. Moreton-Robinson (2006) argues that within postcolonial contexts such as Australia, whiteness as an invisible norm, operates through racialized disciplinary knowledge's and practices to preclude the recognition of Indigenous sovereignty, in particular, Indigenous rights to land and self determination. Moreton-Robinson (2006) concludes that what is critical to such analysis includes among others, an examination of anthropological discourse on land tenure and representation in legislation and the courts, media analysis of representations of Indigenous sovereignty and land rights, and analysis of government policy concerning land rights and native.title.

Underlying such analysis is a focus on representations of "race" in political discourse and media reporting on 'Indigenous issues' which have represented 'black' and 'white' in an oppositional relationship since the early 1990s. While blackness is represented as a "racial" Other, whiteness is portrayed as mainstream, ordinary, and employed as a symbolic marker of Australian identity. Similarly, the non-white other is commonly represented as being synonymous of un-Australian values. For example, newspaper reporting on Indigenous land rights has a common narrative embedded in a representation of "race" as a threat to Australian values and heritage. This is also illustrated in the Government response to native title, when in May 1997 John Howard sought to address the fears of farmers and claimed that his Government would guarantee certainty of land title for farmers (Gale, 2005). Correspondingly, reporting and political debate on violence in remote Indigenous communities placed an emphasis on what was represented as a national emergency.

Following Michel Foucault (2003) this analysis focuses on the discourse and "race" associated with what Foucault describes as "normalizing society", as the colonizing discourse of sovereignty intersects with the discourse of human sciences, namely normalization. In this instance, mechanisms of coercions are founded on what is prescribed as rights of sovereignty along with and what is constituted as a process of normalization. The focus of this research was on representations of Aboriginality and the way in which this shaped both public debate and political responses to Indigenous violence in remote Indigenous communities in Australia.

The Politics of Division

The first wave of media reporting on Indigenous violence against women and children in remote communities became the focus of attention during May 2006 (ABC, 2006). For the Howard Government it clearly positioned such violence as a law and order issue. John Howard sought to position the agenda of public debate with his comments on Indigenous Affairs, asserting that the Government spent hundreds of millions on Indigenous programs and more money was not the answer. The Howard Government employed the metaphor of pouring millions of dollars into Aboriginal Affairs, seeking to focus on law and order rather than on more funding. There were also claims that there is nothing new in many of the reports on the level of violence in Indigenous communities. For example, the death of Indigenous women in the Northern Territory was front page news in September 2002 with editorials calling for action and not just words from Governments. (Toohey, 2002:1)

The extensive media coverage of Indigenous violence during 2006 began with a report on the incidence of violence in remote Aboriginal communities by a Crown Prosecutor in Alice Springs in the Northern Territory. Media commentators such as Christopher Pearson (2006:30) referred to the "rape of young girls" and sexual initiation practices, and quoted anthropologists on "...pre-contact past or even in the era of modified traditional tribal adaptation is a matter of historical record". A feature of this reporting is the representation of Aboriginality as culturally deficit. The level of violence in remote communities was an outrage. Western culture is represented as being the foundation of law and order where the protection of the innocent and the vulnerable are its touchstones, in contrast with "traditional" societies that are depicted as being less advanced. Such an approach advocates policies that restricts cultural practices and the recognition of traditional law, and places an emphasis on law and order in communities through increased numbers of police officers in remote communities.

Government intervention is seen as a way of breaking the pattern of neglected children, reflected in an article in *The Australian* which claims that child welfare is destroying families as "...kids woke up every morning to an empty refrigerator and a bunch of drunks who had kept them awake all night" and the argument put forward by the Indigenous Affairs Minister, Mal Brough, that "It is not the money that is doing the damage but, rather, what it is being spent on." (Koch, 2006a:11) Many articles placed a greater level of responsibility on the role and responsibility of governments to intervene. This is reflected in an article published in *The Australian* claiming that there had been many reports tabled in parliament and information provided to government departments and officials, including the Prime Minister, and very little action had taken place. Noel Pearson, the Director of the Cape York Institute for Policy and Leadership, is quoted as saying that any abuse against children is "...totally reprehensible and not acceptable in any community" and argued that there had been no response by government following requests for intervention. (Koch, 2006c:15)

A feature of this reporting was the representation of Indigenous women and children as innocent victims of violence. For example, one article argued for "...the federal Government to declare a state of emergency ...and to employ the army or a civil service volunteer corps to provide viable settlements with proper facilities" (Rothwell, 2006:17).

Similarly, the front page image of a toddler in a nappy with the caption of "rape victim" accentuates both the act of violence and innocence of the victims. This article concludes with the comment that "...even in communities where the victims are fighting back ...the sexual abuse and domestic violence continues" (Koch, 2006b:1).

This is the most prominent representation of Aboriginality as being subject to a cycle of violence due to the economic, social, and cultural context of remote communities that have become welfare dependant and vulnerable to substance abuse. Debate in response to such serious problems places an emphasis on government intervention to address health, housing, education and employment, but places greater emphasis on addressing the perceived problems associated with a culture of welfare dependency.

Much of the reporting on violence in remote communities places a greater level of emphasis on the capacity of Indigenous communities to respond to the crisis and Indigenous perspectives and alternative approaches to addressing such violence. Very few articles included discussion on related issues of Indigenous governance, or Indigenous rights.

Creating the Crisis

This paper is based on analysis of the available discourses on Indigenous violence in remote communities. It includes both political and media discourse based on media releases by political leaders, along with speeches and interviews with Government Ministers, and media reporting based on newspaper reporting. Media Monitors note that there were over 22,000 media items on Indigenous communities in one week of media coverage of the national emergency in newspapers and electronic media (Ricketson, 2007). This analysis is based on both hard copy newspaper articles on media reporting and electronic *Newsbank* newspaper archives using key words associated with the reporting on Indigenous issues.

The sample period for the reporting on Indigenous violence was from newspapers published between June and July 2007 with an emphasis on the major national newspaper, *The Australian* and *The Weekend Australian*, along with other major regional newspapers such as *The Age* and the *Sydney Morning Herald*. Over four hundred newspaper articles published in Australia's national and regional newspapers during the period examined made reference to "Indigenous violence".

Political debate and reporting on violence in remote Indigenous communities includes a range of competing ideological perspectives. These include, Discourse of panic and paternalism; the 'problem' of past policies and welfare dependence; Addressing disadvantage; and Protecting Indigenous rights and self-determination.

National Emergency: Discourse of Panic and the 'Problem'

The predominant theme in both statements by the Howard Government and media reporting on Indigenous violence in remote communities was founded on a discourse of panic, along with a paternalism that focused on the protection of innocent children. For example, one front page story in *The Age*, under the headline, *National Emergency: PM*

Acts, illustrates both the panic and paternalism as the Government intervention is represented as an unprecedented response to 'indigenous child sex crisis'. (Schubert, Murphy and Murdoch, 2007:1,4) Similarly, in an editorial in *The Australian* under the headline, *Howard Finds Fertile Ground for Support: Strong Leadership has Got Voters' Attention*, there is an emphasis on both the national emergency and the electoral support for Government intervention. (Editor, 2007:13) The stress on crisis intervention is also illustrated by Noel Pearson (2007a:23) in an article under the headline of *Action Only Way Forward*, in which he argues that intervention is the only way forward to protect children when communities and past policies have failed. The 'problem' is represented as one of a culture of dependency on welfare, and the solutions are interventions that seek to break the cycle of dependency.

Many articles presented a national emergency that required intervention as discussed above, and media reporting focused on the 'problem' of past policies and welfare dependence. The focus on the culture of welfare dependence, along with past 'failed' policies that contributed to dependency resulting in the level of violence in remote communities shifts any debate from the Howard Government and the lack of what can be seen as adequate funding for health, housing, education, and employment in remote communities. For example, in many articles such as one front page story by Steven Lewis (2007:1) under the title of *Tough Love for Aboriginal Communities*, the problem is aligned with welfare dependency. Similarly in another article by prominent Indigenous leader, Noel Pearson (2007b:26) under the title of *An Abyss Beyond the Bottle*, substance dependency is identified as a major problem associated with welfare dependency. This perspective is also illustrated in an article by Ashleigh Wilson (2007:11), titled, *Brough wants to 'finish the job'*, in which the crisis demands dramatic intervention. Reminiscent of past arguments around a culture of poverty debates from the 1960s the reporting on Indigenous violence as a 'national crisis' places an emphasis on a culture of dependency. However such debates do not contribute to substantive policy outcomes, while outrage over past neglect similarly places an emphasis on non-Indigenous intervention. This is explored in the following section which focuses on a second major theme in the reporting on the national emergency, that of addressing Indigenous disadvantage.

Addressing Disadvantage

While there was significant media attention on a culture of dependency and associated Aboriginal violence there was less attention drawn to the need for increased levels in spending on health, housing, education and employment. However, some reporting did acknowledge the link between substance abuse, and the dramatic disparity in the levels of health, housing, education, and employment opportunities in remote communities. Similarly, within such debates it is highlighted that specific changes are required to engender hope for a future for Indigenous young people, in particular, through opportunities in education and employment.

From this perspective on remote communities there is an acknowledgement of the need for broad public support for increased spending and the support of all levels of Government through public endorsement for further spending on infrastructure and services. Similarly, there has been no shortage of voices highlighting the injustice of the inequality being experienced by Indigenous Australians, including the Human Rights and Equal Opportunity Commission, and the World Council of Churches among others. This perspective also notes that while the Howard Government may not be judged on the resistance to make a formal apology for the history of the removal of Indigenous children from their families, however in hindsight there may be widespread debate on the level of institutional neglect in funding that compromised basic human rights in health, housing and education.

For example, in the article titled, *National Emergency: PM Acts*, Misha Schubert, Katharine Murphy, and Lindsay Murdoch (2007:1,4) reflect on the significant calls for Governments to address underlying issues related to violence in remote communities, namely the levels of disadvantage in health, housing, education and employment. Similarly other articles such as *Children 'Traded for Alcohol'* (Kearney, 2007:6) and *Violence Behind the Silence* (Skelton, 2007:8), highlighting the need to address a broad range of issues.

From this perspective, key issues that are identified as making a difference include governance, education, health, housing, and employment. Education and training programs at a remote community level on community governance and relations between different levels of government is an essential part of breaking the nexus of communities being dependent on non-Indigenous administrators and advisors. While there is also extensive debate on welfare dependence in remote communities, from this perspective it is also seen as crucial for remote communities to become more independent through training Indigenous young people in community governance as both a future employment opportunity as well as diminishing the continued reliance on non-Indigenous community administrators.

This perspective also places an emphasis on the clear link between substance abuse and violence and the dramatic disparity in the levels of health, housing, education, and employment in remote communities and a shift towards addressing such underlying issues as an essential component in addressing the national 'crisis'. While this was not the most prominent perspective in the reporting on violence in remote communities it was a significant feature embedded within the debates along with a third perspective that highlighted the ongoing significance of self-determination and Indigenous rights in relation to the independence required to address the issues underlying the violence in remote communities.

Indigenous Rights and Self-determination

A contrasting approach to the reporting on the violence in remote communities focused on what is identified as the ongoing need include community consultation and a level of self-determination in developing policy responses and implementing programs to address the 'crisis'. As highlighted in the Northern Territory Government report on the protection of Aboriginal children recommends, community consultation is represented as a key to the success of any new policy direction and programme delivery as communities endorse and implement community based initiatives for change (Wild and Anderson, 2007). From this perspective, changes in policy need to include Indigenous representation of remote communities in making recommendations to all levels of Government. Similarly, it is also seen as essential to include consultation with communities in the determination of priorities over the allocation of funding for infrastructure and services. From this third perspective, it is identified that self-determination through substantive consultation is the only way in which the allocation of resources can be effective in making a difference for remote communities.

A significant aspect of the debate is on what is seen as a sustainable community and the continued funding of services to such communities.

Indigenous Australians in remote communities may not be forced to leave their communities, but with little hope for sustainable levels of funding for essential services, many Indigenous people from remote communities may be forced to live on the margins of larger regional towns or cities. Under the present level of state, territory, and federal funding, without dramatic increases in public spending for basic infrastructure and the delivery of services, and with a long-term commitment to such funding, then many remote communities will not be seen as sustainable. For example, Katharine England and Deborah Bogle (2007) in an article under the headline of *Place of Hope and Desperation*, highlight the role of communities to take control over their own lives to gain a hope for a future. Similarly, Patrick Dodson (2007:9), in *The Age*, highlights that *An Entire Culture is at Stake* as the current Government intervention includes no long-term economic and social development. Long term vision is also seen to offer hope, whereas from this perspective, present Government intervention offers very little hope for improved long-term quality of life for Aboriginal people in remote communities, or as Dodson concludes any government policy or programme needs to include substantive Aboriginal participation in decision making.

Crisis Politics

The political debate and media reporting on the emotive issue of violence involving Indigenous children echoed the frenzied debates surrounding native title during the 1990s. Similar pronouncements of a national crisis followed the High Court decisions on Indigenous rights to land in 1992, and again in December 1996 following the High Court Wik judgment during the first year of the Howard Government. The media reporting and political discourse on violence in remote communities was inseparably linked with 'traditional' Aboriginal culture and in conflict with what are seen as acceptable norms and values of Australian, and more broadly 'western' liberal democratic societies. The dramatic and at times described as 'draconian' Federal Government intervention has been represented as being in the national interest and an immediate requirement for the protection of children, in line with the expected norms of any modern liberal society such as Australia.

The political announcement of a national crisis also fed the myths that continue to circulate throughout the community that Indigenous

Australians are welfare dependent and receive special treatment from governments and the courts, reflecting past failed policies on Indigenous Affairs in Australia. This was highlighted in the first wave of reporting and political pronouncement on Indigenous violence in 2006. Taking the lead from the Prime Minister, in the first wave of media reporting on violence in remote communities, Mal Brough as Minister for Indigenous Affairs, claimed that there was a "culture of fear" and a "black mafia" operating in remote Indigenous communities. (Madigan, 2006:49, 52)

Appearing to be tough on crime has become a popular response by both federal and state governments around Australia. Not surprisingly, with the second wave of media reporting on the plight of Indigenous women and children in remote communities in 2007 the Howard Government argued that there was a national emergency that required unprecedented action, including unprecedented levels of military and police presence in remote Indigenous communities. There was no shortage of graphic headlines and depictions in the media of child abuse, and widespread violence highlighting the national 'crisis'.

Failed past policies were linked with what was depicted as 'special' rights of Indigenous Australians associated with native title to land and self determination. These past policies were identified as being part of the 'problem' and the linking of land title issues with the Federal government intervention was represented as being integral to an overall shift in policy to redress the problem of violence in remote communities and the protection of children.

While the past shifts in policy associated with the 1967 referendum received widespread public support, this was seen as redressing past wrongs and the problem of a perceived contradiction in the quality of life and treatment of Indigenous Australians, seemingly inconsistent with human rights and expectations for any group within a modern liberal democratic nation state. However, further political reforms under both the Whitlam Labor Government of the early 1970s and the Fraser Liberal Government of the late 1970s was then represented are pushing the pendulum of fairness too far in favor of Indigenous groups and inconsistent with the fair treatment of all citizens in a liberal democracy.

The subsequent High Court decisions on Indigenous rights to land was then represented in political debate and media reporting as being in fundamental conflict with the interests of ordinary Australians who had worked hard to advance the national interest, both through mining and the pastoral industry. In contrast with the 1967 referendum there was significant opposition to native title rights and the Howard Government fueled such opposition and sought to redress the balance—and restore the rights of miners and farmers and protect the national interest.

While claiming that the recent Government intervention is protecting Indigenous children and their future well being, the actions and legislation also sought to restore the balance, consistent with amendments to the native title legislation introduced by the Howard Government in the first year of office in 1997. The Howard Government has defended its actions and shift in policy in the name of the rights of Indigenous children while also implementing significant changes in both policy and legislation, defending charges of promoting the interests of mining companies and instigating actions that are 'racially' motivated.

While representing Indigenous violence as both a crisis and the result of past failed policies, it has been possible for the Howard Government to implement such policies without facing either an electoral backlash, or being seen as acting in ways that are inconsistent with liberal democratic norms that include both fair and just treatment and policies of anti-discrimination. For over ten years in office, the Howard Government has implemented major changes in Indigenous policy, including the mainstreaming of Indigenous services and abolishing the independent structure and administration of services through the democratically elected Indigenous body of Aboriginal and Torres Sbrait Islander Commission (ATSIC). Similarly, amendments to the native title legislation, has been achieved without any significant electoral backlash, and in many instances attaining an electoral advantage. This has been possible through representing such changes as both redressing the balance and responding to past failed policies, all in the name of protecting Indigenous children and in the national interest.

Although recent public debate has highlighted the need to significantly increase public funding for Indigenous health, housing, education, and employment, amidst such debate there has also been significant blame attributed to both Indigenous culture, and a culture of dependence on welfare, along with failed past policies of self-determination, self management, and Indigenous rights to land. It is difficult to maintain hope in a future that is able to achieve broad public support for Indigenous rights to land and self-determination while such policies are under such a sustained attack through both the media reporting and contemporary political representation of Indigenous issues.

References

Behrendt, Larissa. 2003. *Achieving Social Justice: Indigenous Rights and Australia's Future*. NSW: The Federation Press.

Behrendt, Larissa. 2006. 'Indigenous Policy: No Quick Fix', in *Australian Policy Online*, http://www.apo.org.au/webboard/results.chtml?filename_num=80532 (accessed June 2006)

Bunda, Tracey. 2006. "Self-determination: Actualising the space", in *Gas Worby and Lester-Irabinna Rigney eds.,Sharing Spaces: Indigenous and Non-Indigenous Responses to Story, Country, and Rights*, Perth: Australian Research Institute, Curtin University of Technology, pp. 449–460.

Cunneen, Chris. 2007. 'Riot, Resistance and Moral Panic: Demonising the Colonial Other', in Scott Poynting and George Morgan eds., *Outrageous! Moral Panics in Australia*, University of Tasmania, Hobart: ACYS Publishing, pp. 20–29.

Foucault, Michel. 2003. *Society Must Be Defended: Lectures at the College De France 1975–76*, translated by David Macey. London: Penguin Books.

Gale, Peter. 2004. 'Refugee Crisis and Fear: Populist Politics and Media Discourse', *Australian Journal of Sociology*, vol. 40, no. 4, December, pp. 321–340.

Gale, Peter. 2005. *The Politics of Fear: Lighting the Wik*. Sydney: Pearson Education.

Gale, Peter. 2006. Compassion and Fear—Convergence and Divergence: Politics and the Media. Paper presented to the Indian Association for the Study of Australia Conference on Australia and India: Convergences and Divergences. January.

Goot, Murray and Tim Rowse. 2007. *Divided Nation? Indigenous Affairs and the Imagined Public*. Melbourne: Melbourne University Press.

Grossman, Michele. 2003. After Aboriginalism: Power, Knowledge and Indigenous Australian Critical Writing', in Michele Grossman ed. *Blacklines: Contemporary Critical Writing by Indigenous Australians*. Melbourne: Melbourne University Press, pp. 1–24.

Hall, Stuart, Chas Critcher, Tony Jefferson, John Clarke, and Brian Roberts. 1978. *Policing the Crisis*. London: Macmillan.

Hall, Stuart. 1997. "The Work of Representation" in Stuart Hall ed., *Representation: Cultural Representations and Signifying Practices*. London: Sage Publications, pp. 1–74.

Howard, John. 1997. *Opening Address to the Australian Reconciliation Convention*, Melbourne, 26 May. http://www.pm.gov.au/media/index.cfm?type=2 (accessed August 2007).

Howard, John. 2006. Address to the National Press Club, Parliament House, Canberra, 25 January. http://www.pm.gov.au/media/index.cfm?type=2 (accessed August 2007).

Howard, John. 2007. Joint Press Conference with the Hon Mal Brough, Minister for Families, Community Services and Indigenous Affairs, Canberra, 21 June. http://www.pm.gov.au/media/index.cfm?type=3 (accessed August 2007).

Human Rights and Equal Opportunity Commission. 1997. *Bringing them home: National Inquiry into the Separation of Aboriginal and Torres Strait Islander Children from their Families*. Canberra: Australian Government Publishing Service.

Langton, Marcia. 1997. "Pauline as the Thin End of the Wedge", in Philip Adams ed., *The Retreat From Tolerance: A Snapshot of Australian Society*. Sydney: ABC Books.

Manning, Peter. 2003. *Dog Whistle Politics and Journalism: Reporting Arabic and Muslim people in Sydney newspapers*. Australian Centre for Independent Journalism, Sydney: University of Technology Sydney.

Morris, Megan. 2001. "Introduction" in Megan Morris and Brett deBary eds., *"Race" Panic and the Memory of Migration*. Hong Kong: Hong Kong University Press, pp. 1–18.

Morrissey, Michael. 2006. 'The Australian State and Indigenous People 1990–2006' in *Journal of Sociology*, vol. 42, no. 4, pp. 347–354.

Moreton-Robinson, Aileen. 2006. 'Towards a New Research Agenda? Foucault, Whiteness and Indigenous Sovereignty', *Journal of Sociology*, vol. 42, no. 4, pp. 383–395.

Wild, Rex, and Pat Anderson, 2007. *Report of the Northern Territory Board of Inquiry into the Protection of Aboriginal Children from Sexual Abuse*, Darwin: Northern Territory Gov.ernment.

Newspaper References

ABC, 2006. "Culture of violence revealed in central Australia", ABC News Online, May16, http://www.abc.net.au/news/newsitems/200605/s1639145.htm

Dodson, Patrick. 2007. 'An entire Culture is at Stake', in *The Age, Insight*, Saturday 14 July, p. 9.

Editor, 2007. 'Howard Finds fertile Ground for Support: Strong Leadership has got voters' attention', in *The Australian*, Tuesday 10 July, p. 13.

England, Katharine and Deborah Bogle. 2007. 'Place of Hope and Desperation', in *The Advertiser, Review*, Saturday, 30 June, pp. 8–10.

Harin, Adele. 2006. 'Money Spent on Votes, Not Aborigines', in *The Sydney Morning Herald*, 27 May, p. 37.

Kearney, Simon. 2007. 'Children 'traded for alcohol', in *The Australian*, Thursday, July 12, p. 6.

Khadem, Nassim. 2006. 'Aboriginal sex Abuse row grows – Call for evidence on paedophile claims', in *The Age*, 18 May, p. 3.

Koch, Tony. 2006a. 'Circuit Breaker', in *The Australian*, 2 May, p. 11.

Koch, Tony. 2006b. 'Eight years ago, this picture brought calls for action. But nothing happened', in *The Australian*, 17 May, p. 1.

Koch, Tony. 2006c. 'Dirty Big Secret', in *The Australian*, 17 May, p. 15.

Lewis, Steven. 'Tough love' for Aboriginal communities, in *The Australian*, Monday 18 June, p. 1.

Madigan, Michael. 2006. 'Culture of Violence', in *Courier Mail*, pp. 49, 52.

Overington, Caroline and Ashleigh Wilson. 2006. "Desperation that forced a hand", in *The Weekend Australian*, 20 May, p. 1.

Pearson, Christopher. 2006. 'Law of Diminishing abuse', in *The Weekend Australian*, 27–28 May, p. 30.

Pearson, Noel. 2007. Action only way forward, in *The Weekend Australian, Inquirer*, 7-8 July, p. 23.

Pearson, Noel. 2007. 'An Abyss beyond the bottle', in *The Weekend Australian*, 14–15 July, p. 26.

Ricketson, Matthew. 2007. 'Saturation Coverage', in *The Age*, 30 June, p. 12.

Rothwell, Nicolas. 2006. 'Cry of the innocent', in *The Weekend Australian*, 20-21 May, p. 17.

Schubert, Misha, Katharine Murphy and Lindsay Murdoch. 2007. 'National emergency: PM acts', in *The Age*, Friday, 22 June, pp. 1, 4.

Skelton, Russell. 2007. 'Violence behind the silence', in *The Age, Insight*, Saturday 7 July, p. 8.

Skelton, Russell, Nassim Khaddem and Melissa Fyfe. 2006. 'Urgent call: send troops now to NT – Doctors say 1500 vulnerable children are at risk of abuse by warring gangs', in *The Age*, 20 May, p. 1.

Toohey, Paul. 2002. 'Territory shame: the grim scale of blacks killing each other', in *The Australian*, 26 September, p. 1.

Wilson, Ashleigh. 2007. 'Brough wants to 'finish the job'', in *The Weekend Australian*, 7-8 July, p. 11.

9

Changing Patterns of Language Socialization in Inuit Homes[1]

Martha B. Crago, Betsy Annahatak and Lizzie Ningiuruvik

In Northern Quebec, there is a wide river that flows for many miles until its waters reach Ungava Bay. One woman who has lived most of her life on the shores of this river likened the recent cultural changes in the lives of Inuit to the water of the river, perpetually moving and flowing across a bed of time. Life must evolve—it always does—and Inuit, she felt, were adapting the course of their river to meet the flow of time. This article describes certain changes and adaptations that have occurred in the socialization of young Inuit children. The focus is on how mothers, young and old, communicate and have communicated with their children—on how they have guided their children's language use and interwoven it into their children's growth as cultural members situated in historical time.

Three bodies of literature contributed to the research on which this article was based. First, a substantial body of literature on language socialization of children in a variety of societies has developed over the last two decades (Blount, 1972; Boggs, 1985; Clancy, 1986; Crago, 1988; Demuth, 1986; Eisenberg, 1982; Fischer, 1970; Harkness, 1977; Heath, 1983; Miller, 1982; Ochs, 1988; Philips, 1983; Schieffelin, 1990; Scollon and Scollon, 1981; Smith-Hefner, 1988; Ward, 1971; Watson-Gegeo and Gegeo, 1986). By documenting how each culture has different patterns of caregivers' communication with young children, these language socialization studies have produced key information on how children in various groups develop their cultural membership as they learn and use language with the people in their lives. This article reports on data taken from a language socialization study of Inuit children in Northern Quebec.

---

1. This article has been reprinted from the *Anthropology and Education Quarterly* 24(3):205–223 with the permission of the author and the publisher.

An intersecting body of research has documented the deleterious effects of educational instruction that ignores the difference between the communicative interaction that certain minority-culture children experience at home and at school (Erickson, 1987; Heath, 1983; Philips, 1983; Tharp and Gallimore, 1988). Going to school for many minority-culture children can be seen as a form of secondary socialization in which they have to learn new ways of interacting and communicating that are discontinuous with their home environments (Duranti and Ochs, 1988; Tharp et al., 1984). Research that focuses on the language socialization of children in their homes and on the effects of the imposition of the dominant culture's communicative interaction within the school has, for the most part, been done without addressing (i) whether the communicative patterns of the school extend into and influence communication in the home, and (ii) in what way families adapt or redefine their communicative interactions with their children in response to and in preparation for school. Heath (1990), one of the few researchers who has conducted a longitudinal study of language socialization in homes and schools, has pointed out that home patterns of language socialization can be dramatically disrupted in situations of rapid social change. When the caregiver-child communicative interactions in one of the communities she studied were rendered almost unrecognizable in scarcely more than 15 years' time, Heath concluded that:

> we must run the risk of demonstrating that fewer and fewer individuals in some minority groups define themselves in terms of webs of significance that they themselves spin, and many may be caught without understanding, interpreting, or transmitting anything like the cultural patterns into which they themselves were socialized (Heath, 1990:517).

Unlike Heath's study, most ethnographic studies of language socialization and classroom interaction have, for the most part, been conducted in a single circumscribed time period. This ahistorical perspective has produced very few clues about the process of evolution and little material for understanding change. Changes over time merit attention because they can lead to information on shifting patterns of domination and control.

The third body of literature that informs this article concerns domination and control issues in relationship to language and to education. Bourdieu and Passeron (1990) have described the resources that are necessary for competition in the school and the marketplace as a form of cultural capital. Without holding the forms of capital of the dominant society, children from nondominant cultures are often at risk for failure in school. The importance of language as a form of cultural capital has been underlined by Gal (1989). Patterns of communicative interaction can also be interpreted as crucial holdings for success in the marketplace, schools, and negotiating tables of the dominant society. Such linguistically linked patterns of dominance are likely to come into play in the process of cultural change.

This article, then, describes a study of communicative interaction between four young Inuit children and their families. In particular, it addresses the effects of cultural change, including the introduction of schooling, on the communicative interaction of caregivers and young children by focusing on the differences between the behaviour and stated concepts of two generations of mothers.

The Study

The research on which the article is based was a two-year-long ethnographic study of the communicative interaction of four Inuit children and their families living in Quaqtaq and Kangirsuk, Quebec.

Data Sources

Data for the study were collected using ethnographic methods. They were derived from three sources: 80 hours of transcribed and translated videotapes of four target children and their families, 20 ethnographic interviews of Inuit women, and several hundred pages of observation and informal interview notes. The principal body of data was collected from June 1985 to July 1987.

The People of the Study

Videotapes were made of four Inuit children and their families; two of the children were boys and two were girls. Children selected for the study came from unilingual (Inuktitut) and unicultural (Inuit) homes and were between 12 to 24 months old. The family constellations of these children were as follows (see Table 9.1): Nora and Annie, the mothers in Family 2 and Family 4, were young women, whereas Qaajia and Eva were older mothers of adopted children. Custom adoption is a common practice in both of these communities.[2] At the time of the study, 40 percent of the children in Quaqtaq and 37.5 percent of the children in Kangirsuk had been adopted in or out of their families. Two of the families lived in Kangirsuk and two lived in Quaqtaq. This meant that a boy, a girl, a young mother, and an older mother came from each of the two communities. Nora lived with her extended family; Annie's family, on the other hand, was a small nuclear family, a phenomenon that has only recently emerged in northern Quebec as the number and type of housing units have expanded. The combination of adoption by the two mothers in their late forties and early childbearing by the mothers in their late teens meant that the maternal caregivers in this study spanned three decades and at least two generations. The older mothers were born in igloos, never went to school, and spoke only Inuktitut; the younger ones had lived their entire lives in houses, had attended school from the age of six, and spoke English in one case, French and English in the other.

Permission to videotape these four families was negotiated by the two Inuit authors of this article, who served as research advisor and research coordinator for the project. No families that were approached refused this permission. The permission included the right to show the tapes for educational purposes. This meant that tapes might be shown outside of the community and also to certain members of the community as a vehicle for obtaining reactions and reflections on certain child-rearing practices (see Crago, 1988 for further details on this procedure and on the analysis of the videotapes). Sections of the tapes are now routinely used in Inuit teacher training courses to demonstrate the nature of language socialization in that culture. In addition to the children and their families who were taped, ethnographic interviews of 20 women out of the 45 women living in Quaqtaq were conducted by Lizzie Ningiuruvik in Inuktitut. These 20 women ranged in age from 18 to 65 and were randomly selected from the whole population of women of this age in Quaqtaq. They are subdivided into a group of older women (45 years and older) and a group of younger women (18 to 45 years of age). Quotations that follow in this article are taken from interviews of these two groups and include comments by 19 of the 20 women that were interviewed.

---

2. Custom adoption involves adoption arranged within the Inuit community without the intervention of government social service agencies. It is a longstanding cultural practice existing for a variety of reasons.

Table 9.1 Family Constellations.

	Present in Family Home	*Age*	*Comment*
Family 1 (KANGIRSUK)			
Grandfather	x	81	
Mother (Qaajia)	x	57	
GIRL CHILD	x	1	Adopted in from Brother 3
Brother 1		32	Adopted out
Brother 2		29	
Brother 3		25	Father of target child
Sister 1	x	14	Adopted in
Family 2 (KANGIRSUK)			
Grandfather	x	45	
Grandmother	x	42	
Aunt 1	x	22	
Aunt's boyfriend	x	23	
Mother (Nora)	x	20	
BOY CHILD	x	1	
Uncle 1	x	19	
Uncle 2	x	17	
Aunt 2	x	14	
Uncle 3		13	Adopted out
Uncle 4	x	11	
Uncle 5	x	6	Adopted in
Uncle-Brother 5	x	<1	Mother's child adopted by grandmother
Cousin	x	<1	
Family 3 (QUAQTAQ)			
Mother (Eva)	x	52	
BOY CHILD	x	1	Adopted in
Brother 1	x	25	Adopted in
Brother 2	x	22	Adopted in
Sister 1	x	18	Adopted in
Brother 3	x	13	Adopted in
Family 4 (QUAQTAQ)			
Father	x	22	
Mother (Annie)	x	21	
GIRL CHILD	x	1	
Brother		3	Adopted out

Finally, observation notes were made of the same four families featured on the videotapes. In addition, a variety of episodes and encounters with other people in the two communities formed a part of the observation notes. These included the actions and reactions of Martha Crago's own non-Inuit children, aged 3, 8, and 10, to Inuit and Inuit's reactions to her children and her parenting.

The three authors of this article were all involved in the research. The research advisor, Betsy Annahatak, has lived in Kangirsuk and worked as a teacher and pedagogical counselor for the local school board for over 20 years. The research coordinator, Lizzie Ningiuruvik, has lived all her life in Quaqtaq and worked for the school board for many years as a teacher, teacher training instructor, and commissioner. These women's native language is Inuktitut, but they are also fluent speakers of English. The non-Inuk investigator, Martha Crago, was a lecturer at McGill University in the area of language development and language disorders at the time that this study was conducted. She has also worked as a consultant and teacher training instructor for the Kativik School Board, taught in Inuit teacher training, and administered a project of adapted audiological service delivery for Inuit children with Otitis Media.

The Two Communities: A Brief Description and History

The Inuit territory of Northern Quebec covers 563,515 square kilometres or approximately one-third of the province of Quebec. Kangirsuk is approximately 1,000 miles north of Montreal and had a population of 325 in 1986; Quaqtaq is approximately 100 miles north of Kangirsuk and had a population of 200 in 1986.

History of Schooling

The first school in these two communities was a small Catholic mission school opened in 1947. It was not until 1960 that the Canadian government opened federal schools in Quaqtaq and Kangirsuk. When the first government school was built in Kangirsuk, Inuit families still lived nomadically on the land. Going to school in these first years meant that children as young as five years old were removed from their families and taken to the present-day location of the village of Kangirsuk. There, they were lodged in a residence from fall until spring and educated in English. In the space of a few years, families began to move off the land and settle near the school in order to be able to live with their children. At first, the families lived nearby the school in tents and igloos; later, they built shacks and small houses. In the mid-1960s, the federal government began building houses for the Inuit of Ungava Bay.

In 1967, a second school, run by the provincial Direction Général du Nord du Québec (DGNQ), was opened in Kangirsuk. It differed from the federal school by offering French language instruction and kindergarten taught by Inuit teachers in Inuktitut. The two schools, the federal and provincial, operated in parallel until the James Bay Agreement was signed in 1975. This latter was a financial land claims settlement that gave Inuit regional and municipal control over their schools.

The Present Day

Since 1976, teaching in Northern Quebec has come under the jurisdiction of the Inuit-controlled Kativik School Board. This board oversees schools in all 14 of the settlements. It has an Inuk director general and a large number of Inuit educators and others on staff. At the time of the research, the Kangirsuk school had 10 Inuit counselors and teachers out of a staff of 18 in addition to the Inuk who was the center director; the Quaqtaq school was headed by an Inuk principal with a staff of 6 Inuit out of a total of 12 teachers. Despite Inuit control of educational authority, many of the educational practices in the Kativik schools, especially in the classrooms with non-Inuit teachers, are modeled after mainstream practices. At the time of the study, the school board did not offer orientation courses to new non-native teachers, and the vast majority of these teachers had not had any training courses pertinent to teaching in the Inuit context. Hence, there were very limited opportunities for non-Inuit teachers to obtain information on the Inuit culture, language, or even on Inuit teachers' classroom practices. As a consequence, their teaching did not reflect such knowledge. The school board as a whole was just beginning to realize the cultural roots and impact of teaching and, as a consequence, had not yet effected any change in this area for the schools that it controlled. This study was one the first steps in documenting cultural patterns relevant to education. Later research documented Inuit teacher classroom discourse (Eriks-Brophy and Crago, 1994) and non-Inuit teacher classroom discourse (Eriks-Brophy and Crago, 2003).

In the communities of Kangirsuk and Quaqtaq, the Ungava Bay dialect of Inuktitut is spoken by all Inuit residents. It is spoken for all formal and informal transactions that take place between Inuit. Many of the people in these two communities who are under 40 years of age speak English, while many of those over 40 speak virtually no second language. In both communities, Inuktitut is the language of instruction for kindergarten through second grade.

In the space of 25 years, a great deal has changed. The Inuit of Quaqtaq and Kangirsuk who once lived in family groupings scattered across vast tracts of land are now clustered in villages, living in southern-Canadian-style homes. Commercial enterprise, schools, governmental agencies, and long-distance transportation are a part of their village way of life. The remainder of this article will describe certain changes in communicative interaction that have taken place in Inuit homes and relate them to the cultural change that has taken place at a societal level.

Changes in Communicative Interaction: Differences between Younger and Older Mothers

The changes that have occurred in the communicative interaction of Inuit caregivers with their young children are reflected in the differences in language socialization patterns of younger and older mothers. A number of such patterns will be described and considered in the light of Inuit mothers' interpretations of their meaning.

Aqausiit: Affectionate Verses

Aqausiit are rhythmical verses that Inuit mothers have traditionally sung or chanted to their babies. Many women that were interviewed recognized that increasingly fewer people *aqaq* their babies in this traditional way. Only a small group of younger and older mothers reported that they still used or had ever used aqausiit for their children. Aqausiit re dyadic; each child-adult pair has its own unique set of words or nonsense words that the adult sings or chants to the child. One older Inuk woman that we interviewed said, "Most children had *aqausiq*, the same one attached to them, repeated by everyone and loved by everyone."

Aqausiit are a way of showing affection to a child. Two other women from the older group described their sense of this way of talking to children as follows:

> To me it means a way of loving a child, I think that's what it is. I feel like saying something like that when I feel affection towards a child.

The mother's way of showing happiness. She does it to show love to her baby.

Aqausiit are highly rhythmical and embody an early interactional communicative mode between caregivers and children. Children, it was reported, recognize their own chant and express pleasure physically by smiling, bouncing, and cooing in return. Most importantly, all the aqausiit that were recorded for this study convey a loving, playful sense not only in their content but also in the manner in which they are sung and chanted to the child.

The increasing disappearance of the aqausiit saddened these three older women:

> I just know some from long ago but regretfully not from our own family.
> I could not really aqaq so that's sad about me.

Well, they used to aqaq their children better than now. Nowadays we do not hear almost anybody aqaq a child because the way of talking to a child has changed. In those days their way of talking to children may have been better.

Only a handful of younger women that we interviewed aqaqed their babies. In fact, one younger woman did not know what an aqausiq was; another thought it was a way of sharing a joke. None of the caregivers in the four families I videotaped said aqausiit to their children—neither the younger mothers nor the older ones. The reason aqausiit have been abandoned was poignantly described by one mother from the younger group: "You can't do it when you feel anxious. We are too anxious these days. We have to get up and run off to work in the morning." The disappearance of the aqausiit from most households is one indicator of cultural change in the communicative interaction between caregivers and their children.

Nilliujuusiq: Affectionate Talk

Another form of affectionate talk, *nilliujuusiq*, has outlasted the aqausiit and still has considerable frequency of occurrence among today's Inuit in Quaqtaq and Kangirsuk. In a number of loving situations, women talked to their children in a loud, raucous voice. The two older mothers who were videotaped, Qaajia and Eva, used this voice or occasionally a soft, whispery one to chant phrases or add a string of nonsense syllables onto sensible words and grammatical constructions. Qaajia described her behaviour like this: "It is just my way of speaking, my way of loving her."

Similar descriptions of affectionate talk came from the interviews. When asked whether she spoke to her children differently than to adults, another older woman said that she did,

> because we tend to have affectionate ways of talking to them when they are babies. That is the sort of way I have when they are small, talking to them affectionately and not using my normal way of talking because we talk to them in that way when they are small and they know our way of talking and they recognize it.

Two other women, when asked how they talked to their children, said:

> I just love them and talk to them in that way. I don't talk real talk to my babies.
> I would answer the child even trying to talk in the child's language from feeling a surge of love for my child.

Of the two young mothers that were videotaped, only Annie occasionally used language that resembled affectionate talk. She added short, single, syllables onto a few of her words. In the interviews, other young mothers spoke of affectionate talk differently than the older mothers. When asked if they used this kind of talk with their children, they said things like "Only sometimes," and "I only tell them things for children but trying to mean something." Both Qaajia and Eva had teenage daughters who did a considerable amount of caregiving for their younger siblings. Neither of these girls used affectionate talk while taking care of their younger siblings.

Information from the videotapes and from the interviews, then, showed that there is less use of nilliujuusiq by young mothers with their children than by older mothers with their children. One of the authors of this article felt that this form of talk is done more by mothers with their second or third child, at a point when they are more experienced and more at ease as a mother. Two older women, however, reported using affectionate talk with their first children when they were young mothers.

"Baby Words": A Special Vocabulary for Young Children

Inuit refer to a specialized vocabulary that is used with young children as "baby words" (*piaraujausiit*) and the caregivers' way of talking as "baby talk" (*piaraujautuq*). In all four families, this vocabulary was used both by and to the children. The baby word vocabulary was also heard in almost every home in Quaqtaq and Kangirsuk that had small children. The words are remarkably consistent across households. Baby words have phonologically simpler roots than their adult equivalents.

The use of baby words is age-related, not language-stage-related. One Inuit kindergarten teacher told us that 5-year-old children in her class tease other children their age who still use baby talk. The general consensus of Inuit teachers was that this vocabulary fades out at about 3 to 3½ years old.

Some of the young mothers we interviewed expressed disdain for this specialized vocabulary. One of them described the difference between herself and the older mothers in this way: "When the older people talk,

> to them, they baby talk and they aqaq them more." Others, when they were asked about how they talked to their small children, said:

> By talking to them well, *not* acting like a child to them.

Just like that, just the same words. I talk to her in the same way I usually talk.

I think that if children would be talked to plainly, as they are growing up, that they are learning to talk well by not talking baby talk when talking to them.

Only one of the older women interviewed said that she did not use baby talk to her children. She is married to a non-Inuk. Her statement reflected an awareness of the Inuit way of speaking to children, a way she says she no longer uses: "I just make the words easy, but not baby talk, using real words when I talk to my children. I used to talk the way Inuit do. Now I talk to them just like an adult."

Her statement is in sharp contrast with this statement by Eva, one of the older mothers we videotaped:

I use a way of talking that is more suitable for a child his age [pointing to her two-year-old]. I talk in a way not meant for an adult. The language would be too heavy if I talked to him as I would to an adult. When they are first learning to understand we should not talk in such a way to them.

Eight of the other ten older women concurred with her. Two of them said:

I don't talk real talk to my babies.

When they are small I use a special way of talking and follow his ability to learn to recognize that special way of talking that is different from the way of talking to an adult.

These older women, then, expressed the need to use a specialized vocabulary with their children. They found it appropriate to differentiate the way that they talked to children from the way adults are talked to. Younger women did not share their perceptions. For them the distinction between adult talk and child talk was not considered to be useful or desirable. This difference between the younger and the older women seems to be another indication of cultural change in communicative interactions with young Inuit children.

Appropriate Exclusion

Because young Inuit children are present in many multiage situations, they are exposed to a great deal of talk by older people. In our study, children were expected not to participate with or to ask questions of adults who were speaking together. One older Inuk woman explained it this way:

> It is not so much that the children should not interrupt but that they should not participate in adult conversation…to prevent them getting involved with adult stuff before they are mature enough.

Making sure that children are not exposed to things for which they are not ready is a communicative modification that some older Inuit women said helps to keep children from ideas and ways that are not appropriate for them.

Younger women had quite different conceptions of keeping children from interfering in adult conversations. Only one of the 10 women under 35 years old remembered times when she was not supposed to talk. Those times, she said, were when adults were telling stories. The reactions of the younger women were in direct contrast to those of the older women. All of the older women described the unacceptability of children interfering in adult conversation.

Bearing this difference in mind, the videotapes were inspected to see if the two children of young mothers were more involved in adult conversation than the two children of older mothers. Annie's child, who lived alone with her parents, asked many questions of them by the time she was two years old. In one section of a videotape, Annie and the child were sitting at a table eating. Her mother talked throughout the meal with her, trying to get her to say "yum." While watching this tape, an older Inuk woman said, "She doesn't seem to know how to eat silently with her daughter." Nora was also a young mother. Her son asked many questions of her and of his uncles and aunts, all of whom were under 20 years old. They, as in the case of the previous child, responded to his questions. Nora's son would interrupt his mother if she sat talking to one of her friends. He also conversed with his mother as they walked along the road outside. This was in striking contrast to numerous situations where children his age sat or walked with their older parents in complete quiet.

The Role of Comprehension in Language Learning

When the women in Quaqtaq were interviewed, the majority of the women over 45 stated that one could determine whether a child had learned language by whether the child understood what was said. The women in the younger group, on the other hand, indicated that they judged language learning on the basis of production (Crago, 1992). Furthermore, Inuit children are socialized to become useful participants in their society by encouraging them to understand and to follow directives. Directives to Inuit children are delivered in the imperative form and are designed to elicit action. Children's ability to understand and to do what is asked is valued behaviour. Eva described her way of teaching a child to talk as follows:

When I'm eating, I tell them to eat, saying "apaapalaurit" (eat). For the bottle I tell them to drink from the bottle, saying "amaamalaurit" (drink), for they quickly learn to understand the word.

One of the authors of this article reported:

> Giving tasks to children is very important as early as the child can understand. My grandmother used to say very often when a child had reached a certain stage, "He now can do this." "He now can get this for me." "He now can make tea for me." During the course on Inuit values in 1987, the elder who served as the resource person made us aware that as early as possible one should start asking the child to get things for you and the tasks should get harder as the child grows.

She also reported that some men in her community have described language loss in these terms: "These children are losing their language. They don't understand what we ask them to do." One form of acceptance into the social world, then, is marked for Inuit children by their learning to interpret and follow the directions given to them by their caregivers. The early comprehension of directives is part of the process of acquiring cultural membership, of becoming an appropriate Inuk who knows how to learn by looking and listening.

Use of Questions

Traditionally, Inuit children have not been encouraged to participate in conversations with adults. In fact, their questions are usually ignored. One woman commented about Martha Crago's daughter who was visiting Northern Quebec from Montreal: "I found that when I was home with her and the other children that she talked a lot and asked questions of the adults. We don't like our children to ask questions of adults." Children are not expected to ask many questions of adults, nor are many questions asked of them by adults. On the 80 hours of videotapes, very few questions were asked of the four children to which adults knew the answers. Qaajia and Eva, the two older mothers, asked their two small children only one kind of question: "What's the matter?" when the children were crying. Even that was done rarely, and there were many instances when one of the children cried and was not asked what the problem was. On the other hand, the two young mothers, Nora and Annie, asked their children questions to which they already knew the answers. The most frequent one was, "Who's this?" while pointing to a relative or visitor. The second most frequent one was "Whose is this?" while pointing to an object. Annie and Nora's children were also asked "How old are you?" A visiting *Qallunak* (non-Inuk) audiologist said that on her first trips to Northern

Quebec she wanted her Inuk colleague to ask children questions in Inuktitut such as "Where's your nose?" or "Where's your mouth?" to test their comprehension. She said the children just looked at the Inuk hearing specialist and often did not answer. This Inuk hearing specialist, a young mother herself, said that she had noticed that children needed to be able to answer questions like that in school, so she had begun teaching her child to reply to such test questions. She claimed that "the younger women talk more like that to their children."

Second Language and Politeness Routines

Annie and Nora as well as Qaajia's and Eva's daughters often engaged young Inuit children in imitative routines in which the child was instructed to repeat after the more competent person. These repetition routines are used to teach young children how to greet their relatives and other people of their community (Crago and Eriks-Brophy, 1993). They were also regularly used by the two young mothers to teach their children English phrases and numbers. On videotape, these routines were accomplished in dyads, except occasionally when a child would be instructed to use an English politeness term in a triadic situation.

Traditionally, Inuit politeness conventions in Kangirsuk and Quaqtaq did not consist of saying specific words. Nevertheless, in modern Inuktitut there are words for "thank you" (*nakurmik*) and "you're welcome" (*ilali*). These are not frequently used by Inuit to each other. The only time a child was asked to repeat the word *nakurmik* was when it was being addressed to the Qallunak researcher. However, Annie's daughter was asked by her parents to repeat "thank you" and "please" in English on a number of occasions. These repetitions were not structured into multiple turn-taking events and were asked for in the context of particular situations. There were no instances on videotape of this child's parents using English or Inuktitut politeness words with each other. The efforts to teach *Qallunaat* (non-Inuk) conventions such as politeness words may indeed be one of the important social interactional skills in school. One white teacher candidly described her first months of teaching Inuit children: "By November I was ready to strangle them. I thought I would go crazy if I didn't hear a 'please' or a 'thank you' come out of their mouths." This reaction reflects a more complex interface that exists between second-language teaching and Inuit patterns of communicative interaction (see Crago, 1992 for a detailed description of this interface).

All the young mothers that were interviewed, except for two, said they spoke a certain amount of English to their children. They explained, in comments like the following, that their reason for doing so was to prepare their children for school:

> So that when she goes to school in English she will understand some, and also that she will not have too much of a hard time.

Since he's always hearing TV, he's learning in English and the other children are learning in English too, so I worry that he'll be behind in learning English.

None of the older women taped, interviewed, or observed spoke English to their children or to others. Despite the English spoken by the younger mothers, there were two quite separate domains of language use in Kangirsuk and Quaqtaq. Second language was identified with school; Inuktitut was identified with home and, to some degree, with the early elementary years of school.

Differences between Inuit and Qallunaat

Qallunaat are not seen as having the same ways of communicating with their children as Inuit. Opinions on this matter emerged in the interviews when women were asked to comment on the differences between Inuit and Qallunaat ways of talking to children. Three of the ten older women who were interviewed described these differences as follows:

> I do not understand fully what they are saying to the child, but they talk to the child as if they are talking to an adult, that seems to be their difference through feeling their way of talking.

The Qallunaat talk to their children as if they were not babies, as if they were mature.

They talk like they were talking to an adult, sometimes even using hard words.

One older woman attributed the difference to Qallunaat having more education than Inuit: "The Qallunaat ways are different and they have learned and they are more educated about the child having to be talked to in real words." This was the same woman who had decided that she would no longer talk to her children as Inuit do with baby words, but would instead use adult words. Very much to the contrary, other older women found that the difference in their communication patterns and beliefs and those of the Qallunaat teachers represented a significant problem (Crago, 1992). Inuit, then, saw their ways of relating to children as different from the Qallunaat way of talking to children. The ways of accommodating communication to the Inuk child were not the same and not perceived of as the same as the Qallunaat way of communicating with small children. Indeed, Inuit patterns of communicative interaction stem from the differences in their beliefs about childhood, the status of the child, and what they think is the appropriate way to bring up a child as an Inuk.

The Meaning of Change

With the evolution of the Inuit culture, there are indications of changes occurring in the communicative interactions of Inuit caregivers with their children. Aqausiit exist almost exclusively in people's memories. Many younger women expressed disdain about using baby words and indicated a lack of awareness that children's interference in adult conversation was an undesirable behaviour. Mothers in the younger and older groups differed in their concepts about whether production was the key evidence for language learning. Younger mothers engaged with their children in question-and-answer routines as well as teaching them Qallunaat politeness conventions and English words. These interactions set these mothers apart from the older ones. Certain women attributed the changes in communication to the advent of schools and the infiltration of Qallunaat ways into their communities. Indeed, younger parents appeared to have experienced and, to some extent, studied the schools and adapted certain of their communicative patterns to suit them.

What do these changes in the communicative interaction of Inuit caregivers mean? According to one theoretical interpretation, the results can be interpreted as showing that the economic, cultural, and political aspects of the majority culture have prevailed over those of the minority culture (Gal, 1989; Heller, 1990; Mehan, 1987). Inuit mothers, in turn, can be seen as having responded to this dominance either (1) by making adjustments whose significance they do not fully understand (Heath, 1990) or (2) by attempting to give their children the resources (cultural capital) to deal in the "marketplace" of schools and the dominant culture (Bourdieu and Passeron, 1990; Gumperz, 1982). An alternative view of these results might be that Inuit families are, to a certain degree, in control of their own destinies and have chosen to adapt their childrearing in view of the dramatic social and cultural changes that have surrounded them for the last 20 years. In this interpretation, their adaptations represent the social construction of a new identity. The process could be seen as one of redefinition (Gallimore et al., 1989; Super and Harkness, 1986).

It is our opinion that evidence from this study is best interpreted as representing a combination of phenomena. Loss and change are certainly taking place and their significance is not always fully understood. Several comments by younger women indicated that they lack awareness of what is being lost as they have abandoned certain socialization practices; older women, on the other hand, expressed awareness of the significance of the change. The erosion of certain forms of communicative interaction between Inuit caregivers and their children, therefore, cannot be exclusively interpreted as families redefining themselves in the modern world. Rather, it appears as though the pressures of modern living have altered the time, space, and manner in which Inuit people do their parenting, obliterating certain traditional practices.

Combined with this lack of awareness, however, is some degree of conscious decision making on the part of certain Inuit caregivers to prepare their children to participate in the communicative conventions of school. The ability to participate in the dominant instructional modes of question-and-answer routines and the ability to show respect for teachers by using Qallunaat politeness terms have come to be viewed by younger Inuit mothers as important resources for Inuit children to take to school with them. Helping children to learn these skills can, in this way, be seen as adaptation to the reality of schooling. It seems that some Inuit mothers are shaping some of their interactions to encompass the melding of their traditional culture with modern-day realities. In this process, they are redefining what they think is important for their children to learn. They are aware of the speech conventions of school and they want their children to be able to do trade in that world. Delpit (1988) described similar sentiments among Alaskan natives and American blacks.

The process of redefinition should not be one-sided. Schools also must involve themselves in the process, and this includes schools that have native self-governance. Although the present research does not document the nature of communicative interaction in the classroom, the studies of minority-culture education mentioned at the outset of this article have shown how culturally unadapted and unsuccessful many educational practices are when used with minority-culture children. Ignoring the strength of the relationship between communication and culture and ignoring the evidence supporting meaningful cultural adaptation of education has meant that non-mainstream children have been expected to adapt their communicative patterns to the ways of the dominant culture (Crago, 1992). Even in the context of the Kativik School Board, where Inuit control the school authority, it is important that educational redefinition take place at several levels, including at the levels of cultural patterns of interaction and language use.

After the establishment of self-governance, then, there is not only a need for educational redefinition but also the need to create a definition of Inuit education. The transformation of schooling by minority populations is receiving increasing attention (Falgout and Levin, 1992; Lipka, 1991). The ways in which Inuit teachers transform communicative interaction in their classrooms (Crago and Eriks-Brophy, 1993; Eriks-Brophy and Crago, 1994) should help to clarify the nature of educational practices that originate in the Inuit population. The recognition of the value of such practices, by both natives and non-natives, should enhance native pedagogy as it moves to its own center of control and away from a position of subordination.

Finally, this article, by inspecting certain Inuit socialization practices and their changes over time, has attempted to show how important such practices are in the Inuit culture. We believe that the real value of understanding how and why these socialization practices are changing is that it enhances the possibility that Inuit can exert increased control over their own process of change.

Acknowledgments. The research presented in this article was supported by grant #8614 from the Toronto Sick Children's Hospital Foundation and funds provided by the Faculty of Medicine of McGill University and Kativik School Board. We would like to give thanks to Elisabeth Handsley, Shanley Allen, Alice Eriks-Brophy, and Wendy Hough for help in preparing the manuscript and to anonymous reviewers whose comments added greatly to the quality of our efforts.

Our deepest debt is to the families of Kangirsuk and Quaqtaq, who helped us to learn about their ways of raising children.

References

Blount, Benjamin. 1972. 'Aspects of Luo Socialization', *Language in Society* vol. 1, pp. 235–248.

Boggs, Stephen T. 1985. *Speaking, Relating and Learning: A Study of Hawaiian Children at Home and at School*. Norwood, NJ: Ablex.

Bourdieu, Pierre, and Jean-Claude Passeron. 1990. *Reproduction in Education, Society and Culture*. London: Sage Publications.

Clancy, Patricia M. 1986. "The Acquisition of Communicative Style in Japanese", in B. B. Schieffelin and E. Ochs, eds., *Language Socialization across Cultures*. Cambridge: Cambridge University Press.

Crago, Martha B. 1988. *Cultural Context in Communicative Interaction of Young Inuit Children*. Unpublished doctoral dissertation, McGill University, Montreal.

——. 1992. 'The Sociocultural Interface of Communicative Interaction and L2 Acquisition: An Inuit Example', TESOL *Quarterly*, vol. 23, no. 3, pp. 487–506

Crago, Martha B., and Alice Eriks-Brophy. 1993. "Culture, Conversation, and the Co-construction of Interaction: Implications and Applications for Intervention", in J. Duchan, L. Hewitt, C. Reynolds, and R. Sonnenmeier eds., *Pragmatics: From Theory to Therapy*. Englewood Cliffs, NJ: Prentice Hall.

Delpit, Lisa D. 1988. 'The Silenced Dialogue: Power and Pedagogy in Educating Other People's Children', *Harvard Educational Review*, vol. 58, no. 2, pp. 78–95.

Demuth, Katherine. 1986. "Prompting Routines in the Language Socialization of Basotho Children", in B. B. Schieffelin and E. Ochs, eds., *Language Socialization across Cultures*. Cambridge: Cambridge University Press.

Duranti, Alessandro, and Eleanor Ochs. 1988. "Literacy Instruction in a Samoan Village", in Eleanor Ochs, ed., *Culture and Language Development*. Cambridge: Cambridge University Press.

Eisenberg, Ann. 1982. *Language Acquisition in Cultural Perspective: Talk in Three Mexican Homes*. Unpublished doctoral dissertation. University of California, Berkeley.

Erickson, Frederick. 1987. 'Transformations and School Success: The Politics and Culture of Educational Achievement', *Anthropology and Education Quarterly* vol. 18, no. 4, pp. 335–357.

Eriks-Brophy, Alice, and Martha B. Crago. 1994. 'Transforming Classroom Discourse: An Inuit Example', *Language and Education*, vol. 8, no. 3, pp. 105–122.

——. 2003. 'Variation in instructional discourse features: Cultural or Linguistic? Evidence from Inuit and non-Inuit Teachers of Nunavik', *Anthropology and Education Quarterly*, vol. 34, no. 4, pp. 1–25.

Falgout, Suzanne, and Paula Levin. 1992. 'Transforming Knowledge: Western Schooling in the Pacific', *Anthropology and Educational Quarterly*, vol. 23, no. 1, pp. 3–9.

Fischer, J.S. 1970. "Linguistic Socialization: Japan and the United States", in R. Hill and R. Konig, eds., *Families in East and West*. The Hague: Mouton.

Gal, Susan. 1989. 'Language and Political Economy', *Annual Review of Anthropology*, vol. 18, pp. 345–367.

Gallimore, Ronald, T. Weisner, S. Kaufman, and L.P. Bemheimer. 1989. 'The Social Construction of Ecocultural Niches: Family Accommodation of Developmentally Delayed Children', *American Journal of Mental Retardation*, vol. 94, no. 3, pp. 216–230.

Gumperz, John J. 1982. *Discourse Strategies*. Cambridge: Cambridge University Press.

Harkness, Sarah. 1977. "Aspects of Social Environment and First Language Acquisition in Rural Africa", in C. E. Snow and C. A. Ferguson, eds., *Talking to Children*. New York: Cambridge University Press.

Heath, Shirley Brice. 1983. *Ways with Words: Language, Life and Work in Communities and Classrooms*. Cambridge: Cambridge University Press.

——. 1990. "The Children of Trackton's Children: Spoken and Written Language in Social Change", in W. Stigler, R. A. Shweder, and G. Herdt, eds., *Cultural Psychology: Essays on Comparative Human Development*. Cambridge: Cambridge University Press.

Heller, Monica. 1990. *The Politics of Codeswitching: Processes and Consequences of Ethnic Mobilization*. Third Workshop of the European Science Foundation Network on Codeswitching. Brussels, Belgium.

Lipka, Jerry. 1991. 'Toward a Culturally Based Pedagogy: A Case of One Yu'pik Eskimo Teacher', *Anthropology and Educational Quarterly*, vol. 22, no. 3, pp. 202–223.

Mehan, Hugh. 1987. "Language and Schooling", in G. Spindler and L. Spindler, eds. *Interpretive Ethnography of Education at Home and Abroad*. Hillsdale, NJ: Laurence Erlbaum Associates.

Miller, Patricia. 1982. *Amy, Wendy and Beth: Learning Language in South Baltimore*. Austin, TX: University of Texas Press.

Ochs, Eleanor. 1988. *Culture and Language Development: Language Acquisition and Language Socialization in a Samoan Village*. Cambridge: Cambridge University Press.

Philips, Susan U. 1983. *The Invisible Culture: Communication in Classroom and Community on the Warm Springs Indian Reservation*. New York: Longman Inc.

Schieffelin, Bambi B. 1990. *The Give and Take of Everyday Life*. Cambridge: Cambridge University Press.

Scollon, Ron, and Susan Scollon. 1981. *Narrative, Literacy and Race in Interethnic Communication*. Norwood, NJ: Ablex Publishing.

Smith-Hefner, Nancy J. 1988. 'The Linguistic Socialization of Javanese Children in Two Communities', *Anthropological Linguistics*, vol. 30, no. 2, pp. 166–198.

Super, C., and S. Harkness. 1986. 'The Developmental Niche: A Conceptualization at the Interface of Child and Culture', *International Journal of Behaviour Development*, vol. 9, pp. 1–25.

Tharp, Roland G., and Ronald Gallimore. 1988. *Rousing Minds to Life: Teaching, Learning, and Schooling in Social Context*. Cambridge: Cambridge University Press.

Tharp, Roland G., C. Jordan, G. E. Speidel, K. Hu-Pei Au, T. W. Klein, R. P. Calkins, K. C. M. Sloat, and Ronald Gallimore. 1984. "Product and Process in Applied Developmental Research: Education and the Children of a Minority", in M. E. Lamb, A. L. Brown, and B. Rogoff, eds., *Advances in Developmental Psychology*. Hillsdale, NJ: Lawrence Erlbaum Associates.

Ward, Margaret. 1971. *Them Children: A Study in Language Learning*. New York: Holt, Rinehart and Winston.

Watson-Gegeo, Karen A., and David W. Gegeo. 1986. "The Social World of Kwara'ae Children: Acquisition of Language and Values", in J. Cook-Gumperz, W. A. Corsaro, and J. Streeck, eds., *Children's Worlds and Children's Language*. New York: Mouton de Gruyter.

10

Borders and Aboriginal Identity Construction in Canada: Everyday, Cultural, Legal, and Political Activisms

Margery Fee

Although Aboriginal peoples in Canada frequently assert that the Canada-US border is meaningless to them as a colonial construct, in fact the border has often been used as a site of identity construction by Aboriginal activists in crossing the literal border as well as writing fiction, performing cultural events, initiating legal cases and devising political theory about it.[1] The border asserts the dominance of two settler nations; those Aboriginal people contesting its power assert their identity as members of pre-existing nations whose territories and rights of movement extend across it. Activists assert sovereignty in attempting to cross the border without the documentation required of citizens, or taking goods freely across the border without paying duty, or in refusing to answer questions or submit to searches, or in maintaining family, cultural and spiritual ties across the border in the face of ever-tightening security. They also rethink borders at a theoretical and fictional level to reveal how arbitrary and destructive they have been and continue to be for those in a colonial relationship to the state. One feature common to many of these actions is the use of the current Canada-US border to reveal what that border has overlaid and denied and to refuse to accept it as applying to Aboriginal peoples, whose identities both include and transcend Canadian identity.

---

1. Aboriginal is the broadest legal term describing indigenous people in Canada, and includes Indian, Inuit and Metis people (Constitution Act, 1982). 'First Nations' usually refers only to those groups whose members are registered under the Indian Act, that is, Status Indians. In the US, the usual terms are Native American or (to distinguish and include the peoples that Canada calls Inuit), American Indian and Alaska Native.

Thomas King's "Borders" demonstrates this: in this story a Blackfoot woman travelling south with her son is turned back from the US border because she won't say she is Canadian, but insists she is Blackfoot; when she tries to go back across the border, still insisting she is Blackfoot, the Canadian border guards won't let her back in. The Canadian border guard says "I'd be proud of being Blackfoot if I were Blackfoot. But you have to be Canadian or American" (King, 1993a:138–139). Mother and son spend a few days in the limbo of a parking lot, making the point that Blackfoot territory and identity has been overwritten by American and Canadian state power. There is a media frenzy, someone in a suit turns up and does something not clear to the child-narrator, and they are allowed to go to Salt Lake City and return without saying they are Canadian or American. The point is that for Blackfoot people, the border is a fiction that can be resisted. This does not mean that Aboriginal people can't have secondary ties to their country of citizenship, however. Indeed, even the most militant nations will negotiate with the Canadian state, but only *as* nations, usually relying on treaties made with Britain in the past and turning to international agencies, such as the United Nations, if negotiation and lawsuits fail.

In 1969, Pierre Trudeau's Liberal government proposed, in a White Paper, to abolish the Indian Act, which had governed the lives of many Aboriginal Canadians since 1876, defining them as wards of the state, forcing their children into abusive residential schools and denying them the right to vote until 1960. The White Paper proposed to assimilate Aboriginal people into the general population, repudiating all treaties and land claims as well as federal responsibility for Aboriginal affairs. However, the Indian Chiefs of Alberta, led by Harold Cardinal, produced a response in 1970, known as "Citizens Plus" or the "Red Paper", that made it clear that most First Nations people did not want to be forced into choosing to be either Indian or Canadian. They insisted that they retain their Aboriginal rights *and* have Canadian citizenship, a right which was subsequently upheld in the Constitution Act of 1982 (Cairns, 2000:67–68).

Because Quebec refused to sign the Constitution Act of 1982, there have been two subsequent attempts to negotiate Quebec's inclusion, the Meech Lake Accord (which failed in 1990, partly because of Aboriginal disagreement) and the Charlottetown Accord (which did not pass in a national referendum held in 1992). Phil Fontaine, then head of the Assembly of Manitoba Chiefs, pointed out that Aboriginal opposition did not come from a wish to deny French-speaking Quebec recognition as a distinct society: "We recognize that and support that. But if Quebec is distinct, we are even more distinct. That's the recognition we want, and will settle for nothing less" (qtd. Dickason, 1997:387). He further added:

> We, the original people of this country, have inherited through the original traditions of our forefathers 55 distinct original languages. Fifty-two of these distinct original languages of Canada are on the brink of extinction. Unlike you, we cannot retrieve these languages from our mother country. Unlike you, Canada is our mother country. (qtd. Dickason, 1997:387)

In "Borders" one can see the "Citizens Plus" concept at work. Indeed, the mother in "Borders" is a Canadian nationalist of the annoying kind; she and her son dress up to go across the border "for my mother did not want us crossing the border looking like Americans" (King, 1993a:133); when her daughter gets brochures that say that "Salt Lake City was one of the best places in the whole world" the mother replies that "People in Salt Lake City are probably sending away for brochures about Calgary and Lethbridge and Pincher Creek right now" (King, 1993a:139).

This story may seem simply an amusing conceit written by a California-born part-Cherokee Canadian who knows the paradoxes of the border from personal experience, but Bruce G. Miller makes it clear that this story is a distillation of a common experience. He quotes an American border official who says "Lots of times Indians won't tell us what country they are from. Coast Salish believe both countries are their country. Indians often say they are resident of both. We ask them 'where is your longhouse' [in an effort to determine residency]" (Miller, 2006:59). Clearly many Aboriginal people regard crossing the border as a opportunity for "everyday activism," a place to assert their difference.

In "The 'Really Real' Border and the Divided Salish Community" Miller outlines the details of a legal case, *Robert Watt v. E Liebelt and the Minister of Citizenship and Immigration* which resulted from Watt's appeal of his deportation in 1993 from Canada; Robert Watt was an enrolled member of the Colville Confederated Tribes in the United States. He had been appointed by Salish elders to act as "the guardian of a sacred burial site in British Columbia" (Miller, 1996/97:67). The

Arrow Lakes band, on whose territory the site was located, had been declared extinct by the Canadian government in 1953 because the last resident had died; most of its members had previously become members of the Colville Confederated Tribes, although they were still regularly using the land (ibid: 57). The Constitution Act of 1982, subsection 35 (2) of Canada states "In this Act, 'aboriginal peoples of Canada' includes the Indian, Inuit, and Métis peoples of Canada." Watt's counsel argued that the word "includes" means that the definition could be read as including more than these peoples of Canada, particularly since "the Supreme Court of Canada has held that Section 35 of the Constitution Act is to be interpreted generously and liberally" (ibid: 67). In other words, they argue that "all Aboriginal people living along the US-Canada border should be included under Section 35 as Aboriginal peoples of Canada" (ibid: 67). In a subsequent appeal of the case, "The Canadian courts . . . commented without finding that a US Native American citizen could claim the aboriginal right of free passage, if she or he could establish a sufficient geographical "nexus" to Canada" (Gastle, 2002:20–21). Thus, this case has left an opening for subsequent court cases to establish free passage and freedom from deportation out of Canada for transborder indigenous peoples.

This case is part of a longstanding struggle on the part of Aboriginal people in Canada and Native Americans and indeed, of indigenous peoples in Mexico, (Luna-Firebaugh, 2002) to make the international border into a new borderland. Defined as "the contested boundaries between colonial domains" (Adelman and Aron, 1999:816), a borderland is a space "where indigenous peoples played imperial rivals off against each other" (ibid: 817). After the American War of Independence ended in 1783, Britain abandoned many of its Indian allies; some moved to Canada, most notably those Mohawks associated with the famous war leader Joseph Brant (1743–1807). Renewed hostilities later in the decade also ended badly for Indian allies of Britain. However, the Jay Treaty (also known as the Treaty of London or the Treaty of Friendship, Commerce and Navigation), 1794, did make concessions for border crossing:

> Article III of the Jay Treaty declared the right of aboriginal peoples (people indigenous to Canada and/or the US) to trade and travel between the United States and Canada, which was then a territory of Great Britain. This right was restated in

> section 289 of the 1952 [US] Immigration and Naturalization Act, currently codified as 8 U.S.C. § 1359: Nothing in this title shall be construed to affect the right of American Indians born in Canada to pass the borders of the United States, but such right shall extend only to persons who possess at least 50 per centum of blood of the American Indian race. ('Jay Treaty', 2008)

Because control of the definition of who qualifies as Aboriginal or American Indian is in the power of the Canadian and American states, which use different criteria, it can be difficult for individuals with identification acceptable to one jurisdiction to use it in the other one. Further, the Canadian government maintains that the terms of this treaty between the US and Britain were abrogated by the War of 1812, and does not recognize it, although the Treaty of Ghent, 1814, states that relations between each country and the "tribes or nations of Indians" would return to what it had been in 1811, provided all hostilities ceased. Nonetheless, border officials usually accept a tribal membership card from Native Americans or a Status card from Canadian Indians as sufficient to cross, without proof of blood quantum (Luna-Firebaugh, 2002:163). Border officials have extensive powers, and for someone who doesn't "look Indian" it is harder to use these document unsupported by others (American Indian Law Alliance).

Mohawks (part of the Six Nations, also known as the Iroquois Confederacy, or the Haudenosaunee Confederacy) have several reserves near or on the US border in Ontario (Tyendinaga and Akwasasne) and in Quebec (Akwasasne, Kahnawake, Kahnesatake). Mohawks have always crossed the border regularly, in recent times often to find employment (they are famous as ironworkers, who played a major role in building the skyscrapers of New York). In 1927, the US Supreme Court, in a case brought by a Kahnawake ironworker, Paul K. Diabo, ruled that Article 3 of the Jay treaty "exempted Native people from US immigration laws" (George-Kanentiio, 2006:27). Since September 2001, border regulations have tightened considerably, and since January 2007, the US has required all Canadians to carry a passport when crossing the border by air and to provide two pieces of government issued photo ID if crossing by land (Miller, 2006). Until June 2009, an Indian Status card can be used to cross the border and there is some expectation that Indian Status cards and various forms of American tribal identity cards will be accepted after that date as well. However, some nations wish to issue their own identity papers, rather than using state-issued ones.

Angie Barnes, the Grand Chief of Akwesasne in a letter to the US Bureau of Customs and Border Protection, notes that "The Mohawks of Akwesasne are uniquely situated on islands and mainland between the United States and Canada. Older than both of these countries, the traditional homeland of this ancient pre-contact Mohawk community is currently dissected by the international border. To further complicate matters, two of the districts within our community that are located within 'Canada' are only accessible by roads in the United States" (Barnes, 2005). Members of this community cross the border many times a day and the requirement that they carry a passport (an expensive document) would be a hindrance to their daily life. Currently, "as a sovereign nation and a member of the international community, the Haudenosaunee are adhering to international security standards rather than those established by the United States" (Haudenosaunee, 2008). The US Department of Homeland Security has stated "that they will continue to accept the Red Cards and all other Indian Nation issued photo I.D. until at least June 2009" (ibid). By making it a practice to travel on their "Red Cards" and the Haudenosaunee passport, and insisting that these will conform to international requirements, rather than those imposed by the US Department of Homeland Security, the Mohawk assert their status as a sovereign nation.

Aboriginal people have not found the Canadian or the American governments so willing to adhere to another clause in the Jay Treaty which allowed "Indians" "freely to carry on trade and commerce with each other" and to take personal effects across the border without paying duty. In 2001, the Supreme Court of Canada ruled in *Mitchell (a Mohawk Grand Chief)* v. *MNR (Ministry of Natural Resources)* that Mitchell could not take goods across the border for trade with other Aboriginal people without paying duty on the grounds that such trade had not been an essential feature of Mohawk culture in the past. The Court did not deal with the issue of free transmission of personal goods, which is also covered in the Jay Treaty. The Assembly of First Nations proposes to take "Canada before international courts and international forums for its failure to recognize and respect aboriginal and treaty border crossing rights" (Assembly of First Nations, 2001).

The freedom to cross the border is important not just for work or for trade, but also for the maintenance of family, cultural and ceremonial ties. In his novel *Green Grass, Running Water*, King includes another brief story about a Blackfoot family crossing the border on the way to a dance (King 1993b:256–257). Their dance costumes are confiscated because they have eagle feathers on them (the issue of preserving endangered species has been used to block ceremonial practices, although the species have only become endangered since European incursion). Eventually, after much media attention, the costumes are returned by their member of parliament (who thinks they are Cree): the costumes have been walked on, stuffed into green garbage bags, the feathers broken (ibid: 283). The threat that sacred objects and people in certain ritual states will be violated as they cross the border is a long-standing one: Salish spirit dancers cannot be looked at directly, for example, without being put into spiritual danger and "masks and other regalia cannot be handled by non-dancers" (Miller, 1996/97:69). Nor are these dancers allowed to talk to non-initiates about these issues, which means that their behaviour may mark them as suspect. Some customs officials are aware of this—the border official in *Green Grass* is a summer student. Here King asserts the importance for the Blackfoot and other cross-border nations of being able to cross the border without having their personal possessions searched, a provision of the Jay Treaty. Ceremonial life is crucial to Aboriginal identity and so is maintaining cross border ceremonial ties with other members of one's cultural group.

The border has—not surprisingly—been an important site of identity construction for the mainstream societies as well, with settler Canadians smugly contrasting their peaceful ways with violent American ones:

> In the Canadian narrative, Americans went west aggressively to fulfill their Manifest Destiny; Canadians did so defensively out of a manifest duty to protect the Native peoples north of the forty-ninth parallel from the cruel fate that Americans imposed south of it. The American West represented the apogee of autarchic individualism; the Canadian West apotheosized the orderly transplantation of community and government institutions. Vigilante justice misruled the American West; in Canada the incorruptible North-West Mounted Police meted out the Queen's law evenhandedly to all. (Thompson, 2006:xii)

So the American symbol was the cowboy, the Canadian, the Mountie (an officer of the North-West Mounted Police, later, the Royal Canadian Mounted Police).

In two important early works by Aboriginal writers in Canada, one can see some of the ideas outlined above—the United States is depicted as a dangerous, lawless place. In 1969, Native Americans seized Alcatraz Island, and engaged in protests led by the American Indian Movement (AIM), the most famous ones being the seizure of the Bureau of Indian Affairs building in Washington in 1972 and the 71-day standoff at Wounded Knee in 1973: many of these protests involved violence and two were left dead at Wounded Knee (Smith and Warrior, 1996). But what is contrasted in these novels with the violence and danger inherent in these protests is not Canada, the so-called 'peaceable Kingdom,'[2] but indigenous territory on both sides of the border. In Jeannette Armstrong's *Slash* (1985), Tommy Kelasket crosses the border from Canada into the United States, participates in the occupation of the Bureau of Indian Affairs and ends up in jail. He is confused and angry, unable to come to terms with the chaos of the militant life except during a brief respite where he spends time with a Native American elder. In Thomas King's *Green Grass, Running Water*, Lionel Red Dog crosses the border and is caught in a car loaded with guns meant for the protestors at Wounded Knee. Although he had no knowledge of the guns, he is sent back to Canada, where he is fired from his job at Indian Affairs. Both characters come from cross-border nations: Tommy (nicknamed Slash) is Okanagan, Lionel is Blackfoot. After these excursions into violent activism, both characters return home. Because neither character learns much from the activist events they participate in—indeed, both are damaged by the incidents—the novels appear to argue for a need to work through an Aboriginal identity in the modern world *before* leaping into politics. Once he is home, Slash refuses to join in any political meetings, even though his wife Maeg is heavily involved in having Aboriginal rights included in the Canadian Constitution (brought to Canada from Britain in 1982). Lionel's participation in the Sun Dance leads—at the age of 40—to his first small activist move in preventing George Morningstar

2. William Kilbourn (1970) and Northrop Frye (1971: 249) both used this expression to characterize myths about Canada; the phrase is based on a biblical prophesy (Isaiah 2:4 and 11:6) and a painting on this theme by an American painter, Edmund Hicks, in 1930.

from taking photographs of the dancing without permission. The emphasis on the need to learn to live as an Okanagan or a Blackfoot before engaging in politics is important in both novels; thus, the most respected figures in the novels are elders—the Four Old Indians and Pra-cwa, the head of the traditional Okanagan.

This is not to say that the novels have no political position. Armstrong's novel comes out strongly against Native involvement in the patriation of the Constitution as a threat to sovereignty: Slash says "We don't need anybody's constitution, what we have is our own already. We hold rights to the land and to nationhood. We just need to have it recognized" (Armstrong, 1985:241). Both novels support a development of a distinctive, communal and firmly grounded cultural perspective before any decision is made about political initiatives. The fear in both novels is that rights that should be inalienable will be traded for short-term concessions that will leave future generations without land or culture.

Neither writer advocates simple passive resistance or the model of civil disobedience, however. Eli, Lionel's uncle, left the reserve to become an English professor, and after retirement returned to live in his mother's cabin, which is blocking the spillway of a dam that had been built without Blackfoot consent on their territory (most dams in North America have displaced Aboriginal peoples and disrupted their traditional access to land and water for hunting, gathering, farming and fishing). This protest is a solitary one, and his sister Norma often suggests that he is neglecting other cultural and family duties—particularly providing advice to the hapless Lionel. Eli only succeeds after he stops his emulation of Henry David Thoreau (who promoted the individual conscience as the Centre of Ethico-political Action), advises Lionel and dances at the Sun Dance. When he dies, he is part of the community, and the community moves in to fill the space his death has left. Lionel, who has always wanted to be John Wayne, the movie star cowboy hero, voices his first desire to identify as Blackfoot in saying he wants to take Eli's place and live in his grandmother's house. Significantly, his Aunt Norma says he must wait his turn. Otherwise, individual protest becomes another version of the lone gunslinger/Western individual exemplified by Henry David Thoreau and John Wayne. Lionel must wait to take over the cabin until it is clear that he realizes that John Wayne is not an appropriate role model and he has achieved the wisdom required for such actions.

Similarly, Slash does not just hunker down at home, but turns to working with young people on reducing the effects of colonization on them, rather than making dramatic individual moves. The community as a whole must be involved in political decisions, particularly the elders. In both novels, to take the national or continental political stage alone is to play the white man's game, the game of media frenzies around soon forgotten "actions." The border crossing in both novels serves to show, logically enough, that the farther one is from home, the more likely one is to forget one's roots. This may seem banal, but the lure of pan-Native urban activism destroyed many young people's ties to their families and communities in the sixties—the reaction to this is the focus on home and traditional cultural values found in many Aboriginal literary works, such as Tomson Highway's *The Rez Sisters* and *Kiss of the Fur Queen*, Ruby Slipperjack's *Honour the Sun*, the plays of Drew Hayden Taylor and Richard Wagamese's *Keeper n' Me*.

In recent years, Aboriginal people have been emphasizing the need to move away from state-defined and state-approved identities and organizations. Bonita Lawrence has written a detailed account of how Aboriginal acceptance of state definitions of identity have led to a variety of organizations that—rather than working together to assert definitions that work for Aboriginal people broadly defined—see themselves as in a hierarchy of relationships with the federal government, with Status Indians represented by the Assembly of First Nations at the top. The others include non-status Aboriginal people, those from groups who were overlooked in treaty making or reserve allocation, mixed-race Métis people, and those excluded by various legal mechanisms. (The patriarchal Indian Act ruled that Aboriginal women who married non-Aboriginal men lost their status, while Aboriginal men who married non-Aboriginal women not only retain theirs, but had it bestowed on their wife, children and descendants.) The hierarchy formed partly from government refusal to deal with those excluded, however arbitrarily, from the category of Status Indians, but also from perceptions among Status Indians that given the scarcity of resources the federal government has been prepared to expend on Aboriginal people, including more people in the category would deprive Status Indians. The state has moved more and more to definitions that rely on blood quanta and continues to discriminate against women and those who marry non-Aboriginals, so that some predict Aboriginal people will be legislated out of existence in a few decades (Lawrence, 2004:77–79). Although it is a widespread truism among Aboriginal people that the state engages in widespread "divide and conquer" policies, often these are accepted as a given. Many Indian bands/First Nations control their membership policies, but many find it difficult to provide housing and services for those reinstated by changes in the law. Bill C-31, which attempted to provide equity for Status men and women on marriage did return Status to many women and children. However it remains problematic (Indian Affairs and Northern Development).

Lawrence and another prominent Aboriginal political thinker, John Borrows, advocate a refusal of these colonial definitions and a return to traditional alliances and territories, rather than focusing on the minuscule land base currently controlled by Status Indian bands (First Nations). Lawrence writes:

> The difference between the ancient confederacies and current nationhood assertions through provincial territorial organizations, such as the Nichnawbe-Aski Nation, or the Anishinabek Nation, is that those organizations are groupings primarily organized around specific territorial treaties, which in most instances follow the logic of the colonizer with respect to who was included or excluded in the process. The ancient confederacies reference older realities, where individuals who are currently classified as nonstatus Indians or Métis, could potentially be entitled to citizenship outside of Indian Act categories. (Lawrence, 2004:241)

She notes that efforts to develop a Cree confederacy involves member communities from the United States, which could lead to the production of transborder identities. Her question is whether they will reach out across another border, that between Status and non-Status Aboriginal people, particularly Cree- Métis communities (ibid: 241).

Other First Nations have also reached across the border: "The Blackfoot Confederacy has existed since time immemorial and is comprised of the Piikani Nation, Siksika Nation, Blood Tribe and Blackfeet Tribe (Montana, USA) which have recently renewed their commitment to each other in the (Blackfoot Declaration) OOKAWA SIKSIKAITSIITAPIWA OTOOKUKST'SIMAN" (Blackfoot Issues). The Okanagan-Sylix people have demonstrated against border regulations and perform annual crossborder trips on horseback and by canoe to demonstrate "that the Okanagan-Sylix on both sides of the border remain a strong and unified nation" (Okanagan Nation).

Ceremonies that are open to the public and sports events have also become a way to reaffirm cross-border ties, for example, the active traditional canoe races held in Salish territories in British Columbia (Neel, 1995). Bill Reid (Haida) carved his first traditional canoe in 1985–86, and in 1989 it was paddled up the Seine to Paris, and up the coast of British Columbia to Alaska "to reconnect two nations divided by the imposition of the Canada-US border" (ibid: 2). Neel notes that "The 1989 Paddle to Seattle journey . . . spawned the revival of the great canoes among the ocean-going peoples of the Pacific Northwest" (ibid: 3).

Borrows argues against the current focus on sovereignty on reserve lands only for band members, arguing as well for "Aboriginal control . . . of Canadian affairs" (2002:157) on the basis of the special relationship Aboriginal people have, not just with the tiny pieces of land granted by the colonial government, but with their traditional territories.

> To speak only of Aboriginal control of Aboriginal affairs would disenfranchise most Aboriginal peoples from their traditional lands. Measured separatism would separate many of them from places they hold dear. Why should an artificial line drawn around my reservation bar me from a relationship with the vast areas my ancestors revered? (2002:157)

He notes that "The accommodation of Aboriginal conceptions of citizenship does not come at the expense of promoting more general Canadian citizenship" (Borrows, 2002:156), arguing that the current insecurity aroused by binaristic and separatist notions of identity can be overcome through a reconception of Canadian and Aboriginal citizenships. Indeed, the traditional territories he refers to cross the international border, again pointing to a shift in rethinking identities for Aboriginal people toward a concept of transborder rights beyond the current ones.

Miller notes the "appropriation and reshaping of federal notions of membership and citizenship" on both sides of the international border by Native Americans and Aboriginal Canadians (2006:63), a process that faces considerable difficulty in the face of increasing tightening of the US border since 2001. Nonetheless, such reimaginings that link indigenous groups across the border inspire new ways of thinking about identity, often ways that link old territories with new conceptions about Aboriginal identities and relationships to the state.

References

Adelman, Jeremy and Stephen Aron. 1999. 'From Borderlands to Borders: Empires, Nation-States, and the Peoples in between in North American History', *The American Historical Review*, vol. 104, no. 3, pp. 814–841.

Armstrong, Jeannette C. 1985. *Slash*. Penticton, BC: Theytus.

American Indian Law Alliance. 'Border Crossing Rights between the United States and Canada for Aboriginal People.' http://www.ptla.org/wabanaki/jaytreaty.htm#Cross%20Border (access on 19/04/2008)

Assembly of First Nations. Resolution 28, 2001. http://www.afn.ca/article.asp?id=2969 (access on 19/04/2008)

Barnes, Angie. 2005. Letter to US Bureau of Customs and Border Protection. *INDIAN TIME*, vol. 23 no. 44 - Kentenko:wa / November 3. Edition 4 http://members.aol.com/miketben1/passport2.htm (access on 19/04/2008)

"Blackfoot Confederacy Border Crossing Issues." 2002. http://www.afn.ca/resolutions/2002/aga%202002/res16e.htm (access on 19/04/2008)

Borrows, John. 2002. *Recovering Canada: The Resurgence of Aboriginal Law*. Toronto: University of Toronto Press.

Cairns, Alan C. 2000. *Citizens Plus: Aboriginal Peoples and the Canadian State*. Vancouver: University of Vancouver Press.

Dickason, Olive Patricia. 1997. *Canada's First Nations: A History of Founding Peoples from Earliest Times*. 2nd ed. Toronto: Oxford University Press.

Frye, Northrop. 1971. *The Bush Garden*. Toronto: Anansi.

Gastle, Charles M. 2002. 'Shadows of a Talking Circle: Aboriginal Advocacy before International Institutions and Tribunals' Dec. 2. http://www.esteycentre.ca/Shadowsofatalkingcircle_final.pdf (access on 19/04/2008)

George-Kanentiio, Douglas M. 2006. *Iroquois on Fire : A Voice from the Mohawk Nation.* foreword by Vine Deloria. Westport, Conn. : Preager.

'Haudenosaunee Confederacy Makes Important Strides on Border Crossing Issue.' 2008. http://www.ailanyc.org/Bordercrossing.htm (access on 19/04/2008)

Indian and Northern Affairs Canada. 1996. *Royal Commission on Aboriginal Peoples.* http://www.ainc-inac.gc.ca/ch/rcap/index_e.html (access on 19/04/2008)

Jay Treaty. Wikipedia. http://en.wikipedia.org/wiki/Jay_Treaty#Aboriginal_rights, (access on 19/04/2008). For a scanned copy in English and French, see http://www.canadiana.org

Kilbourn, William, ed. and intro. 1970. *A Guide to the Peaceable Kingdom.* Toronto: Macmillan.

King, Thomas. 1993a. 'Borders', *One Good Story, That One*. Toronto: HarperCollins, pp. 129–145.

King, Thomas. 1993b. *Green Grass, Running Water*. Toronto: HarperCollins.

Lawrence, Bonita. 2004. *"Real" Indians and Others: Mixed-Blood Urban Native Peoples and Indigenous Nationhood*. Vancouver: University of British Columbia Press.

Luna-Firebaugh, Eileen. 2002. 'The Border Crossed Us: Border Crossing Issues of the Indigenous Peoples of the Americas', *Wicazo Sa Review*, vol. 17, no. 1, pp. 159–181.

Miller, Bruce G. 2006. "Conceptual and Practical Boundaries: Indians/First Nations on the Border of Contagion in the Post- 9–11 Era", in Sterling Evans, ed., *The Borderlands of the American and Canadian Wests: Essays on Regional and Trans-boundary History*. Lincoln, NB: University of Nebraska Press, pp. 49–66.

Miller, Bruce G. 1996/97. 'The "Really Real" Border and the Divided Salish Community', *B.C. Studies*, no. 112, pp. 63–79.

Neel, David. 1995. *The Great Canoes: Reviving a Northwest Coast Tradition*. Vancouver: Douglas & McIntyre.

Okanagan Nation. 'K'al?alqw -Across the Line' http://www.acrosstheline.ca/about/index.php (access on 19/04/2008)

Smith, Paul Chaat and Robert Warrior. 1996. *Like a Hurricane: The American Indian Movement from Alcatraz to Wounded Knee*. New York: New Press.

Thompson, John Herd. 2006. "Foreword". in Sterling Evans, ed. *The Borderlands of the American and Canadian Wests: Essays on Regional and Trans-boundary History*. Lincoln, NB: University of Nebraska Press, pp. xi-xxii.

11

Indigenizing Human Rights: First Nations, Self-Determination, and Cultural Identity

Ashwani K. Peetush

Introduction

In this paper, I argue that, with regard to Indigenous identity, there is a profound irony at work in the purportedly emancipatory power of human rights discourse. On the one hand, it is clear that this discourse has made, and continues to make, a significant contribution in helping Aboriginal peoples to articulate their claims for cultural recognition and struggle for freedom and self-rule. On the other hand, I contend that this discourse has a detrimental effect. I argue that the discourse of rights brings along with it powerful theoretical under pinnings, assumptions, and institutions that are at odds with and that undermine what most Native communities in Canada take to be an essential component of their cultural identities and self-understandings. I contend that at the heart of this issue are profound philosophical tensions about notions such as the self, community, and agency. That is, the core tensions rest on ideas that most Canadians take to be basic or unquestionable. I show that such assumptions are not only not basic or unquestionable, but, in fact, biased towards Western liberal ideals. I argue that dialogue in this context requires understanding that human rights, or any form of a global ethic, needs to be recast within Indigenous self-understandings and beliefs if such a dialogue is to be authentically intercultural and fruitful.[1]

---

1. Let me emphasize that this issue is not simply limited to Aboriginal communities in Canada but applies to all Indigenous populations globally. Indeed, I would argue that it applies to most formerly colonized peoples of the world.

Aboriginal Freedom and Human Rights

Individual rights discourse has been, and is, a source of empowerment for Indigenous and other formerly colonized nations. For example, according to the United Nations Declaration on the Granting of Independence to Colonial Countries and Peoples (adopted in 1960): "The subjection of peoples to alien subjugation, domination and exploitation constitutes a denial of fundamental human rights, is contrary to the Charter of the United Nations and is an impediment to the promotion of World peace and co-operation" and that "all peoples have the right to self-determination; by virtue of that right they freely determine their political status and freely pursue their economic, social and cultural development" (articles 1 and 2). The right to self-determination or self-rule has provided a powerful philosophical and political ideal that under girds formerly colonized peoples' claim to political and territorial sovereignty. Unfortunately, historically, the right of self-determination has been generally applied to overseas colonies and not to internally colonized peoples and nations, further marginalizing Indigenous populations. Such an application has been criticized as arbitrary and unjust, as Indigenous communities constitute peoples who have been unjustifiably dispossessed of their lands and have had their cultures almost destroyed.

Recognizing the arbitrary nature of the application of the former declaration, the United Nations recently extended the right of self-determination to Aboriginal communities by ratifying the Declaration on the Rights of Indigenous Peoples (DRIP) in September 2007, forty-seven years later. Interestingly, I should point out that Canada, the United States, New Zealand and Australia all voted against the ratification. All four countries have significant native populations. I would argue that DRIP represents a major development in thinking about Aboriginal communities and cultures from a Western liberal perspective. The Declaration recognizes the right of self-determination of Aboriginal peoples (article 3), as well as recognizing their distinct social, political, cultural and legal systems as legitimate. It also recognizes the distinct spiritual relationship to land that most Aboriginal peoples throughout the world claim constitute an essential component of their identity (article 25).

Indigenous activism often relies heavily on the discourse of human rights and it is clear to see why. Human rights discourse is not only helpful to Aboriginal peoples and their plight for self-rule, but has made great strides over the last fifty years. So, where are the purportedly deep problems?

Neo-Colonialism and Human Rights

Let me start by exploring the charge that human rights are part and parcel of a continuing neo-colonial Western agenda. The charge is often rejected out of hand by most Western liberal theorists. The rejection is often based upon two factors. The first is the great advances that human rights have made possible for formerly colonized peoples. Second, Western theorists often conflate any criticism of human rights as a criticism of the underlying ethical content or standards upon which the discourse is based. I would argue that both kinds of responses are misguided. Let me point out that because something has had positive benefit does not mean that it cannot at the same time have negative or even detrimental side effects. Moreover, conflating any criticism of human rights with a relativist rejection of cross-cultural ethical norms of decency is simply mistaken.

Let us explore the relationship between human rights and Western colonization. Many indigenous nations and other non-Western peoples challenge that human rights, as articulated in the declaration by the Universal Declaration of Human Rights (UDHR), are biased towards Western modes of social organization and thought. That is, in short, they are not truly universal or cross-cultural. Furthermore, many argue that the idea that all nations must conform to the UN Charter of Human Rights is a continuation of a Western colonial agenda that uncritically assumes that Western norms set the standards that all other nations need to adopt in order to be considered civilized (Alfred, 1999; Panikkar, 1982; Turpel, 1989–90).

Let me discuss colonialism before I detail these objections. I would contend that one of the most interesting and insidious features of colonialism is how the realm of ideas are used as a means to exclude different peoples and ways of life from participation in important social, economic, and political arenas. A critical insight into colonialism and resistance is that the real force of imperialism consists not in actual colonization, but the colonization of the realm of ideas or consciousness as opposed to physical space. It consists in the uncritical and illegitimate universalization of a narrow and specific perspective of human experience to all of humankind. Western self-understandings, ideas, and ways of life are uncritically presumed to be universal, objective, and neutral and non-Western communities are simply required (or forced) to assimilate to these. Cultural difference is often constructed as deviance and the self-understandings, beliefs, values, practices, and forms of social organization of non-Western nations are considered to be inferior and in need of Western civilization and progress.

This historically alive discourse hinders intercultural dialogue and mutual cooperation and the hope for a just and peaceful social order. It denies the legitimacy of cultural differences and seeks to stamp out diversity in the name of a false universality. The struggle for self-rule and self-determination in its various forms arises out of the struggle against colonial domination and oppression. The struggle for self-rule is an integral component of the process of decolonization. It is a struggle for respect and acceptance of cultural differences and identities and the legitimacy of those differences and identities. I would argue that one of the pivotal moments in this struggle was exemplified by Gandhi's battle for *Swaraj* or self-rule in India. India's independence marks a central shift in colonial consciousness where compliance gives way to resistance. But Gandhi realized, that freedom from oppression cannot simply be achieved by regaining physical territory. Freedom is to be gained through self-rule, and self-respect. That is, it is achieved by having the power to determine, for ourselves, the lives of our communities—according to our own self-understandings.

My central point is that the Native challenge to human rights involves just this: It is about having the power to articulate, balance, and specify cross-cultural and universal human values within the structures of native self-understandings. The Western response has been mostly that such challenges are really about attempting to justify arbitrary political power and tyranny (Donnelly, 1999; Tatsuo, 1999). While this unfounded and hasty generalization may be true in specific instances (example, the Chinese Government), this is certainly not true in all cases. The response fails to take into account a number of serious critical issues with human rights that are at the opposite end of the spectrum from attempting to justify political tyranny.

Individual Rights and Other Trojan Horses

What we may think of as setting us free, may in fact bind us; indeed, this is the nature of false consciousness. The discourse of individual rights, upon which human rights relies, is not benign. I contend that such a discourse presupposes ideas and institutions that undermine

Native identities in crucial respects. In other words, the discourse of rights can act as a social, political, and economic Western Trojan horse of sorts.

Now, according to Little Bear, Boldt and Long, self-rule is necessary for Aboriginal people to "preserve their philosophical uniqueness." They contend that natives require self-rule so that they can live according to their distinct self-understandings and "develop their own intuitions and shape laws to reflect and enhance their traditional cultural values." They do not want a "European Western model of government" simply run by Indians, but "want an Indian government that operates in accordance with traditional principles and customs, one that rests on a spiritual base" (1984:xvi). However, as Justice Mary Ellen Turpel, a philosopher and legal theorist of the Mohawk community, points out, the idea of individual rights, upon which the Canadian Charter and the UDHR are based, is in tension with a pervasive constellation of views of the self, community and agency that ground many Aboriginal cultures (Turpel, 1989–91). Yet, the very reason that Aboriginal peoples seek cultural recognition is because they seek self-rule or self-definition; they ask that their distinct self-understandings be accommodated and, furthermore, respected (Chief Ovide Mercredi, 1993).

Let me examine the manner in which the discourse of individual rights is problematic for Aboriginal peoples. Historically, the idea of Individual rights grows out of a European liberal tradition; rights are based on a particular bundle of perspectives about the nature of the individual and self, and the individual's relationship to other individuals and to society at large. Such perspectives predominately view the relationship between members of a community in terms of a contractual association. Individuals agree to live together for the sake of rational self-interest and mutual benefit. The individual freedom of each member to do what he or she wants is the highest and most important good on such a model of society. Among the social conditions that make individual freedom possible on such a perspective is the individual and private ownership of property. Property rights are foundational to this model; ownership is seen to be a quintessential part of what it means for an individual to be free (that is, its transcendental conditions).

Since individual self-interests often diverge, the state's overriding purpose consists in arbitrating competing demands between various members. It is to ensure that individuals keep their agreements and do not interfere with each other's freedom by harming one another or violating each other's private property. Individual rights are essential to such a framework. They are basic legal tools that individuals possess over and against each other; they are safeguard mechanisms in what is essentially an adversarial and competitive model of human relationships. The purpose of the state or governing power is minimal on such a perspective. The state is supposed to remain neutral with regard to issues such as questions about the good life, ethics and morality, and religion. These are individuals' private business. As such, distinctions between the church and state, law and morality, and the private and the public become paramount. Such a society is decidedly individualistic and common goals are supposed to be limited to the aggregate sum of individual self-interests (example, funding police stations, fire stations, and fixing roads). Apart from this, common goals and aspirations are relegated to private clubs and memberships. While this theoretical model of the good polity bears out more in the United States than in Canada, it still reverberates strongly with Canada's basic legal and political structure.

Although Aboriginal societies are clearly not homogenous, there are a number of recurring paradigms that are historically and philosophically pervasive among many such communities. Aboriginal peoples insist that (along with other non-Western nations, most notably Asian societies) they ground themselves in a more organic view of community. Such a view of the community centers on common or shared goals, values, and traditions. Indeed, almost all Aboriginal peoples in Canada and the United States emphasize the importance of common spiritual principles, which are usually grounded in a close stewardship relationship to the land or "Mother Earth" (Alfred, 1999; Gunn Allen, 1980; Henderson, 1995; RCAP, 1996; Starna, 1988; Tully, 1995). In the Mohawk community, such values are based on principles such as, for example, the *Four Ways*: sharing, strength, kindness, and trust. Society is not thought of as a number of individuals who contract together for the sake of rational self-interest. Other members of society are not seen as possible sources of conflict and competition from whom we therefore need individual rights as protections. Rather, every person's interest is deeply tied to the interest of the other, much like the model of a family. Others' well being is not something separate from one's own well-being, but rather, part and parcel of it.[2] Members

---

2. One practical manifestation of such an idea is how many Aboriginal peoples conceptualize justice for a crime in terms of "healing," rather than punishment.

necessarily share goals in common that are not simply the sum of individual self-interests. On such a model, the duty we have towards each other, rather than the individual rights we have over and against one another, best conceptualizes the relationship of the self to other selves and the community.

As importantly, individual freedom is not defined as freedom from interference, but rather as freedom to participate in the shared life of the community. This stems from the highly deliberate and participatory nature of most native communities in Canada. Nor is individual freedom connected to the private ownership of property in any sense analogous to a Western liberal society. In fact, Aboriginal perspectives of land and "property" differ vastly from individual private ownership, emphasizing sharing and stewardship rather than individual consumption and possession.

Indeed, one may go so far as to argue that the very idea of "human" rights presupposes a metaphysical framework in which the unit of moral and political agency, or the self, relevant to ethical consideration, is limited to the human being. This view of self and agency is biased toward Euro-Western cultures and certainly not widely shared. According to most Indigenous traditions, the self includes the environment, the trees, the animals, and the eco-system. The human being does not stand in the same privileged ontological or epistemological position, such that we need to devise a separate ethic solely for him.

Now, a key difficulty in attempting to negotiate and enter into dialogue with non-Aboriginal peoples is the rigidity with which basic concepts, such as individual rights, are held. The parameters, or the prerequisite of simply entering into dialogue are already set by the normative framework of the other (Western) party. Such a framework is uncritically presumed as somehow neutral and universal. I would urge that the problems only begin here and get worse as any questioning of the framework itself is interpreted as tantamount to rejection of the supposed "dia"-logue itself – which in fact is a monologue in most cases. I take it that a paramount issue in intercultural dialogue, and living in a culturally diverse world, is the understanding and acknowledgement that axiomatic concepts, such as the self and its relationship to the community, what it is to be a political and moral agent, may not be shared and may need explicit discussion and dialogue. Without such an understanding, concepts and the institutions they embody risk the danger of becoming hegemonic and an imposition on those who do not share them. As Raymond Williams once argued, we need to understand that in intercultural dialogue with the other, the most basic concepts, the concepts from which we begin, should not be understood as given, but as problems open to discussion and dialogue (Turpel, 1989–91:14). Only then can we begin to make real progress.

Objections

Let me now consider various objections to the idea that the discourse of individual rights is problematic for Aboriginal nations.

Immediately, many will point out that Aboriginal peoples themselves often use the discourse of individual rights; in fact, they have done so for many years and continue to do so. While I agree that this is true, I urge that one must be careful about what lesson to draw from this usage. I would argue that most Aboriginal people use this discourse not because they desire to be on the road to becoming Westernized and liberalized, but because it is the only discourse available to them to which the majority of non-Aboriginal peoples will listen. That is, if they did not make their claims using the language and tools of the dominant party they would not get very far. We should not take this use as evidence of assimilation; indeed, the First Nations have resisted assimilation into Canadian society for hundreds of years and continue to do so.

Another objection has it that my argument assumes a picture of cultures as monolithic, unchanging, and impermeable. We know that this is not the way that the real world works; identities are always changing, in flux and a hybrid of various cultures in the modern world. My picture (and that of the First Nations) is essentialist and rides roughshod over the various differences that exist between Aboriginal peoples and communities themselves. There is no such thing as "Aboriginal Identity," so the post-modern view goes.

I would urge that while it is true that cultures change, influence one another, and are acted upon internally and externally, does not mean that there are no enduring cultural identities or that there may be no overriding beliefs, values, or family resemblances among these, that are pervasive to a culture. To argue such would be to distort lived experience. Of course, the degree and nature of family resemblances among various beliefs and values depends on the nature of the aspect and culture under examination. I have no doubt that the American population as a whole diverge across a range of measurements (religion, ethnicity, world views). But even across such a heterogeneous population, there are significant agreements on a host of traditions and values. For example, individuality, freedom, democracy, and consumerism are held in rather high esteem by the majority of Americans, notwithstanding other differences. Now, most Aboriginal nations in Canada are much more homogenous, especially when it comes to beliefs and values about the connection between land and spirituality. To generalize the kind of heterogeneity that exists across Canada or America to the First Nations is to distort the actual experience and voices of such nations themselves. The current sloppy use of the in-vogue post-modern anti-essentialist picture is as distorting as the careless use of the essentialist picture, if not more.

Furthermore, the post-modern picture unwittingly denies political legitimacy to key claims regarding cultural identity and self-rule of formerly colonized peoples and unwittingly paves the road to conceptual domination since the supposed "hybrid" and "cosmopolitan" identity become simply other words for Western identity (a good example of this is Waldron, 1992).

Let us say that one recognizes the distinct traditions of Aboriginal peoples and their cultures. There is still a critical objection that is made by liberal theorists, which some believe is devastating. This is that one can argue that any adequate set of constitutional or human rights norms requires adopting the idea of individual rights, and furthermore, a liberal democratic framework (Tatsuo, 1999; Fukuyama, 1992). One cannot have anything resembling human rights without also at the same time adopting rights discourse and the framework of a liberal society.

I think that not only is this gravely mistaken but the wrong-headed approach to attempting to reach agreement on some form of a global cross-cultural ethic. I would argue that we can separate out cross-cultural ethical standards from the manner in which they are articulated, institutionalized, and applied. It is clear that Aboriginal peoples are not objecting to the idea that rape and genocide are morally heinous, or that discrimination is wrong, or that slavery (and colonialism for that matter) ought to be prohibited. Morality and ethics was not invented in the West or by Western liberal philosophers. In the global context, what is important in arriving at an agreement on ethical standards is precisely to focus on what actions are to be prohibited or prescribed, regardless of how such prohibitions and prescriptions are articulated, institutionalized and metaphysically justified. In fact, as John Rawls himself argues in the *Law of Peoples* (1999, and Jacques Maritain before him), we should expect such differences in justification given the nature of global diversity. My reasons as a Christian, or a Mohawk, or a Buddhist for thinking that murder and rape are wrong will no doubt be different than yours as an atheist. This need not be worrisome as long as we can establish agreement on norms, and also nurture the drive to sympathetically understand from where the other is coming, culturally, epistemologically, and metaphysically.

Deeper Differences: Post-secular Society

One might wonder then, is the Aboriginal criticism of rights discourse a difference that really makes a difference? In other words, is it not simply a matter of superficial differences among various communities? I would argue that the differences do in fact run deep and wide, and here we enter the domain of what many find intensely controversial. Rejecting the discourse of individual rights, for most Aboriginal communities, comes as part and parcel of rejecting the basic tenets of a liberal model of society as the normative standard to which they need to adhere. Along with this is the rejection of foundational liberal ideals, such as secularism and the separation between church and state and property rights. It is to argue that the UDHR, as it stands, is thoroughly problematic since it brings along with it such liberal ideals as axiomatic. Rawls anticipated this objection, and argued that human rights ought to be conceived of as a set of special or urgent rights, which the UDHR arguably does not do. Human rights ought not to be conflated with liberal constitutions and conflated with the list of individual rights that one finds in such societies.

Let me discuss such differences in more detail. For one thing, in contrast to liberal societies, for the majority of Aboriginal peoples, land is not conceptualized as private property or as a fungible commodity. It is not seen as something that one can buy and sell, like an automobile. Rather, it is thought of as part and parcel of one's very concept of self—it is what defines agency and being in the world. It is not difficult to understand why, if this is one's conception of land, one might see the very idea of selling land as offensive. I would argue that Aboriginal objections to the liberal idea that land should be thought of as private property and that private property is a basic human right

(UDHR, article 17) is no longer seen to be as controversial as it once was. Or, at the very least, the United Nations have, in ratifying DRIP, accepted as much. This however is not the case with the rejection of secularism.

Almost all Aboriginal groups in Canada are expressly non-secular. Spirituality is an inextricable and essential part of the very social fabric of most of these societies (Lyons, 1980; Svensson, 1979). For liberal theorists, and a predominant understanding of human rights norms, this is a major point of contention. It is often assumed that, without debate, secularism is somehow the very life breath of tolerance. It is the only road to cultural amity and the acceptance of pluralism (both internal and external). One can understand why this is the case in the West. Secularism, and liberalism for that matter, arose in Europe due to the wars between religions. The dominant understanding of such religious doctrines at that time (and perhaps even now) lacked the internal resources to allow for peaceful co-habitation and existence of diversity (hence, for example, the Crusades).

Yet, this history should not presume to delimit the resources for tolerance in other societies. In a "Billion Gandhis," Ashis Nandy contends that "to go to an Indian village to teach tolerance through secularism is a form of obscene arrogance to which I do not want to be a party" (Nandy, 2004). Tolerance in the lives of ordinary villagers is grounded in religion, "however superstitious, irrational and primitive they may seem to be to progressive, secular Indians." Rather than seeking to graft the Western idea of secularism as a solution to religious factions (which is not working), we should rather look to indigenous resources that resonate at a deep level with the majority of the population, and which have worked for thousands of years. Indeed, Nandy points out that in India, in the last fifty years, less than 4 per cent of all victims of communal or religious riots have been in villages, where 75 per cent of the population lives, and 96 per cent in cities, where only 25 per cent of the population lives. As Indian history attests, Indian cultures and traditions have sufficient internal resources for tolerance. There are alternative post-secular theoretical routes to the development of tolerance and respect, and one should not be so arrogant as to assume that only secularism can lead to communal peace (example, Asoka, Akbar, Kabir, Gandhi). Indeed, it may be that in imposing an alien secular structure on a society that one can run into deep problems, as this concept may not be rooted in culture or tradition or belief, often making it impossible to implement successfully (Taylor, 2007).

The First Nations in Canada are not willing to abandon their religious and spiritual ways of life, as they claim that these are foundational to their identities and the lives of their communities (RCAP, 1996). As long as such communities can provide basic protections for the life, integrity and well-being of their members, then I would argue that such groups constitute acceptable forms of polity that ought to be recognized and respected. There is more than one form of an acceptable social organization. Because a society is not liberal or secular does not mean that it is a form of mob-rule grounded in the arbitrary abuse of political power. I would emphasize that we not be so blinded as to equate all non-liberal and non-secular societies as *a priori* being anti-liberal and non-constitutional. Liberalism is not identical to constitutionalism (Graham Walker, 1997). Aboriginal groups are certainly constitutional; they have specific laws and ethical codes that constrain the use of political power, yet such laws are based on spiritual teachings.[3]

Unity in Diversity

A last key criticism is as follows: accommodating and recognizing cultural differences and diversity, and what this requires, will lead to disunity and disintegration (Tully, 1995:195–196; Taylor, 1993:182–185, 197–200; Kymlicka, 1995:173–192). A political community is founded on bonds of trust between members, a mutual sense of belonging, understanding, a sense of concern, and a willingness to make sacrifices if necessary. Recognizing various identities threatens to undermine the conditions that make possible such virtues and could result in disintegration. With the affirmation of self-government, Aboriginal peoples no longer have a reason to affirm a common identity with the rest of Canada since they have their own community. Why should the rest of Canada care about these groups when they do not seem to share any enthusiasm for being a part of the country anyway? The recognition of cultural differences and diversity only adds to such problems. It puts too much emphasis on differences and not enough on commonalities, which will inevitably result in the breakup of the country.

One of the problems with this objection is the implicit connection it makes between unity and uniformity on the one hand, and disunity

3. Indeed, democracy as we know it today has been historically and conceptually influenced by the deliberate forms of democracy of the First Peoples of North America.

and cultural diversity on the other. But unity, a sense of trust and belonging, does not necessarily arise only in conditions of cultural uniformity. In fact, the attempt to impose such uniformity and assimilate others actually leads to disunity and strife. It is difficult to generate a sense of trust, belonging, understanding, among one's compatriots by forcing them to fit into a Western cultural mold. It is difficult to generate a sense of mutual respect without recognizing their ways of life. The history of colonialism shows at least this much.[4] This is what those who make the above objection do not make explicit: what are the alternatives to cultural recognition? Indeed, if it is a lack of respect and recognition that causes tension and disunity in a multicultural environment, how is further denying it supposed to resolve the problem? How is this supposed to lead to any genuine unity, or sense of trust, or belonging, or concern between peoples?

On the other hand, a sense of belonging and trust can indeed be cultivated and nurtured by accommodating and recognizing peoples' differences, by trying to sympathetically understand and appreciate their ways of life. If Aboriginal peoples and their traditions are respected and recognized, and if they have enough power in the definition of the lives of their communities, if they have an effective voice in the relationship with the Canadian government and non-Aboriginal Canadians, then the chances are much stronger that they will begin to develop a sense of common identification with the larger community of which their cultures are a part. But denying recognition will certainly not lead to a climate of trust, which the colonial history of Aboriginal peoples in Canada too readily shows. When constitutional arrangements are grounded in a dialogue, when it reflects one's own traditions, when one has an effective voice in such arrangements, there is no inherent conflict in being a member of two communities. This is where the path to peace lies.

---

4. As James Tully argues: "The imposition of uniformity does not lead to unity but to resistance, further repression and disunity. The proof is the dismal record in practice. . . . Aboriginal peoples are exemplary. Every imaginable means of destruction of their cultures and assimilation into uniform European ways has been tried. Yet, after five hundred years of repression and attempted genocide, they are still here and as multiform as ever. The other cultures I have mentioned have suffered suppression and assimilation as well. They too have resisted . . . for cultural recognition is a deep and abiding human need. The suppression of cultural differences in the name of uniformity and unity is one of the leading causes of civil strife, disunity and dissolution today" (1995:197).

Conclusion

Human rights present one of the most admirable efforts in the aid of the downtrodden, the weak, and those without a voice. Such rights continue to empower us in the struggle against colonial tyranny, domination and oppression. They contribute to the struggle for self-rule for indigenous peoples around the globe, and the rebuilding of indigenous identities. I would urge however that we be careful that the tools themselves not become an instrument of cultural domination; the discourse of individual rights is only one way of formulating cross-cultural ethical standards. The underlying ethical aspirations may as well be grounded in differing Indigenous cultural identities and traditions; these are many paths towards the same destination. In terms of our differences, I would urge that the path to peace lies in a commitment to dialogue and understanding. It is only through such a dialogue that we can meet the challenges that face our diverse world.

References

Alfred, Taiaiake. 1999. *Peace, Power, Righteousness: An Indigenous Manifesto.* Toronto: Oxford Press.

Donnelly, Jack. 1999. "Human Rights and Asian Values: A Defense of "Western" Universalism", in Joanne R. Bauer, Daniel A. Bell, eds., *The East Asian Challenge For Human Rights*. New York: Cambridge University Press.

Fukuyama, Francis. 1992. *The End of History and the Last Man*. New York: Free Press.

Gunn Allen, Paula. 1980. "Iyani: It Goes This Way,' in G. Hobson, ed., *The Remembered Earth: An Anthology of Contemporary American Indian Literature*. Albuquerque: University of New Mexico Press.

Henderson, James Sakj Youngblood. 1995. 'Mikmaw Tenure in Atlantic Canada', *Dalhousie Law Journal*, vol. 18, pp. 196–294.

Kymlicka, Will. 1995. *Multicultural Citizenship: A Liberal Theory of Minority Rights*. Oxford: Clarendon Press.

Little Bear, L., M. Boldt, and J. Long. 1984. *Pathways to Self-Determination: Canadian Indians and the Canadian State*. Toronto: University of Toronto Press.

Lyons, Oren. 1980. "An Iroquois Perspective", in Christopher Vecsey, and Robert W. Venables, eds., *American Indian Environments: Ecological Issues in Native American History*. Syracuse: Syracuse University Press.

Mercredi, Chief Ovide. 1993. "First Nations and Self-Determination", in K.E. Mahoney and P. Mahoney, eds., *Human Rights in the Twenty-First Century*. Boston: Martinus Nijhoff.

Nandy, Ashis. 2004. 'A Billion Gandhis', *Outlook India*, 21 June.

Obomsawin, Alanis producer and director, and Wolf Koenig, producer. 1993. *Kanehsatake: 270 Years of Resistance* [Film], available from National Film Board of Canada, Montreal, Quebec.

Panikkar, Raimundo. 1982. 'Is the Notion of Human Rights a Western Concept?' *Diogenes*, vol. 120, pp. 75–102.

Rawls, John. 1999. *The Law of Peoples: With the Idea of Public Reason Revisited.* Cambridge, Mass.: Harvard University Press.

Royal Commission on Aboriginal Peoples. 1996. *Restructuring the Relationship.* vol. 2, part one. The Government of Canada.

Royal Commission on Aboriginal Peoples. 1996. *Restructuring the Relationship* vol. 2, part two. The Government of Canada.

Starna, William A. 1988. "Aboriginal Title and Traditional Land Use: An Anthropological Perspective", in Christopher Vecsey and William A. Starna, eds., *Iroquois Land Claims*. Syracuse: Syracuse University Press.

Svensson, Frances. 1979. 'Liberal Democracy and Group Rights: The Legacy of Individualism and its Impact on American Indian Tribes', *Political Studies*, vol. 27, no. 3, pp. 421–439.

Tatsuo, Inoue. 1999. "Human Rights and Asian Values: A Defense of "Western" Universalism", in Joanne R. Bauer, Daniel A. Bell, eds., *The East Asian Challenge For Human Rights*. New York: Cambridge University Press.

Taylor, Charles. 1993. *Reconciling the Solitudes: Essays on Canadian Federalism and Nationalism*. Montreal: McGill-Queen's University Press.

Taylor, Charles. 2007. *A Secular Age*. Cambridge, Mass.: Belknap Press of Harvard University Press.

Tully, James. 1995. *Strange Multiplicity: Constitutionalism in an Age of Diversity.* Cambridge: Cambridge University Press.

Turpel, Mary Ellen. 1989–90. 'Aboriginal Peoples and the Canadian Charter: Interpretive Monopolies, Cultural Differences.' *Canadian Human Rights Yearbook*, vol. 6, pp. 3–45.

Waldron, Jeremy. 1992. 'Minority Cultures and the Cosmopolitan Alternative', *University of Michigan Journal of Law Reform*, vol. 25, no. 3, pp. 751–793.

Walker, Graham. 1997. "The Idea of Nonliberal Constitutionalism", in Ian Shapiro and Will Kymlicka, eds., *Ethnicity and Group Rights*. New York: New York University Press.

Bibliography

Adams, Phillip and Lee Burton. 1997. *Talkback: Emperors of Air*, St. Leonards, NSW: Allen & Unwin.

Adelman, Jeremy and Stephen Aron. 1999. 'From Borderlands to Borders: Empires, Nation-States, and the Peoples in between in North American History', *The American Historical Review*, vol. 104, no. 3, pp. 814-41.

Alfred, Taiaiake. 1999. *Peace, Power, Righteousness: An Indigenous Manifesto*. Toronto: Oxford Press.

Aguirre Beltrán, Gonzalo. 1992. *El proceso de aculturación y el cambio socio-cultural en México*, México, D.F.: Fondo de Cultura Económica Obra Antropológica, 6 .

Albert, Bruce. 1997. 'Territorialité, Ethnopolitique Et Développement: À Propos Du Mouvement Indien En Amazonie Brésilienne' in *Cahiers Des Ameriques Latines*, 23. Paris: Éditions De L'IHEAL, pp. 177-211.

——. 2000. "Associações indígenas e desenvolvimento sustentável na Amazônia brasileira" in Carlos Alberto Ricardo ed., *Povos Indígenas no Brasil, 1996-2000*. São Paulo: Instituto Socioambiental, pp. 197-207.

Almeida, Rubem Ferreira Thomaz De. 1991. 'O Projeto Kaiowá-Nandera: Uma Experiência De Etnodesenvolvimento Junto Aos Guarani-Kaiowá E Guarani-Nandera Contemporâneas Do Mato Grosso Do Sul'. Dissertação De Mestrado Em Antropologia Social. Rio De Janeiro: Museu Nacional, PPGAS.

Alves, Jean Paraizo. 2007. Em Busca da Cidadabia: Escolarização e Reconhecimento de Identidades Indígenas em dois Países Americanos Brasil e México . PhD dissertation presented at the Centro de Pesquisa e Pós-Graduação sobre as Américas: Doutorado em Ciências Sociais, CEPPAC/ Universidade de Brasília.

An-Na'im, Abdullahi Ahmed. 1992. "Towards a Cross-Cultural Approach to Defining International Standards of Human Rights: The Meaning of Cruel, Inhuman, or Degrading Treatment or Punishment", in Abdullahi Ahmed An-Na'im, ed., *Human Rights in Cross-Cultural Perspectives*. Philadelphia: University of Pennsylvania Press, pp.21-43.

Armstrong, Jeannette C. 1985. *Slash*. Penticton, BC: Theytus.

Arruti, José Maurício. 1997. 'A emergência dos 'remanescentes':notas para o diálogo entre indígenas e quilombolas.' *Mana*, vol. 7, no. 2, Rio de Janeiro, pp. 7-38.

——. 2006. "Etnogêneses Indígenas" in B. Ricardo and F. Ricardo, eds. *Povos Indígenas no Brasil: 2001-2005.* São Paulo: Instituto Socioambiental, pp. 50-54.

Assembly of First Nations. 2001. Resolution 28, 2001. http://www.afn.ca/article.asp?id=2969 access on 19/04/2008

Assembly of First Nations. 2002. 'Blackfoot Confederacy Border Crossing Issues.' Resolution16E/2002.http://www.afn.ca/resolutions/2002/aga%202002/res16e.htm access on 19/04/2008

Attwood, B. 2003. *Rights for Aborigines*, Sydney: Allen and Unwin.

Attwood, B. and A. Markus, 1999. *The Struggle for Aboriginal Rights: A Documentary History*. Sydney: Allen and Unwin.

Attwood, B. and F. Magowan, eds. 2001. *Telling Stories: Indigenous History and Memory in Australia and New Zealand*. Sydney: Allen and Unwin.

Bailey, F. G. 1960. *Tribe, Caste and Nation: A Study of Political Activity and Political Change in Highland Orissa*. London: Manchester University Press.

Baines, Stephen G. 1991. *'É a FUNAI que sabe': a frente de atração Waimiri-Atroari.* Belém, Museu Paraense Emílio Goeldi/CNPq/SCT/PA.

——. 1993a. 'A Política Indigenista Governamental e os Waimiri-Atroari: Administrações indigenistas, mineração de estanho e a construção da 'autodeterminação indígena' dirigida' *Revista de Antropologia*, vol. 36, São Paulo, pp. 207-237.

——. 1993b. 'O Território dos Waimiri-Atroari e o indigenismo empresarial' *Ciências Sociais Hoje, 1993*, São Paulo, pp. 219-243.

——. 1995. 'Os Waimiri-Atroari e a invenção social da etnicidade pelo indigenismo empresarial.' *Anuário Antropológico/94*, Rio de Janeiro: Tempo Brasileiro, pp. 127-159.

——. 1996. "A Usina Hidrelétrica de Balbina e o deslocamento compulsório dos Waimiri-Atroari." in Sonia Barbosa Magalhães, Rosyan de Caldas Britto and Edan Ramos de Castro. *Energia na Amazônia*, Vol. II, Belém: Museu Paraense Emílio Goeldi/ Universidade Federal do Pará/ Associação de Universidades Amazônicas, pp. 747-759.

——. 2000. 'Imagens de liderança indígena e o Programa Waimiri-Atroari: índios e usinas hidrelétricas na Amazônia' *Revista de Antropologia.* vol.43, no.2, pp. 141-163.

Balandier, Georges. 1951. 'La Situation Coloniale: Approche Théorique' in *Cahiers Internationaux De Sociologie,* vol. 11, pp. 44-79.

Barel, Yves. 1969. 'Le Social et Ses Territories'. in F. Auriac and R. Brunet eds., *Espaces, Jeux & Enjeux*. Sydney: Allen & Unwin.

Barnes, Angie. 2005. 'Letter to US Bureau of Customs and Border Protection'. *INDIAN TIME*, vol. 23 no. 44 - Kentenko:wa / November 3. Edition 4 http://members.aol.com/miketben1/passport2.htm access on 19/04/2008

Barth, Fredrik. 1969. *Ethnic Groups and Boundaries: The Social Organisation of Cultural Difference*. Boston: Little Brown & Co.

Bartlett, Richard. 1998. 'Casenote—Delgamuukw', *Indigenous Law Bulletin*, vol.4, no.9, p.17.

Bartra, Roger. 1987. *La jaula de la melancolía. Identidad y metamorfosis del mexicano*. México, D.F.: Editorial Grijalbo.

Bauman, Zygmunt. 2006. *Modernidad Líquida*. Buenos Aires: Fondo de Cultura Económica.

Behrendt, Larissa. 2003. *Achieving Social Justice: Indigenous Rights and Australia's Future*. NSW: The Federation Press.

——. 2006. 'Indigenous Policy: No Quick Fix', in *Australian Policy Online*, http://www.apo.org.au/webboard/results.chtml?filename_num=80532 accessed June 2006

Beilharz, Peter. 1996. 'Citizens of Cities', *Thesis Eleven*, Issue 46, August, pp. 89-95.

Benhabib, S. 2002. *The Claims of Culture: Equality and Diversity in the Global Era,* Princeton: Princeton University Press.

Benhabib, Seyla. 1992. *Situating the Self: Gender, Community, and Postmodernism in Contemporary Ethics*. New York: Routledge.

Berndt, R. 1981. *Aboriginal Sites, Rights and Resource Development*. Perth: University of Western Australia Publications.

Blount, Benjamin. 1972. 'Aspects of Luo Socialization', *Language in Society* vol.1, pp. 235-48.

Boggs, Stephen T. 1985. *Speaking, Relating and Learning: A Study of Hawaiian Children at Home and at School*. Norwood, NJ: Ablex.

Bonfil Batalla, Guillermo. 1995 [1972] 'El concepto de indio en América: una categoría de la situación colonial' in *Obras escogidas de Guillermo Bonfil*. Vol. 1, pp. 337-357. México: INI-INAH.

——. 1990. *México Profundo. Una civilización negada*. México, D.F.: Editorial Grijalbo/Conaculta Los Noventa.

Borrows, John. 2002. *Recovering Canada: The Resurgence of Aboriginal Law*. Toronto: University of Toronto Press.

Bourdieu, Pierre and Jean-Claude Passeron. 1990. *Reproduction in Education, Society and Culture*. London: Sage Publications.

Bourdieu, Pierre. 1984. 'La Délègation et le Fetichisme Politique'. *Actes de La Recherche en Sciences Sociales,* vol. 52/53, pp. 49-55.

Bowen, John R. 2000. 'Should We Have a Universal Concept of 'Indigenous Peoples' Rights'?' *Anthropology Today.* vol.16, no.4, August, p.12.

Bricker, Victoria Reifler. 1989. *El cristo indígena, el rey nativo*. translated by Cristina Paschero. México: Fondo de Cultura Económica.

Bunda, Tracey. 2006. 'Self-determination: Actualising the Space', in Gus Worby and Lester-Irabinna Rigney eds., *Sharing Spaces: Indigenous and Non-Indigenous Responses to Story, Country, and Rights*. Australian Research Institute, Perth: Curtin University of Technology, pp. 449-60.

Burdon, Peter. 2006. 'Above the Law? Roxby Downs and BHP Billiton, *Friends of the Earth* Adelaide, 1 May 2006, <http://www.geocities.com/olympicdam/indenture1.html>

Burns, Allan F. 1983. *An Epoch of Miracles. Oral Literature of the Yucatec Maya.* Austin: University of Texas Press.

Cairns, Alan C. 2000. *Citizens Plus: Aboriginal Peoples and the Canadian State.* Vancouver: University of Vancouver Press.

Cardoso de Oliveira, Roberto, 1994. 'O movimento dos conceitos na antropologia' *Revista de Antropologia*, São Paulo, vol. 36, 1994, pp. 13-31.

——. 1964. *O Índio E O Mundo Dos Brancos*. 2 Ed. São Paulo: Livraria Pioneira Editora. Há Uma 4ª Edição Da Editora Da Unicamp, De 1994, Incluindo Um Posfácio .

——. 1976. *Identidade, Etnia, e Estrutural Social*. São Paulo: Livraria Pioneira Editora.

——. 2000. 'Ação indigenista, eticidade e o diálogo interétnico' *Estudos Avançados*, vol.14 40, pp. 213-30.

Carvalho, José Murilo De. 1987. *Os Bestializados: O Rio De Janeiro E A República Que Não Foi.* 2.Ed. São Paulo: Companhia Das Letras.

Caso, Alfonso. 1958. *Indigenismo*. México: Instituto Nacional Indigenista Culturas Indígenas.

Clancy, Patricia M. 1986. 'The Acquisition of Communicative Style in Japanese', in B. B. Schieffelin and E. Ochs, eds., *Language Socialization across Cultures.* Cambridge: Cambridge University Press.

Clifford, James. 1997. *Routes. Travel and Translation in the Late Twentieth Century* Cambridge: Harvard University Press.

Coe, P. 1994. 'ATSIC: Self Determination or Otherwise', *Race and Class*. vol.35, no.4, April-June, p.37.

Cohen, R. and S.M. Rai, eds. *Global Social Movements*, London: The Athlone Press.

Correia, Cloude de Souza. 2007. *Etnozoneamento, Etnomapeamento e Diagnóstico Etnoambiental: representaçõies cartográficas e gestão territorial em terras indígenas no estado do Acre*. Tese de doutorado em Antropologia Social, DAN, Brasília: Universidade de Brasília.

Council for Aboriginal Reconciliation. 2000. *Reconciliation: Australia's Challenge, Final report of the Council for Aboriginal Reconciliation to the Prime Minister and the Commonwealth Parliament,* available at: http://www.austlii.edu.au/au/other/IndigLRes/car/2000/16/

Cox, Helen et al. 1994. "Two Laws, One Land", in Bourke et al, *Aboriginal Australia*. Brisbane: University of Queensland Press.

Crago, Martha B. 1988. *Cultural Context in Communicative Interaction of Young Inuit Children*. Unpublished doctoral dissertation, McGill University, Montreal.

——. 1992. 'The Sociocultural Interface of Communicative Interaction and L2 Acquisition: An Inuit Example', TESOL *Quarterly*, vol.23, no.3, pp. 487-506

Crago, Martha B., and Alice Eriks-Brophy. 1993. "Culture, Conversation, and the Co-construction of Interaction: Implications and Applications for Intervention", in J. Duchan, L. Hewitt, C. Reynolds, and R. Sonnenmeier eds., *Pragmatics: From Theory to Therapy*. Englewood Cliffs, NJ: Prentice Hall.

Cunha, Manuela Carneiro da, ed. 1992. *História dos índios no Brasil.* São Paulo: Companhia das Letras.

Cunneen, Chris. 2007. 'Riot, Resistance and Moral Panic: Demonising the Colonial Other', in Scott Poynting and George Morgan. eds., *Outrageous! Moral Panics in Australia*. University of Tasmania, Hobart: ACYS Publishing, pp 20-29.

Dean, B. and J.M. Levi, eds. 2003. *At the Risk of Being Heard: Identity, Rights and Postcolonial States*. Ann Arbor: The University of Michigan Press.

Delpit, Lisa D. 1988. 'The Silenced Dialogue: Power and Pedagogy in Educating Other People's Children', *Harvard Educational Review*, vol.58, no.2, pp. 78-95.

Demuth, Katherine. 1986. "Prompting Routines in the Language Socialization of Basotho Children", in B. B. Schieffelin and E. Ochs, eds., *Language Socialization across Cultures*. Cambridge: Cambridge University Press.

Díaz Polanco, Héctor. 2006. *Elogio de la diversidad: globalización, multiculturalidad y etnofagia*. México: Siglo XXI Editores.

Dickason, Olive Patricia. 1997. *Canada's First Nations: A History of Founding Peoples from Earliest Times*. 2nd ed. Toronto: Oxford University Press.

Donnelly, Jack. 1999. 'Human Rights and Asian Values: A Defense of "Western" Universalism', in Joanne R. Bauer, Daniel A. Bell, eds., *The East Asian Challenge For Human Rights*. New York: Cambridge University Press.

Douzinas, C. 2000. *The End of Human Rights: Critical Legal Thought at the Turn of the Century*, Portland: Oxford.

Duranti, Alessandro, and Eleanor Ochs. 1988. 'Literacy Instruction in a Samoan Village', in Eleanor Ochs, ed., *Culture and Language Development*. Cambridge: Cambridge University Press.

Dyer, Richard. 1997. *White*. London: Routledge.

Education and Health Standing Committee WA . 2007. *Initiatives in the Remote Indigenous Communities of Cape York*. Report, No 7.

Eisenberg, Ann. 1982. *Language Acquisition in Cultural Perspective: Talk in Three Mexican Homes*. Unpublished doctoral dissertation. University of California, Berkeley.

Erickson, Frederick. 1987. 'Transformations and School Success: The Politics and Culture of Educational Achievement', *Anthropology and Education Quarterly* vol.18, no.4, pp. 335-57.

Eriks-Brophy, Alice, and Martha B. Crago. 1994. 'Transforming Classroom Discourse: An Inuit Example', *Language and Education*, vol.8, no.3, pp. 105-22.

Eriks-Brophy, Alice, and Martha B. Crago. 2003. 'Variation in instructional discourse features: Cultural or Linguistic? Evidence from Inuit and non-Inuit Teachers of Nunavik', *Anthropology and Education Quarterly*, vol.34, no.4, pp. 1-25.

Escárcega, Silvia y Stefano Varese, eds. 2002. *La ruta mixteca*. México: Universidad Nacional Autónoma de México-Programa México Nacion Multicultural.

Escobar, Arturo and Sonia Alvarez E. eds. 1992. *The Making of Social Movement in Latin America: Identity, Strategy and Democracy*. Boulder: Westview Press.

Falgout, Suzanne, and Paula Levin. 1992. 'Transforming Knowledge: Western Schooling in the Pacific', *Anthropology and Educational Quarterly*, vol.23, no.1, pp. 3-9.

Ferguson, James. 1995. *The Anti-Politics Machine: 'Development, 'Depoliticization, and Bureaucratic Power in Lesotho.* Cambridge: Cambridge University Press.

Fischer, J.S. 1970. "Linguistic Socialization: Japan and the United States", in R. Hill and R. Konig, eds., *Families in East and West*. The Hague: Mouton.

Fisher, William F. 1997. 'Doing Good? The Politics and Antipolitics of NGO Practices', *Annual Review Anthropology*, vol. 26, pp.439-64.

Fleras, A. 1999. "Politicising Indigeneity: Ethno-Politics in White Settler Dominions," in P. Havemann, ed., *Indigenous People's Rights in Australia, Canada and New Zealand*. Auckland: Oxford University Press.

Fleras, Augie and J.L. Elliott. 1992. '*The Nations Within': Aboriginal-State Relations in Canada, the United States and New Zealand.* Toronto: Oxford University Press.

Foucault, Michel. 2003. *Society Must Be Defended: Lectures at the College De France 1975-76*, translated by David Macey. London: Penguin Books.

Frye, Northrop. 1971. *The Bush Garden*. Toronto: Anansi.

Fukuyama, Francis. 1992. *The End of History and the Last Man*. New York: Free Press.

Gal, Susan. 1989. 'Language and Political Economy', *Annual Review of Anthropology*, vol.18, pp. 345-67.

Gale, Peter. 2004. 'Refugee Crisis and Fear: Populist Politics and Media Discourse', *Australian Journal of Sociology*, vol. 40, no. 4, December, pp. 321-340.

——. 2005. *The Politics of Fear: Lighting the Wik*, Sydney: Pearson Education.

Gallimore, Ronald, T. Weisner, S. Kaufman, and L. P. Bemheimer.1989. 'The Social Construction of Ecocultural Niches: Family Accommodation of Developmentally Delayed Children', *American Journal of Mental Retardation*, vol.94, no.3, pp. 216-30.

Galvão, Eduardo. 1978. *Encontro De Sociedades*, Rio De Janeiro: Paz E Terra

Gamio, Manuel. 1960 [1916]. *Forjando Patria*. México: Editorial Porrua.

Gastle, Charles M. 2002. 'Shadows of a Talking Circle: Aboriginal Advocacy before International Institutions and Tribunals' Dec. 2. http://www.esteycentre.ca/Shadowsofatalkingcircle_final.pdf access on 19/04/2008

George-Kanentiio, Douglas M. 2006. *Iroquois on Fire: A Voice from the Mohawk Nation.* foreword by Vine Deloria. Westport, Conn.: Preager.

Gluckman, Max and E. Devons, 1968. "Inter-Hierarchical Roles: Professional and Party Ethics in Tribal Areas in South And Central Africa" in J. Swartz Marc, ed., *Local-Level Politics.* Chicago: Aldine.

Goot, Murray and Tim Rose. 2007. *Divided Nation? Indigenous Affairs and the Imagined Public*. Melbourne: Melbourne University Press.

Grossman, Michele. 2003. "After Aboriginalism: Power, Knowledge and Indigenous Australian Critical Writing", in Michele Grossman ed., *Blacklines: Contemporary Critical Writing by Indigenous Australians*. Melbourne: Melbourne University Press, pp 1-24.

Grupioni, Luís Donizete Benzi. 1999. *Diretório De Associações E Organizações Indígenas No Brasil*. INEP/MEC E MARI/UIP.

Gumperz, John J. 1982. *Discourse Strategies*. Cambridge: Cambridge University Press.

Gunn Allen, Paula. 1980. 'Iyani: It Goes This Way,' in G. Hobson, ed., in *The Remembered Earth: An Anthology of Contemporary American Indian Literature*. Albuquerque: University of New Mexico Press.

Gutmann, A. ed. 1994. *Multiculturalism,* Princeton, Princeton University Press.

Hall, Stuart, Chas Critcher, Tony Jefferson, John Clarke, and Brian Roberts. 1978. *Policing the Crisis*. London: Macmillan.

Hall, Stuart. 1997. "The Work of Representation" in *Representation: Cultural Representations and Signifying Practices*. London: Sage Publications, pp. 1-74.

Handler, Richard and Jocelyn Linnekin. 1984. 'Tradition, Genuine or Spurious', *Journal of American Folklore*, vol.97 no.385, pp. 273-290.

Hanson, Allan. 1989. 'The Making of the Maori: Culture Invention and Its Logic,' *American Anthropologist*, vol. 91, pp. 890-902.

Harkness, Sarah. 1977. 'Aspects of Social Environment and First Language Acquisition in Rural Africa', in C. E. Snow and C. A. Ferguson, eds., *Talking to Children*. New York: Cambridge University Press.

Harvey, David. 2005. *The New Imperialism*, New York: Oxford University Press.

Havemann, P. ed. 1999. *Indigenous People's Rights in Australia, Canada and New Zealand.* Auckland: Oxford University Press.

Haywood, J. 2003. "The Waitangi Tribunal in the Treaty Settlement Process," in R. Miller, ed., *New Zealand Government and Politic*s, 3 rd edition, Auckland: Oxford University Press.

Heath, Shirley Brice. 1983. *Ways with Words: Language, Life and Work in Communities and Classrooms*. Cambridge: Cambridge University Press.

Heath, Shirley Brice. 1990. "The Children of Trackton's Children: Spoken and Written Language in Social Change", in W. Stigler, R. A. Shweder, and G. Herdt, eds., *Cultural Psychology: Essays on Comparative Human Development*. Cambridge: Cambridge University Press.

Heller, Monica. 1990. *The Politics of Codeswitching: Processes and Consequences of Ethnic Mobilization*. Third Workshop of the European Science Foundation Network on Codeswitching. Brussels, Belgium.

Henderson, James Sakj Youngblood. 1995. 'Mikmaw Tenure in Atlantic Canada', *Dalhousie Law Journal*, vol.18, pp. 196-294.

Hirsch, Eric and Michael O'Hanlon, eds. 1996. *The Anthropology of Landscape. Perspectives on Place And Space*. Oxford: Clarendon Press.

Hirsch, Eric. 1996. 'Introduction: Landscape: Between Place and Space', in Eric Hirsch and Michael O'Hanlon. *The Anthropology of Landscape. Perspectives on Place and Space*. Oxford: Clarendon Press, pp.1-30.

Hobsbawm, Eric. 1983. "Introduction: Inventing Traditions" in E. Hobsbawm and T. Ranger eds., *The Invention of Tradition*, Cambridge: Cambridge University Press.

——. 1984 [1983]. "Introdução: A Invenção das Tradições" in Eric Hobsbawm and Terence Ranger, eds. *A Invenção das Tradições*. Rio de Janeiro: Paz e Terra.

Homborg, Alf and Mikael Kurkiala. 1998. *Voices of the Land: Identity and Ecology in the Margins*, Lund: Lund University Press.

Howard, Catherine V. 2002. 'A domesticação das mercadorias: estratégias Waiwai' in Bruce Albert and Alcida Rita Ramos, *Pacificando o branco: cosmologias do contato no norte-amazônico*. São Paulo, Editora UNESP, Imprensa Oficial do Estado, pp. 25-56.

Howard, John. 1997. *Opening Address to the Australian Reconciliation Convention*, Melbourne, 26th May. http://www.pm.gov.au/media/index.cfm?type=2 accessed August 2007

——. 2006. Address to the National Press Club, Parliament House, Canberra, 25th January. http://www.pm.gov.au/media/index.cfm?type=2 accessed August 2007

——. 2007. Joint Press Conference with the Hon Mal Brough, Minister for Families, Community Services and Indigenous Affairs, Canberra, 21 June. http://www.pm.gov.au/media/index.cfm?type=3 accessed August 2007

Human Rights and Equal Opportunity Commission. 1997. *Bringing Them Home: National Inquiry into the Separation of Aboriginal and Torres Strait Islander Children from their Families*. Canberra: Australian Government Publishing Service.

Iglesias, Marcelo Piedrafita. 1993.*O Astro Luminoso*. Dissertação De Mestrado Em Antropologia Social. Rio De Janeiro: Museu Nacional/PPGAS.

Indian and Northern Affairs Canada. 1996. *Royal Commission on Aboriginal Peoples.*http://www.ainc-inac.gc.ca/ch/rcap/index_e.html access on 19/04/2008

Ivanitz, M. 2002. "Democracy and Indigenous Self-Determination," in A. Carter and G. Stokes eds., *Democratic Theory Today: Challenges for the 21 St Century*, Cambridge: Polity Press.

Ivison, D., P. Patton and W. Sanders, eds. 2000. *Political Theory and the Rights of Indigenous Peoples*. Cambridge: Cambridge University Press.

Jackson, Jean. 1995. 'Culture, Genuine and Spurious: The Politics of Indianness in the Vaups, Colombia', *American Ethnologist*, vol. 22, no. 1, pp.3-27

Jay Treaty. Wikipedia. http://en.wikipedia.org/wiki/Jay_Treaty#Aboriginal_rights, access on 19/04/2008. For a scanned copy in English and French, see http://www.canadiana.org

Kilbourn, William, ed. 1970. *A Guide to the Peaceable Kingdom*. Toronto: Macmillan.

King, Thomas. 1993a. 'Borders', *One Good Story, That One*. Toronto: HarperCollins, pp. 129-45.

——. 1993b. *Green Grass, Running Water*. Toronto: HarperCollins.

Klandermans, B. and H. Johnston eds. 1995. *Social Movements and Culture*, London: UCL Press.

Knight, Alan. 1990. 'Racism, Revolution and Indigenismo: México, 1910-1940', in Richard Graham, ed. *The Idea of Race in Latin America*. Austin: University of Texas Press, pp. 71-113

Kymlicka, Will. 1995. *Multicultural Citizenship: A Liberal Theory of Minority Rights*. Oxford: Oxford University Press.

Langton, Marcia. 1997. "Pauline as the Thin End of the Wedge", in Philip Adams ed., *The Retreat From Tolerance: A Snapshot of Australian Society*: Sydney, ABC Books.

Lawrence, Bonita. 2004. *'Real' Indians and Others: Mixed-Blood Urban Native Peoples and Indigenous Nationhood*. Vancouver: University of British Columbia Press.

Lima, Antônio Carlos Souza. 1995. *Um Grande Cerco De Paz*. ANPOCS. Petrópolis: Ed. Vozes.

Linnekin, Jocelin. 1992. 'On the Theory and Politics of Cultural Construction in the Pacific', *Oceania*, vol. 62 no. 4, pp.249-263.

Lipka, Jerry. 1991. 'Toward a Culturally Based Pedagogy: A Case of One Yu'pik Eskimo Teacher', *Anthropology and Educational Quarterly*, vol.22, no.3, pp. 202-23.

Lipschutz, A. 1956. *La comunidad indígena den América y en Chile*. Santiago de Chile: Editorial Universitaria.

Little Bear, L., M. Boldt, and J. Long. 1984. *Pathways to Self-Determination: Canadian Indians and the Canadian State*. Toronto: University of Toronto Press.

Löfgren, N. 1995. 'Common Law Aboriginal Property Rights', *Aboriginal Law Bulletin*, vol.3, no.77.

Luciano, Gersem José dos Santos. 2006. 'Projeto é como branco trabalha; as lideranças que se virem para aprender e nos ensinar': experiências dos povos indígenas do alto rio Negro. Dissertação de Mestrado apresentada ao Programa de Pós-Graduação em Antropologia Social do Instituto de Ciências Sociais da Universidade de Brasília, Brasília, DF.

Luna-Firebaugh, Eileen. 2002. 'The Border Crossed Us: Border Crossing Issues of the Indigenous Peoples of the Americas', *Wicazo Sa Review*, vol. 17, no. 1, pp. 159-81.

Lyons, Oren. 1980. "An Iroquois Perspective", in Christopher Vecsey, and Robert W. Venables, eds., *American Indian Environments: Ecological Issues in Native American History*. Syracuse: Syracuse University Press.

Macintyre, Stuart and Anna Clark. 2003. *The History Wars*. Carlton, Victoria: Melbourne University Press.

Macklem, Patrick. 1993. 'Distributing Sovereignty: Indian Nations and Equality of Peoples', *Stanford Law Review* vol. 45, pp. 1311-1367.

Maddison, S. and S. Scalmer. 2003. "Passionate Actors: Tension and Conflict in the Life of Social Movements", in Corrigan et al. eds. *New Times, New Worlds, New Ideas: Sociology Today and Tomorrow,* Refereed conference proceedings, 4-6 December, University of New England, The Australian Sociological Association.

——. 2006. *Activist Wisdom: Practical Knowledge and Creative Tension in the Life of Social Movements*. Sydney: UNSW Press.

Maddock, K. 1984. "Aboriginal Customary Law", in P. Hanks and B. Keon-Cohen, eds., *Aborigines and the Law.* Sydney: Allen and Unwin.

Mallon, Florencia E. 1995. *Peasant and Nation. The Making of Postcolonial Mexico and Peru*. Berkeley: University of California Press.

Manning, Peter. 2003. *Dog Whistle Politics and Journalism: Reporting Arabic and Muslim People in Sydney Newspapers*, Australian Centre for Independent Journalism, Sydney: University of Technology.

Markus, Andrew. 2001. *Race: John Howard and the Remaking of Australia*. Crows Nest, NSW: Allen & Unwin.

Martin, K. 2003. "Ways of knowing, being and doing: a theoretical framework and methods for indigenous and indigenist research," in K. McWilliam, P. Stephenson and G. Thompson, eds. *Voicing Dissent*. St Lucia: API Network and University of Queensland Press.

Martins, José De Souza. 1975. *Capitalismo e Tradicionalismo*. São Paulo: Livraria Pioneira.

Mato, Daniel. 1992. 'Disputas en la Construcción de Identidades y 'Literaturas Orales' en Comunidades Indígenas de Venezuela: Conflictos entre Narradores y Papel de Investigadores y Editoriales' *Revista de Investigaciones Folklóricas,* Buenos Aries: Universidad de Buenos Aires. no. 7, pp. 40-47.

May, Benito Aban *et al.*, 1994. *Yum santísima Cruz tun*, (Collection Letras Mayas Contemporáneas), no. 26. Mexico: Instituto Nacional Indigenista.

Maybury-Lewis, D. 1997. *Indigenous Peoples, Ethnic Groups and the State*. Boston: Allyn and Bacon.

——. 2000. 'From Elimination to an Uncertain Future: Changing Policies towards Indigenous Peoples,' in B. Dean, and J.M. Levi eds., *At the Risk of Being Heard: Identity, Rights and Postcolonial States*. Ann Arbor: University of Michigan Press

——. 1967. *The Savage and the Innocent*. Boston: Beacon Press.

Mc William, K., P. Stephenson and G. Thompson, eds. 2,003. 'Voicing Dissent', Editarial. *Jouranl of Australian Atudies,* Lucia 76, pp 1-3.

Mehan, Hugh. 1987. "Language and Schooling", in G. Spindler and L. Spindler, eds. *Interpretive Ethnography of Education at Home and Abroad*. Hillsdale, NJ: Laurence Erlbaum Associates.

Melucci, A. 1995. "The Process of Collective Identity", in H. Johnston and B. Klandermans, eds., *Social Movements and Culture*. UCL Press.

Mercer, David. 1997. 'Aboriginal Self-determination and Indigenous Land Title in Post-Mabo Australia', *Political Geography*, vol.16, no.3, pp.189-212.

Mercredi, Chief Ovide. 1993. "First Nations and Self-Determination", in K.E. Mahoney and P. Mahoney, eds., *Human Rights in the Twenty-First Century*. Boston: Martinus Nijhoff.

Miller, Bruce G. 1996/97. 'The 'Really Real' Border and the Divided Salish Community', *B.C. Studies*, no. 112, pp. 63-79.

Miller, Bruce G. 2006. 'Conceptual and Practical Boundaries: Indians/First Nations on the Border of Contagion in the Post- 9-11 Era', in Sterling Evans, ed., *The Borderlands of the American and Canadian Wests: Essays on Regional and Trans-boundary History*. Lincoln, NB: University of Nebraska Press, pp. 49-66.

Miller, Patricia. 1982. *Amy, Wendy and Beth: Learning Language in South Baltimore*. Austin, TX: University of Texas Press.

Mohawk Nation Council of Chiefs. 2008. 'Haudenosaunee Confederacy Makes Important Strides on Border Crossing Issue.' 3 March 2008.http://www.ailanyc.org/Bordercrossing.htm access on 19/04/2008

Molina Enríquez, Andrés. 1909. *Los grandes problemas nacionales*. México: A. Carranza.

Montemayor, Carlos. 1996. *Chiapas, la rebelión indígena de México*. Mexico City: Joaquín Mortiz.

——. 2000. *Los pueblos indios de México hoy.* Mexico: Temas de Hoy Series, Planeta Mexicana.

Moreton-Robinson, Aileen. 2006. 'Towards a New Research Agenda? Foucault, Whiteness and Indigenous Sovereignty', *Journal of Sociology*, vol. 42, no. 4, pp. 383-95.

——. 2007. 'Witnessing the Workings of White Possession in the Work Place: Leesa's Testimony', *Australian Feminist Law Journal,* vol. 26, pp. 81-93.

Morris, Megan. 2001. "Introduction" in Megan Morris and Brett deBary eds. *'Race' Panic and the Memory of Migration*. Hong Kong: Hong Kong University Press, pp. 1-18.

Morrissey, Michael. 2006. 'The Australian State and Indigenous People 1990-2006' in *Journal of Sociology*, vol. 42, no. 4, pp. 347-54.

Murphy, Robert. 1978. *Headhunters Heritage: Social And Economic Change Among The Munducuru Indians*. New York: Octogon Books.

Nash, June C. 2001. *Mayan Visions: The Quest for Autonomy in an Age of Globalization.* New York: Routledge.

Nandy, Ashis. 2004. 'A Billion Gandhis', *Outlook India*. 21 June.

Navarrete Linares, Federico n.d. 'Discriminación étnica y desigualdades en México: una reflexión histórica' in Elisabetta di Castro ed., *La desigualdad en México: perspectivas interdisciplinarias*. México: Universidad Nacional Autónoma de México.

——. 2004. *Las relaciones interétnicas en México*. México: Universidad Nacional Autónoma de México.

Neel, David. 1995. *The Great Canoes: Reviving a Northwest Coast Tradition*. Vancouver: Douglas & McIntyre.

Nettheim, Garth. 1995. 'Mabo and Legal Pluralism: The Australian Aboriginal Justice Experience', in K. Hazelhurst ed., *Legal Pluralism and the Colonial Legacy*. Avebury: Aldershot.

Niezen, R. 2003. *The Origins of Indigenism: Human Rights and the Politics of Identity*. Berkeley: University of California Press.

Nugent, Stephen. 1993. *Amazonian Caboclo Society: An Essay on Invisibility and Peasant Economy*. Oxford: Berg.

O'Shane, P. 1998. *Aboriginal Political Movements: Some Observations*, 13 th Frank Archibald Memorial Lecture, University of New England, Armidale.

Obomsawin, Alanis. producer and director, and Wolf Koenig, producer. 1993. *Kanehsatake: 270 Years of Resistance* [Film], available from National Film Board of Canada, Montreal, Quebec.

Ochs, Eleanor. 1988. *Culture and Language Development: Language Acquisition and Language Socialization in a Samoan Village*. Cambridge: Cambridge University Press.

Okanagan Nation. 2008. 'K'al?alqw -Across the Line' http://www.acrosstheline.ca/about/index.php access on 19/04/2008

Oliveira, Adolfo Neves de. 2002. 'Fragmentos da Etnografia de uma Rebelião do Objeto: indigenismo e antropologia em tempos de autonomia indígena' *Anuário Antropológico*, Vol. 98, pp. 109-130.

Oliveira, João Pacheco de, ed. 2004. *A Viagem da Volta: etnicidade, política e reelaboração cultural no Nordeste indígena*. 2ª ed. Contra Capa Livraria / LACED.

——. 1979. *A Fronteira e a Viabilidade Do Campesinato Indígena*. Rio de Janeiro: PPGAS.

——. 1988. *'O Nosso Governo': Os Ticuna E O Regime Tutelar*. Rio De Janeiro: Marco Zero/Cnpq.

——. 1989. 'Expedições Científicas em terras Indígenas'. *Boletim da ABA*, Vol. 6, Associação Brasileira de Antropologia.

——. 1993. 'A Viagem de Volta': reelaboração cultural e horizonte político dos povos indígenas no nordeste. *Atlas das Terras Indígenas do Nordeste*. Rio de Janeiro: PETI - Museu Nacional, pp.v-viii.

——. 1999. *A Viagem Da Volta: Etnicidade, Política E Reelaboração Cultural No Nordeste Indígena*. Rio De Janeiro: Contra Capa.

——. 1999. *Ensaios Em Antropologia História*. Rio De Janeiro: Editora UFRJ.

——. 1977. *As Facções E A Ordem Política Em Uma Reserva Ticuna*. Brasília, Universidade De Brasília, Dissertação De Mestrado Em Antropologia Social.

Ortiz, Fernando. 1943. *Etnia Y Sociedad*. Cuba: Editorial De Ciencias Sociales, Pensamiento Cubano .

Ortolan Matos, M. C. 1997. *O Processo De Criação E Consolidação Do*

Movimento Pan-Indígena No Brasil 1970-1980. Mémoire De Maîtrise, Brasilia: Universidade De Brasilia.

Panikkar, Raimundo. 1982. 'Is The Notion of Human Rights A Western Concept?' *Diogenes*, vol. 120, pp. 75-102.

Paz, Octavio 1970 [1950-59] *El laberinto de la soledad*. México: Fondo de Cultura Económica.

Pearson, N. 2005. *The Cape York Agenda*. Cairns: Cape York Institute for Policy and Leadership.

Peirano, Mariza. 1991. 'The Anthropology of Anthropology: The Brazilian Case'. *Série Antropologia,* Vol. 110. Brasília: Unb.

Pereira, Ricardo Neves Romcy. 2007. Comunidade Canafé: história indígena e etnogênese no Médio Rio Negro, Dissertação de mestrado em Antropologia, Universidade de Brasília.

Philips, Susan U. 1983. *The Invisible Culture: Communication in Classroom and Community on the Warm Springs Indian Reservation*. New York: Longman Inc.

Raffestin, Claude. 1986. "Écogénese Territoriale Et Territoriale" in F. Auriac et R. Brunet eds. *Espaces, Jeux & Enjeux*. Paris: Gallimard/Le Seuil, pp. 173-185.

Ramos, Alcida Rita. 2002. "Cutting through State and Class: Sources and Strategies of Self-Representation in Latin America", in Kay B. Warren & Jean E. Jackson, *Indigenous Movements, Self-Representation and the State in Latin America,* Austin: University of Texas Press.

Ranger, Terence. 1984. 'A Invenção da Tradição na África Colonial' in Hobsbawm, Eric and Terence Ranger, eds. *A Invenção das Tradições*. Rio de Janeiro: Paz e Terra.

Rawls, John. 1999. *The Law Of Peoples: With The Idea of Public Reason Revisited.* Cambridge, Mass.: Harvard University Press.

Razack, Sherene. 1994. 'What is to be Gained by Looking White People in the Eye? Culture, Race, and Gender in Cases of Sexual Violence', *Signs,* vol. 19, no.4, pp. 894-923.

Reid, Gerald F. 2007. 'Illegal Alien?: The Immigration Case of Mohawk Ironworker Paul K. Diabo.' *Proceedings of the American Philosophical Society* March 1. www.aps-pub.com/proceedings/1511/151105.pdf

Reina, Leticia. 1986. *Las rebeliones campesinas en México 1819-1906*. México, Siglo XXI Editores Colección América Nuestra, Caminos de liberación.

Ribeiro, Darcy. 1970. *Os Índios e a Civilização*. Rio De Janeiro: Civilização Brasileira.

Ricardo, Carlos Alberto. 1996. 'A Sociodiversidade Nativa Contemporânea No Brasil' in *Povos Indígenas No Brasil. 1991/1995*. São Paulo: Instituto Socioambiental, pp.1-12.

Riviere, Peter. 1972. *The Forgotten Frontier: Ranches of North Brazil*. New York: Holt, Rinchart and Winsdon.

——. 1995. *Absent-minded Imperialism: Britain and the Expansion of Empire in Nineteenth-Century Brazil*. London: Tauris.

Rodrigues, Aryon Dall'Igna. 1986. *Línguas Brasileiras: para o conhecimento das línguas indígenas*. São Paulo: Edições Loyola.

Rodrigues, Carmen Izabel. 2006. 'Caboclos na Amazônia: a identidade na diferença'. *Novos Cadernos NAEA*, vol.9, no. 1, pp. 119-130.

Royal Commission on Aboriginal Peoples 1996. *Restructuring the Relationship*. Vol. 2, part one. The Government of Canada.

Royal Commission on Aboriginal Peoples 1996. Restructuring the Relationship 1996. Vol. 2, part two. The Government of Canada.

Ruiz, Margarito Xib. 1996. "Los pueblos indios y la refundación del estado", in Jesús Ortega Martínez (ed.), *La autonomía de los pueblos indios*, México: Grupo Parlamentario del Partido de la Revolución Democrática, LVI Legislatura de la Cámara de Diputados.

—— and Araceli Burguete. 1996. "Comunidades en estados modernos", in Jesús Ortega Martínez (ed.), *La autonomía de los pueblos indios*, México: Grupo Parlamentario del Partido de la Revolución Democrática, LVI Legislatura de la Cámara de Diputados.

Rutherford, Tony. 2006. 'Native Title Hostility Pointless' *The Western Australian*, 18th October 2006, http://www.thewest.com.au/default.aspx?MenuID=77&ContentID=10238>

Sanders, William. 1993. 'Reconciling Public Accountability and Aboriginal Self Determination/Self Management', *Discussion Paper No. 51*, Centre for Aboriginal and Economic Policy Research, Australia National University.

Schieffelin, Bambi B. 1990. *The Give and Take of Everyday Life*. Cambridge: Cambridge University Press.

Schirmer, Jennifer. 1988. "The Dilemma of Cultural Diversity and Equivalency in Universal Human Rights Standards", in Theodore E. Downing et. al., eds., *Human Rights and Anthropology*. Cambridge, Mass.: Cultural Survival, Inc.

Scollon, Ron, and Susan Scollon. 1981. *Narrative, Literacy and Race in Interethnic Communication*. Norwood, NJ: Ablex Publishing.

Singh, Priti, 2009. "Current Discourse on Indigenous/Tribal Right to Self-government: A Comparative Analysis of Canada and India" in Christopher S. Raj and Marie McAndrew eds., *Multiculturalism: Public Policy and Problem Areas in Canada and India*. New Delhi: Manak.

——. 2000. "Incorporation of Indigenous Peoples' Rights and Development of Participatory Democracy in Colombia Under the 1991 Constitution," in Abdul Nafey, et al eds., *State and Society in Latin America: Challenges of Globalisation*. New Delhi: Commonwealth Publishers.

——. 2001. "Governance of Australia's Aborigines: Some Unresolved Issues" in D. Gopal ed., *Australia in the Emerging Global Order: Evolving Australia-India Relations*. New Delhi: Shipra Publications.

——. 2002. *Governance of Indigenous People in Latin America*. New Delhi: Authors Press.

——. 2003. "Govenance of Aborigines in India and Australia: Policies and

Strategies," in D. Gopal and Dennis Rumley eds., *India and Australia: Issues and Opportunities*. New Delhi: Authors Press.

——. 2005. 'Indigenous Rights and the Quest-(ion) of Participatory Democracy in Latin America' *International Studies*, vol. 42, no. 1, January-March, pp. 61-76.

——. 2006. "Internationalisation of Canada's Indigenous Identity: A Prelude to National Recognition?" Christopher S. Raj and Abdul Nafey eds., *Canada's Global Engagements in the 21st Century and Relations with India*. New Delhi: Manak Publications.

——. 2008. 'The Process of Positive 'Native Title' Determination in Australia: Leading to a 'Negative Title' ?' in D. Gopal ed., *India-Australia Relations: Convergence and Divergence*. New Delhi: Shipra Publications.

——. 2009. "Elusive Justice: Denial Frame for the Tribal Poor in India," in Amita Singh and Nasir Aslam Zahid eds., *Strengthening Governance Through Access of Justice*. New Delhi: PHI Learning.

Smith, Paul Chaat and Robert Warrior. 1996. *Like a Hurricane: The American Indian Movement from Alcatraz to Wounded Knee*. New York: New Press.

Smith-Hefner, Nancy J. 1988. 'The Linguistic Socialization of Javanese Children in Two Communities', *Anthropological Linguistics*, vol.30, no.2, pp. 166-98.

Starna, William A. 1988. "Aboriginal Title and Traditional Land Use: An Anthropological Perspective", in Christopher Vecsey and William A. Starna, eds., *Iroquois Land Claims*. Syracuse: Syracuse University Press.

Stern, Steve. 2001. 'La contracorriente histórica: los indígenas como colonizadores del Estado, siglos XVI a XX' in Leticia Reina, ed. *Los retos de la etnicidad en los estados-nación del siglo XXI*. México, CIESAS, pp. 73-92.

Stocking Jr., G. W. 1991. 'Colonial Situations' in *Colonial Situations: Essays On The Contextualization Of Ethnographic Knowledge*. Madison: The University Of Wisconsin Press.

Stokes, G. and A. Carter, eds. 2001. *Democratic Theory Today: Challenges for the 21 st Century*. Cambridge: Polity Press.

Super, C., and S. Harkness. 1986. 'The Developmental Niche: A Conceptualization at the Interface of Child and Culture', *International Journal of Behaviour Development*, vol. 9, pp. 1-25.

Svensson, Frances. 1979. 'Liberal Democracy and Group Rights: The Legacy of Individualism and its Impact on American Indian Tribes', *Political Studies*, vol. 27, no.3, pp. 421-439.

Tatsuo, Inoue. 1999. "Human Rights and Asian Values: A Defense of "Western" Universalism", in Joanne R. Bauer, Daniel A. Bell, eds., *The East Asian Challenge For Human Rights*. New York: Cambridge University Press.

Taylor, Charles. 1993. *Reconciling the Solitudes: Essays on Canadian Federalism and Nationalism*. Montreal: McGill-Queen's University Press.

——. 1994. "The Politics of Recognition", in Amy Gutmann, ed., *Multiculturalism: Examining the Politics of Recognition*. Princeton, NJ: Princeton University Press.

——. 1999. "Conditions of an Unforced Consensus on Human Rights", in Joanne

R. Bauer, Daniel A. Bell, eds., *The East Asian Challenge For Human Rights*. New York: Cambridge University Press.

——. 2007. *A Secular Age*. Cambridge, Mass.: Belknap Press of Harvard University Press.

Tharp, Roland G., and Ronald Gallimore. 1988. *Rousing Minds to Life: Teaching, Learning, and Schooling in Social Context*. Cambridge: Cambridge University Press.

Tharp, Roland G., C. Jordan, G. E. Speidel, K. Hu-Pei Au, T. W. Klein, R. P. Calkins, K. C. M. Sloat, and Ronald Gallimore. 1984. "Product and Process in Applied Developmental Research: Education and the Children of a Minority", in M. E. Lamb, A. L. Brown, and B. Rogoff, eds., *Advances in Developmental Psychology*. Hillsdale, NJ: Lawrence Erlbaum Associates.

Thiele, S. 2005. 'Sociologists and 'Indigenous Issues," *Nexus*, vol. 17, no. 1, March, pp 13-15.

Thompson, John Herd. 2006. "Foreword" in Sterling Evans, ed., *The Borderlands of the American and Canadian Wests: Essays on Regional and Trans-boundary History*. Lincoln, NB: University of Nebraska Press.

Tilly, C. 1998. 'Social Movements and all Sorts of Other Political Interactions – Local, National and International – Including Identities: Several Divagations from a Common Path, Beginning with British Struggles over Catholic Emancipation, 1780-1829 and Ending with Contemporary Nationalism,' *Theory and Society*, vol. 27, no. 4, pp.453-80.

Todorov, T. 1984. *The Conquest of America: The Question of the Other*, trans. R. Howard. New York: Harper & Row.

Tully, James. 1995. *Strange Multiplicity: Constitutionalism in an Age of Diversity*. Cambridge: Cambridge University Press.

——. 2000. 'The Struggles of Indigenous Peoples for and of Freedom,' in David Ivison, P. Patton and W. Sanders, eds., *Political Theory and the Rights of Indigenous People*. Cambridge: Cambridge University Press.

Turpel, Mary Ellen. 1989-90. 'Aboriginal Peoples and the Canadian Charter: Interpretive Monopolies, Cultural Differences.' *Canadian Human Rights Yearbook* , Vol. 6, pp. 3-45.

Tutino, John. 2001. "Comunidad, independencia y nación: las participaciones populares en las historias de México, Guatemala y Perú" in Leticia Reina, ed. *Los retos de la etnicidad en los estados-nación del siglo XXI*. México: CIESAS, pp. 125-151.

United Nations Economic and Social Council, Preparatory Committee for the World Summit on Sustainable Development, Second Preparatory Session, 28 January - 8 February 2002, E/CN.17/2002/PC.2/6/Add.3

United Nations High Commissioner for Human Rights. 1996 : Draft United Nations Declaration on the Rights of Indigenous Peoples, 1994/45, Office of the United Nations High Commissioner for Human Rights, Geneva. Available at: http://www.unhchr.ch/huridocda/huridoca.nsf/Symbol E.CN.4.Sub.2.RES. 1994.45. En? Opendocument

Valle, Carlos Guilherme do. 1999. "Experiência e semântica entre os Tremembé do Ceará" in Oliveira Filho, João Pacheco de, ed., *A Viagem da volta: etnicidade, política e reelaboração cultural no Nordeste indígena.* Rio de Janeiro: Contra Capa Livraria, pp. 279-337.

——. 2007. Tremembé. *Enciclopédia: Povos Indígenas no Brasil*, Instituto Socioambiental, São Paulo: ISA. http://www.socioambiental.org/pib/epi/tremembe/hist.shtm access on 15/10/2007.

Vasil, R. 1990. *What Do The Maori Want? New Maori Political Perspectives.* Auckland: Random Century.

Velho, Otávio Guilherme. 1972. *Fontes De Expansão E Estrutura Agrária.* Rio De Janeiro: Zahar.

——. 1976. *Capitalismo Autoritário E Campesinato.* Rio De Janeiro: Difel.

Viveiros de Castro, Eduardo, and Lúcia M. M. de Andrade. 1988. "Hidrelétricas do Xingu: o Estado contra as sociedades indígenas" in Leinad Ayer de O Santos, Lúcia M. M. Andrade eds., *As Hidrelétricas do Xingu e os Povos Indígenas.* São Paulo: Comissão Pró-Índio, pp. 7-23.

Waldron, Jeremy. 1992. 'Minority Cultures and the Cosmopolitan Alternative', *University of Michigan Journal of Law Reform*, vol. 25, no.3, pp. 751-793.

Walker, Graham. 1997. "The Idea of Nonliberal Constitutionalism", in Ian Shapiro and Will Kymlicka, eds., *Ethnicity and Group Rights.* New York: New York University Press.

Walzer, Michael. 1997. *On Toleration,* New Haven: Yale University Press.

Ward, Margaret. 1971. *Them Children: A Study in Language Learning.* New York: Holt, Rinehart and Winston.

Warman, Arturo. 2001. *Los indios mexicanos en el umbral del milenio.* México: Fondo de Cultura Económica.

Watson, Irene. 2005. 'Illusionists and Hunters: Being Aboriginal in this Occupied Space', *Australian Feminist Law Journal,* vol. 22, pp.15-28.

——. 2006. "Internationalising, Humanising and Diversifying: The One Nation State", in Baden Offord and Elisabeth Porter eds., *Activating Human Rights,* Bern: Peter Lang European Academic Publishers.

——. 2007a. 'Aboriginal Sovereignties: Past, Present and Future Impossibilities' in Suvendrini Perera ed., *Our Patch, Enacting Australian Sovereignty Post-2001,* Network Books Symposia Series, Australia Research Unit, Curtin University of Technology, pp 23-43.

——. 2007b. 'Aboriginal Women's Laws and Lives: How Might We Keep Growing the Law?' *Australian Feminist Law Journal,* vol. 26, pp. 95

Watson-Gegeo, Karen A., and David W. Gegeo. 1986. "The Social World of Kwara'ae Children: Acquisition of Language and Values", in J. Cook-Gumperz, W. A. Corsaro, and J. Streeck, eds., *Children's Worlds and Children's Language.* New York: Mouton de Gruyter.

Wild, Rex, and Pat Anderson, 2007. *Report of the Northern Territory Board of Inquiry into the Protection of Aboriginal Children from Sexual Abuse.* Darwin: Northern Territory Government.

Windschuttle, Keith. 2002. *The Fabrication of Aboriginal History*. Sydney: Macleay Press.

Wolf, Eric R. 1984. *Europe and the People without History*. Berkeley: California, University of California Press.

Zizek, Slavoj, 1998. "El multiculturalismo o la lógica cultural del capitalismo multinacional" in Fredric Jameson and Slavoj Zizek, *Estudios culturales: reflexiones sobre el multiculturalismo*. Buenos Aires: Paidós, pp. 137-188.

Contributors

Annahatak, Betsy, Coordinator, Curriculum Development, Implementation and Support, Kativik School Board, Quebec.

Baines, Stephen Grant, Professor, Department of Anthropology, Universidade de Brasilia.

Crago, Martha, Vice-Rector, International and Student Life, University of Montreal.

de Oliveira, João Pacheco, Anthropologist, National Museum, Rio de Janeiro.

Gale, Peter, Senior Lecturer, David Unaipon College of Indigenous Education & Research, Division of Education, Arts and Social Sciences, Adelaide.

Fee, Margery, Director, Canadian Studies and Director, Intercultural and Community Programs, University of British Columbia, Vancouver.

Montemayor, Carlos, Professor of Political Sociology, Universidad Nacional Autonoma de Mexico : National Autonomous University of Mexico (UNAM), Mexico City.

Navarrete Linares, Federico, Professor, Instituto de Investigaciones Historicas, Universidad Nacional Autonoma de Mexico (UNAM), Mexico City.

Ningiuruvik, Lizzie, Kativik School Board, Quebec.

Peetush, Ashwani K., Assistant Professor, Department of Philosophy, Wilfrid Laurier University, Waterloo, Ontario.

Singh, Priti, Assistant Professor, Centre for Canadian, US & Latin American Studies, School of International Studies, Jawaharlal Nehru University, New Delhi.

Stavenhagen, Rodolfo, Professor Emeritus, El Colegio de Mexico, Mexico City; UN Special Rapporteur on the Human Rights and Fundamental Freedoms of Indigenous Peoples.

Watson, Irene, Professor, Post-doctoral Research Fellow, Faculty of Law, University of Sydney, Sydney.

Index